Consider the Leaf

Consider the Leaf

Foliage in Garden Design

JUDY GLATTSTEIN

TIMBER PRESS

Portland ~ Cambridge

Published in 2003 by
Timber Press, Inc.
The Haseltine Building
133 S.W. Second Avenue, Suite 450
Portland, Oregon 97204, U.S.A.

Timber Press
2 Station Road
Swavesey
Cambridge CB4 5QJ, U.K.

Manufactured in China by Imago

Library of Congress Cataloging-in-Publication Data
Glattstein, Judy, 1942–
        Consider the leaf : foliage in garden design / Judy Glattstein.
            p. cm.
        Includes bibliographical references (p.).
        ISBN 0-88192-571-3
        1. Foliage plants. 2. Landscape gardening. 3. Leaves. I. Title.

    SB431 .G528 2003
    635.9'75--dc21   2002028697

CONTENTS

❧

Color plates follow pages 48, 96, 160, and 192

ACKNOWLEDGMENTS

Books do not write themselves, and even their authors need assistance. Though content and style (as well as any inaccuracies) are mine, many gardeners and friends provided support. This came in the form of not only information but also comfort and encouragement during those slow patches that every author must deal with. Some individuals are quoted in the text; others are not. This has nothing to do with relative merit and much to do with constraints of space. In gardening, the line between amateur and professional becomes quite blurry in the sense that the nursery staff and garden designers of my acquaintance also love what they are doing for a living. They, and the amateurs, those home gardeners doing it for love, contributed the results of intimate observation and careful thought. Gardeners whose vocation and avocation coincide are among the most fortunate of people. My sincere apologies for the unintentional oversight if I have somehow omitted anyone.

I offer my gratitude to the professionals, in no particular order, who took the time to answer numerous questions, including Dennis Schrader of Landcraft Environments in Mattituck, New York, and Ken Selody of Atlock Flower Farm in Somerset, New Jersey, for allowing me to visit their elegant gardens; Tony Avent of Plant Delights Nursery in Raleigh, North Carolina, and Dan Hinkley of Heronswood Nursery in Kingston, Washington, for providing their own thoughts on using foliage in the garden; Mary Broadhurst and Don Novicky of Young's Nursery in Wilton, Connecticut, for their patience in checking cultivar names and for accompanying me on rambles through the nursery to examine plants; landscape designer Cindy Goulder, based in New York City, for her insights on using plants to bring a sense of nature to an urban setting; and Joe Freeman, chief horticulturist at Cypress Gardens in Cypress Gardens, Florida, and host of the public television gardening program "At Garden's Gate," for helpful information on foliage in the lush tropical environment.

Joe Sharman of Monksilver Nursery in Cambridgeshire, England, generously shared information on variegated perennials that come true from seed, the result of assiduous record-keeping over many years. Holly Shimizu, executive director of the United States Botanic Garden, supplied necessary information in the nick of time. Felder Rushing, gracious plant fanatic and Mississippi extension agent, gave me a glimpse of what it is like in the heart of the South. Bob Brown of Cotswold Garden Flowers in Worcestershire, England, provided a lucid explanation of the "why" of variegation in plants. "The Dalester," Dale Hendricks of North Creek Nursery in Landesberg, Pennsylvania, assured me that he always selects plants based on their foliage simply because he finds that foliage is always a major factor. Patrice Dimino, landscape designer and horticulturist for Hostra University on Long Island, New York, provided thorough information about the university's labyrinth garden and her personal regard for foliage as a factor in her designs.

Many thanks to Dan Heims, "over-the-top" plant fanatic and sports fisherman trolling for that perfect plant, instigator of Terra Nova Nurseries in Canby, Oregon; Allan Armitage, whose knowledge of plants coupled with his standing as professor and author certainly qualify him as a professional but who nonetheless considers himself an amateur, gardening for pleasure; Conni Cross, self-described eclectic designer of four-season gardens, whose fondness for foliage clearly shows not only in her work but also in the plants offered by Environmentals, the Long Island nursery specializing in dwarf rhododendrons and conifers as well as other rare shrubs; Stephanie Cohen from Collegeville, Pennsylvania, "Miss Mighty Mite," for her towering knowledge of plants and their attributes; Frederick H. Ray, retired professor of horticulture at Delaware Valley College, whose information has been instructional but never pedantic, who resides in Springfield, Pennsylvania, and who now thinks of himself as a home gardener; Hans Hansen of Shady Oaks Nursery in Waseca, Minnesota, for helpful information and as a source for excellent plants from a fine nursery; and Jim Avens, superintendent of Buck Gardens in Far Hills, New Jersey, for his viewpoints about foliage as he uses it for a public park as well as in his own garden.

I am grateful to Brent Breckinridge of Tucson, Arizona, who blurs the line between professional and amateur as he includes himself among the clients for his landscape design practice focusing on small gardens for individual homeowners. Flavio Rodrigues, on the grounds staff of PepsiCo, the Pepsi-Cola headquarters in Purchase, New York, generously made an extra effort to provide me with information about the PepsiCo Sculpture Gardens—a heartfelt "thank you" to him for his kindness to an eager author whom he has never met.

I would also like to acknowledge the gardeners who allowed me to explore their personal gardens both in actuality and through their helpful answers to my questions (what do you grow and why? what are your opinions?), which sometimes only engendered more questions. Thanks to Jacque Baclace of Saratoga, California, who took me on a virtual tour of her mountainside garden and discussed how foliage assists in the creation of a garden in a harsh environment; Neal Maillet, simpatico editor and fellow gardener who frequently enjoys using foliage to enhance his young garden in Portland, Oregon; Robert Lee Riffle, enthusiastic amateur gardener (filling in an abandoned swimming pool to create a large planting bed for tropical plants surely qualifies), both for direct information in answer to my questions and as author of a valuable reference, *The Tropical Look*; Melanie Bonacorsa Platosh from Portland, Oregon, who shared with me her pleasure in discovering the helpful attributes of foliage in her small, shady garden; Linny Stovall of Portland, Oregon, who discussed her favorite foliage plants, a diverse range that accommodated her large rural garden in North Plains, Oregon, with sunny sites, shaded sites, and both woodland and a restored meadow garden; Eric Shalit of Seattle, Washington, who finds that foliage offers him the best pretext to truly go wild in the garden; and Jeff Tareila and Risa Sackman of Frenchtown, New Jersey, who were gracious enough to discuss their garden with someone who walked in off the street saying, "I'm writing a book about foliage. Please tell me about your garden."

Thanks to Lew Tucci of Kew Professional Photo Lab in Norwalk, Connecticut, for his expert assistance in making sure the images for this book were as good as they could be. Helen Mageau, librarian at the Frelinghuysen Arboretum in Morristown, New Jersey, is also due recognition for her able assistance with the arboretum's excellent collection of old herbals and for allowing me to plug in and make notes in a thoroughly modern manner.

And to Paul, who cheered me on with encouragement and support when enthusiasm waned, and who provided computer services when my lack of expertise in their mysteries once again bollixed things up, I extend yet again my grateful appreciation and love.

CHAPTER 1

❧

Designing with Foliage

I want a beautiful garden. So do you. We all want lovely gardens—do you know anyone who deliberately sets out to make an ugly one? All too often, though, there is a gap between our hopes and our results. Seduced by pretty flowers, we plant time-consuming gardens that display only passing moments of beauty as plants briefly bloom, then fade. The roses covering the dream cottage have black spot on their leaves and Japanese beetles eating their flowers. I remember a client who asked me with some consternation, "You mean now that the garden is planted I have to take care of it?" Yes, indeed. We plant, then we tend to watering, weeding, fertilizing, mulching, staking, disease and pest protection—on and on. Were I the lady of the manor, with ample funds, more leisure, and a head gardener with support staff, this wouldn't be a problem. In my imagination is a gilded age of opportunity, wherein I drift through the garden on a golden afternoon. I am wearing a flowered dress, wide-brimmed straw hat, and gloves, carrying a basket with a pair of secateurs, and smiling benignly at the gardeners doing the real work. But just like most other gardeners I know, my real costume is a pair of filthy blue jeans and an old tee shirt. Out in the garden, as light fades, I pitch the tools— an 8-pound mattock for hacking at my New Jersey clay and a Weed Wrench to yank out multiflora roses (*Rosa multiflora*)—back into the toolshed and empty assorted 5-gallon Sheetrock buckets filled with lesser rocks and weeds. My time is limited. I cannot afford high-maintenance plants needing special attention in exchange for a two-week bloom period. In fact, even easily grown plants that "pay back" with a two-week period of bloom and nothing more just do not do it for me. I need plants that pay their way. In return for room and board (make that planting room and garden maintenance) I want easy-care plants with extended interest. After all, even in cold-winter regions the growing season lasts for several months. Flowers are great, but I consider them an embellishment for plants with fantastic foliage, the accessories that set off that basic black dress.

In autumn of 1995, when we moved to an unimproved site in western New Jersey, it became clear that I would need good-looking, long-lasting plants whose foliage would provide the primary garden interest, plants that would be attractive for longer than a transient week or two of flower power. As it turns out, this was not an unreasonable expectation. Evergreens, whether woody or herbaceous, have leaves year-round. Deciduous trees and shrubs, as well as the majority of perennials, are in flower for a couple of weeks; yet the selfsame plants have leaves for six or seven months, sometimes longer. Even plants used as temporary additions to the garden last for at least the summer season, June through September. While the majority of tender perennials grown as annuals for seasonal color have been selected for flowers, there are also such popular, reliable foliage selections as coleus (*Solenostemon scutellarioides*), dusty miller (*Senecio cineraria*), polka dot plant (*Hypoestes phyllostachya*), and Persian shield (*Strobilanthes dyeriana*). The word "annual" is used here in the horticultural sense and refers to part-time plants—whether true botanical annuals that germinate, grow, mature, and drop dead in a single growing season, or sensitive perennials that fade with winter's cold or endless summer heat. The intent is that they add their display to the garden for a season, then depart.

As you may have noticed, I like to use the Latin names for plants. If by chance you think people who use Latin names for plants are snobs, I would like to persuade you to reconsider. Perhaps you agree with that prolific author, Anonymous, who wrote, "Latin is a language as dead as it can be. First it killed the Romans, and now it's killing me." I am sure that line of doggerel has more to do with grammar than with plant names. Have you ever stopped to think that rhododendron and *Rhododendron*, iris and *Iris*, and crocus and *Crocus* are identical? Or that lily and *Lilium* are not much of a stretch? In part I prefer to use Latin names to be sure we have the same plant in mind when we discuss something. It is possible for different plants to share the same common name— "loosestrife," for example, refers to both *Lythrum salicaria* and a couple of species of *Lysimachia*. Likewise, one plant might have several common names, which can be upsetting when the plant you think you're buying from a mail-order nursery is not what they intend to send you. More than that, using Latin names shows a certain level of seriousness and professionalism. These names are often descriptive, providing information about what a plant looks like, how it grows, or where it came from. Of course, the taxonomists are always out there, gleefully revising well-known plant genera to something longer, less pronounceable, and harder to spell. But even so, Latin names are more reliable.

Now back to the garden.

Select plants with attractive foliage and their flowers become an added bonus. Choose plants with beautiful flowers and uninteresting foliage, however, and you'll end up with a humdrum garden with a thrown-together look once the flowers fade. Perhaps you have done something like the following (I know I have): pick a grass, any grass, because ornamental grasses are "in" (for the sake of discussion let's use *Calamagrostis* ×*acutiflora* 'Karl Foerster') and then pick a *Hemerocallis* cultivar because of a recent article in a garden magazine. Perhaps the local nursery has some of the newer tetraploid *Iris sibirica* cultivars. And there are those extra specimens of *Liriope muscari* from the garden club plant sale. Good plants all, except what remains once the flowers have faded but a haystack garden? (This is not to say, of course, that grass with grass cannot work effectively.)

Plants chosen for their foliage are more than merely beautiful. They can be problem solvers as well. Jeff Tareila and Risa Sackman, for example, use ornamental grasses to create year-round interest and to keep neighborhood children from cutting across their corner lot. Their house sits on a modest, sunny piece of property in a small New Jersey town on the Delaware River. With a B.S. in ecology, Jeff has a thorough background in plant and habitat interactions, but when it comes to gardening he considers himself an amateur, gardening for personal pleasure. He frequently selects plants for foliage rather than for flowers, finding this fits his personality better and noting that such plants require less maintenance. What qualifies a plant as "having good foliage," in his opinion, is its ability to attract attention in multiple seasons without the need for showy flowers. Jeff and Risa wanted quick results on a limited budget, and ornamental grasses were made to order. The longest planting area on their property is approximately 60 feet long by about 10 feet wide. There are a side entry and a short concrete path between house and sidewalk. Jeff planted *Miscanthus sinensis* cultivars such as white-striped 'Cosmopolitan' and yellow-banded 'Zebrinus' for their height, and five plants of the smaller 'Morning Light' for its elegant airy form, with its thin, fine, narrowly white-striped blades. Eleven plants of the Japanese blood grass *Imperata cylindrica* 'Rubra', in two separate groups, add a warming red accent, and several *Festuca* species create small tussocks of silvery blue. *Pennisetum alopecuroides* forms dense clumps intermediate in size, while *Calamagrostis* ×*acutiflora* 'Karl Foerster' is a vertical accent. A few woody plants—a shrubby holly (*Ilex*), a red-leaved Japanese maple (*Acer palmatum*), and a clump of white birches (*Betula*)—complete the planting. Jeff and Risa are delighted with their garden. Maintenance is minimal. The grasses are shaken free of moisture after a heavy rain, or of snow in winter. Just before growth begins in very early spring, they are cut back. And in return for this modest care, their grasses provide "wonderful foliage effects through all seasons—even in winter."

Another example of the benefits of foliage: woodland plants generally concentrate their bloom time to coincide with maximum availability of sunlight, as during spring, when trees are just leafing out. A savvy gardener who looks beyond bloom and chooses plants with interesting leaves will have an attractive summer garden just made for the shade. How about this common scenario: you plant lots of spring-flowering bulbs, from daffodils (*Narcissus*) to scillas and snowdrops (*Galanthus*), which are great while in bloom but so very shabby all too soon. It is not permissible to fold, braid, spindle, staple, or otherwise knot up bulb foliage, so disguise becomes the answer. Plant attractive leafy plants such as peonies, daylilies, ferns, and hostas to mask the yellowing bulb foliage and to conceal the summer-bare space beneath which they sleep. A mass planting of *Hyacinthoides hispanica* hazes a woodland bank with blue flowers in May. Partner the bulbs with Christmas fern (*Polystichum acrostichoides*), which not only provides a lacy evergreen carpet but additionally traps fallen autumn leaves that tend to blow into the small drainage flow. Additional interest can be created both in and out of the blooming period by planting *Brunnera macrophylla*, whose flowers (like those of forget-me-not) will complement the bulbs' blooms. And afterwards, this perennial's dark green heart-shaped leaves are a charming foil for the dark green fern fronds.

> A savvy gardener who looks beyond bloom and chooses plants with interesting leaves will have an attractive summer garden just made for the shade.

Attempts to find appropriate solutions to problem sites, those with difficult soil conditions, can consume time, effort, money, and plants. Consider a hot, dry, sandy bank, low in fertility, where water sinks with scarcely a trace. So far all we have done is define the parameters. What is needed as a solution are drought-resistant plants with long-term interest that will pretty much care for themselves once established. Suppose we start with *Juniperus virginiana* 'Grey Owl', a slow-growing shrub that eventually reaches 3 to 6 feet tall. Its silver-gray needles will create a finely textured appearance. Pair it with a deciduous shrub such as *Rhus aromatica* 'Gro-Low', a great, tough little plant with attractive, softly hairy trifoliate leaves. Opening a soft green, the aromatic foliage matures to a lustrous deep green in summer and turns a superb orange to flaming red in autumn. Do you feel sumac (*Rhus*) is too trashy a plant and want something with more cachet? Select dusty zenobia (*Zenobia pulverulenta*) with its gray to glaucous blue-green leaves that turn a rich burgundy red in autumn. While deciduous in zones 6 and 7, dusty zenobia is semi-evergreen in zones 8 and 9. A linear leaf would add a pleasing texture, but this site might be too much for most popular grasses. Yucca, on the other hand, would feel right at home. *Yucca filamentosa* has stiff, upright, fairly broad grayish green leaves. One cultivar, *Y. filamentosa* 'Bright Edge', has a bright golden yellow margin to its leaves (see Plate 98). *Yucca filifera* 'Golden Sword' is like a mirror image, with its green-edged leaves and a softer yellow center. These plants solve the problem, and now we even have options to work with.

Jacque Baclace selects plants for their foliage but focuses mainly on their ability to adapt to her site. She wants plants that can fend for themselves and enhance the natural beauty of what she regards as "this special piece of paradise." Jacque gardens at 1500 feet on a small shelf carved out of a south-facing chaparral hillside in Saratoga, California, coping with harsh sun, summer drought, predatory deer, and the difficult situation of renting, rather than owning, her home and garden. Hers is an interesting site: rural, with acres of steep hillside as borrowed scenery, a shaded creek down the hill, and tall conifers that influence her zone 8 to 9 garden. Sometimes she gets snow when her nearest neighbors do not, and the microclimates are variable depending on whether the spot is shaded, open, or sheltered by cliff face. Working with a steep and unstable dirt embankment, and reluctant to allocate resources to build terraces on property not her own, Jacque checks the garden daily to see what has changed: what progress the plants have made, what the deer have eaten, what has slid down the hill.

The chaparral foliage is spiky or thin-leaved. When Jacque selects plants for foliage she does so to create a restful effect, with plants that blend in with the surrounding countryside. Dark green large-leaved plants are not adapted to such sites, nor do they blend in. Deer eat saplings, so trees are not an option. Wormwood (*Artemisia*) and lavender (*Lavandula*) work well, as does rosemary (*Rosmarinus*). Bearded iris thrives in the arid setting, adding swordlike glaucous leaves for structural interest. Jacque's husband, Paul, loves weird plants, so Jacque grows varieties of *Echeveria* and other succulents on the deck, where they are protected from deer (in addition the man-made setting provides a logical distinction between cultivated and natural areas). One of their favorites is *E.* 'Etna', a big, bumpy cultivar with a dinosaurish look. Incidentally, Renee O'Connell of Altman Plants, a large nursery based in Vista, California, hybridized 'Etna', naming several in the series for volcanoes. Jacque and Paul are now looking for 'Vesuvius' and 'Magma' to add to the eruption on their deck.

Succulents have especially appealed to Jacque since she saw them spilling down the hillside at the Getty Museum in southern California. She likes the red of pork and beans (*Sedum rubrotinctum*) and blue succulents combined with echeverias. Yucca Do nursery in Texas has three hardy forms of *Agave* she'd like to try. It is a harsh climate, hard on both plants and gardeners. "I want to emphasize that I put up with a lot of ugly foliage," she says. "When I first moved to the countryside here I thought my rough dirt and dried weedy embankment was ugly. Now my eye is more in tune with the cycles of nature. Summers here are naturally brown. Winter trees and rocks, by contrast, are fluorescent mossy green sculptures. I very much like the promise of winter and spring bulb foliage. I even put up with withering bulb foliage."

Anywhere you garden there are foliage plants just right for you. Many are attractive and functional in sunny situations, while others are just right for the shade. Choose suitable plants for your environment. Foliage can be especially worthwhile in hot and humid Gulf States where summer conditions fry plants. Felder Rushing, a seventh-generation Mississippi gardener, author and columnist, radio personality, and all-around plant enthusiast, says, "When you think south, think palmetto and aucuba, and for shade, the knock-out combo of aspidistra and evergreen holly fern" (that would be *Sabal palmetto* and *Aucuba japonica*, *Aspidistra elatior* and *Cyrtomium falcatum*).

SELECTING AND USING FOLIAGE

When Gertrude Stein cleverly wrote "Rose is a rose is a rose is a rose," she penned an immortal line—one that does not as effectively translate to "Leaf is a leaf is a leaf is a leaf." The fact is, not all leaves are created equal. Setting color aside for the moment, there are structural differences between leaves, both gross and in detail. Making the right choices will result in a better garden.

As soon as you begin to design a flower garden, the unspoken understanding is that there will be color, several colors, possibly even lots of color. Green is an uncommon color in flowers—*Zinnia* 'Envy', *Nicotiana langsdorffii*, and *Moluccella laevis* are three that come to mind. It is very tempting to splash color around with foliage, just as you would with flowers. However, the first steps towards developing an attractive foliage garden should be to select plants with contrasting leaf shapes and to create a dynamic balance of scale by utilizing leaves of different sizes. Only after these aspects of leaf form have been developed would you perhaps advance to colors other than green. Why only perhaps? Just as there is a vogue for monotone flower gardens, such as moon gardens with white flowers, a green garden has just as much, even more, to recommend it. Leaves last; they do not come and go like flowers. Green leaves have an extraordinary range of color. Their shades and hues extend from the warm yellow-green of a chartreuse hosta to leaves the cool blue-green of an arctic sea, from the crisp green of a Granny Smith apple to the British-racing-green of an old Triumph from the 1960s—just the color of the narrowly segmented leaves of bear's foot hellebore (*Helleborus foetidus*).

Plant *Brunnera* species with a midsized hosta and the results are dull; similarities of shape and size provide little visual interest. Pair either brunnera or hosta with a fern or astilbe and the aesthetic appeal takes an effective jump by an order of magnitude. Garden design with foliage is as simple as that. When I'm called in for a garden consultation I often find that people have all the right plants. They just need some simple rearrangement to make the garden look better, to take it from "That's nice" to "Wow!" If you consider the leaf when choosing plants for your garden, you will build a solid foundation. This idea works as effectively for commonplace plants at home centers and chain nurseries as for the latest cutting-edge plant to hit the trendy catalogs. It works for gardens in the hot and humid heart of the South, in the low-rainfall sites of the arid Southwest, in the cool and damp Pacific Northwest—anywhere you happen to live and want to grow plants for pleasure. There may be different plants for different places, but the principles are the same. Just keep in mind that hot summers in the South will fry plants that have no problem with cold winters, and mild Pacific Northwest summers mean tropical *Caladium* species will fail to thrive (but gardeners are always pushing the envelope).

Take the tropical look. It's hot, it's in, it's trendy. I'm not talking about a Trader Vic tiki-hut-with-palm-tree look for your terrace or patio. But a garden in the Bronx can resemble Bermuda, at least in the summer, and perhaps even beyond. Bananas, bamboos, cannas, and palm trees grace gardens where snow is the winter scene. My garden features a Japanese fiber banana (*Musa basjoo*), which is sufficiently cold tolerant to have survived in my New Jersey garden for the last four years. I cut it down to the ground after a hard frost turns the leaves to mush, mulch well, and back it comes every spring. Another, more tender banana spends some summers out in the garden in the pot that provides its winter home, and other summers tipped out and planted directly in the soil. An alternative is to select plants that look tropical even if the plants are not.

Bamboo certainly adds a tropical touch, as do the larger ornamental grasses. Some hostas have huge leaves, such as *Hosta* 'Big Daddy', *H.* 'Big Mama', and *H.* 'Blue Angel'. And then there is butterbur (*Petasites japonicus*). Hardy to zone 5, this is the cold-climate gardener's stand-in for *Gunnera* species. Lush, green, reniform leaves reach 27 to 33 inches across and 22 to 24 inches long, held up on stout stems 24 inches tall. Because butterbur is a traveling plant, I confine mine to an old bathtub sunk to its rim in the ground.

There is a simple technique to push leaf production of certain trees and shrubs from modest to mammoth. If you have ever cut down any of the larger maples, you are probably already aware that unless the stump is treated with a heavy-duty brush killer the tree will respond in a Hydra-like manner, sending up more shoots, and these shoots will have outsized leaves. Ever on the lookout for techniques to manipulate their plants, gardeners make use of this method, called stooling, to create super-sized foliage effects. Take a young empress tree (*Paulownia tomentosa*), just a few years old, or Indian bean tree (*Catalpa bignonioides*)—and if it is the yellow-leaved *C. bignonioides* 'Aurea', so much the showier. In late winter or very early spring, before new growth begins, cut the tree back to within a foot or so of the ground. In response the tree will produce several very straight, extravigorous shoots, and the juvenile foliage will be robust and enlarged. Since *P. tomentosa* and *C. bignonioides* already have large leaves, the results will be striking. Tree of heaven (*Ailanthus altissima*) also responds positively to this technique, with the additional bonus that flowering is eliminated and self-sown seedling trees cannot make pests of themselves. The same technique is used with purple-leaved smokebush (*Cotinus coggygria* 'Royal Purple') at Wave Hill, a marvelous public garden in the Bronx (see Plate 13). The oversized purple leaves create a focal point in the front garden.

Many sumacs (*Rhus*) add a feathery tropical feel to the scruffiest roadside (see Plates 104–107). Though considered trashy and weedy in the United States, sumacs are popular in Europe, where their reliable blazing red fall color performs in even the softest English weather. Staghorn sumac (*R. typhina*) has velvety, hairy twigs and medium green pinnate leaves that are also softly fuzzy when young. Smooth sumac (*R. glabra*) is similar but with smooth twigs and leaves. Shining sumac (*R. copallina*) is perhaps my favorite, with its glossy, dark green, pinnately compound leaves that turn a lustrous purple-bronze in autumn. Silk tree (*Albizia julibrissin*) has an even more finely textured compound leaf, and self-sown specimens of this Asian species, native from Iran to Japan, abound in my part of western New Jersey—no green card, but they have naturalized and made themselves at home.

Eric Shalit is a graphic designer living in Seattle, Washington, with a self-styled tropicalismo garden. It is wedged into the backyard of his larger, quarter-acre urban garden, sharing space with a large playset and woodshed for his two young sons and a 1700-gallon pond and stream. It is the mild (zone 8), maritime Pacific Northwest equivalent of an English garden, less than 1000 feet from Puget Sound and only a short commute from downtown Seattle. He frequently selects plants for foliage rather than flowers, finding foliage more subdued in a visual sense, more at rest, and longer lasting. As Eric notes, natural ecosystems such as woodland or jungle tend to consist more of foliage plants. "I wonder," he says, "if much 'naturalistic' planting tends to be more foliage oriented. You are controlling nature by combining plants from disparate continents, but trying to create a sense of environment/ecosystem. In flower gardening, the human hand is very apparent." He likes plants with strong foliage structure, which he defines as pointy or serrate, or those with an unusual shape. Plants with large leaves, such as gunnera or castor bean (*Ricinus communis*), are favorites.

One June I bought a begonia that would fit right in with Eric's scheme of things. Labeled *Begonia parviflora*, it was one of those tender perennials sold as a summer annual. The fact that I'd never heard of it did little to deter me from driving it home to New Jersey from the Connecticut nursery where I had purchased it. This begonia has interesting fresh green leaves with a jagged edge, arranged in a shingled, overlapping manner on stout stems. By late July it measured over 2 feet tall and was manufacturing leaves more than 14 inches wide and 9 or 10 inches long from petiole to edge. A synonym for this South American begonia, native from Colombia to Bolivia, is *B. gunnerifolia*, which certainly seems appropriate. Kathy Pufahl of Beds and Borders, a wholesale nursery on Long Island that specializes in plants for the summer garden, including *B. parviflora*, told me that for her "it grows 4 to 5 feet tall, flowers in winter and early spring, and is grown primarily for its gorgeous green leaves. I think it prefers some shade from the hot summer sun if for even a few hours." I kept mine on my deck in constant light shade under a poolside-type tent. It grew in a 12-inch-diameter pot but needed something larger before it came indoors at the end of summer.

The tropicalismo garden Eric planted contains treelike windmill palm (*Trachycarpus fortunei*) with feather fronds, bold, blocky-leaved empress tree (*Paulownia tomentosa*), and Japanese fiber banana (*Musa basjoo*). There are about six different kinds of bamboo. "In a corner behind the paulownia," says Eric, "is a young stand (three shoots) of timber bamboo that will someday be very exciting." The tropicalismo garden is a summer thing, but keep in mind that seasons in Seattle are often indistinct and foliage can look very good into November. Eric has put much thought into what he's doing in the garden, and why:

I am in the long-term process of creating an urban park-like setting, an oasis with year-round interest. There are several different factors influencing the design of the gardens. The first is a desire to create an oasis space, a place of comfort and beauty where you can have a sense of the natural world even though we are in the city. Another factor is a love of lush, tropical-like foliage as well as foliage shapes and textures that are dissonant, contrasting with each other. Combinations that wake up the eyes. Some combinations are peaceful and relaxing, some are hot and spicy (stripes and spikes). Another factor is the "wow" factor. When you see the leaves of a paulownia tree or a purple castor bean (*Ricinus*), you can't help but say "wow." It's like having a pet elephant, but with minimal care requirements. Another factor is the curse of the pathological collector, the feeling that you just have to have that plant. A desire to have many different plants, weird plants, unusual plants. This can conflict with the desire to grow really big plants, because space is limited. This has led me to give great plants to friends who provide them with new homes, allowing me to get more plants.

LEAF SHAPES

My husband is an engineer. As such, he is fond of starting a discussion with the statement, "First, define your terms." Let's begin at the beginning, with leaf shapes. When you have an understanding of what is meant when I say that *Rhus aromatica* 'Gro-Low' has a pinnately compound leaf with serrulate edges to the leaflet margins, then we are speaking the same language. While this level of detail is not necessary for every plant I mention, there are times when it will be helpful. Some botanical Latin vocabulary is used to describe details of leaf shape and texture.

A simple leaf consists of a blade attached to its stem by a petiole. Compound leaves have few to many leaflets. If they are arranged like the fingers of your hand, the leaflets are palmate. They have a pinnate arrangement if the leaflets are set along a central axis, like a bird's feather.

Overall, there are three basic leaf shapes: linear, like a grass; lacy, like a fern; and blocky, like a hosta. The most interesting gardens play pattern and shape against one another rather than pairing similar plants as partners. Plant a hosta together with *Brunnera macrophylla* and you still have two shapes too close for comfort. But pair a hosta with a fern and you're getting somewhere. It is not, unfortunately, quite as simple as one, two, three, linear, lacy, blocky, again and again in the same predictable manner. That would lead to rote designs such as those offered in a low-end nursery catalog, and a one-size-fits-all blandness. Static balance may be safe, but it is also dull. Use foliage in an interesting manner with some creativity and originality to arrive at a dynamic garden.

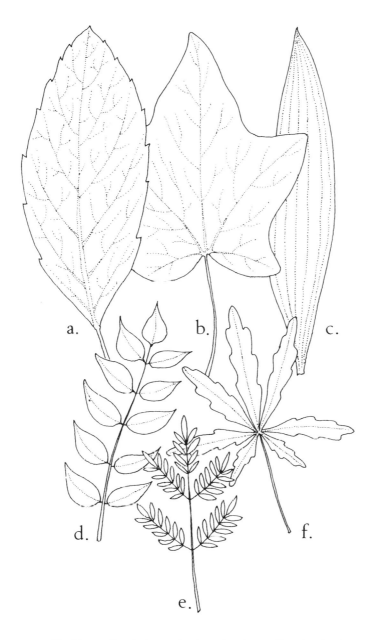

Vein patterns and leaf types. Simple leaves (a–c): a-pinnate venation, b-palmate venation, c-parallel venation. Compound leaves (d–f): d-pinnately compound, e-bipinnately compound, f-palmately compound. Source: Brian Capon, *Botany for Gardeners*.

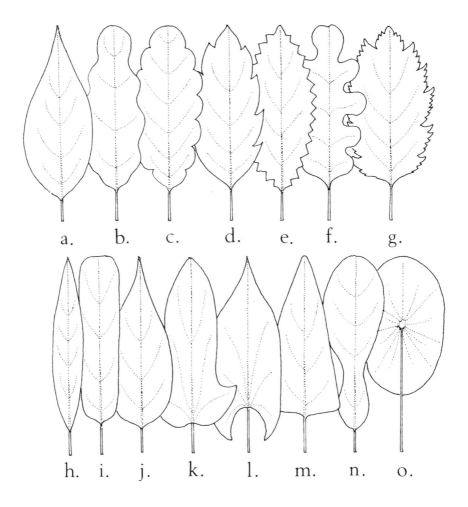

Margin patterns and leaf shapes. Margins (a–g): a-entire, b-sinuate, c-crenate, d-serrate, e-dentate, f-lobed, g-double serrate. Shapes (h–o): h-linear, i-oblong, j-ovate, k-hastate, l-sagittate, m-deltoid, n-spatulate, o-peltate. Source: Brian Capon, *Botany for Gardeners*.

As Mies van der Rohe said in a *New York Times* interview on 19 August 1969, "God is in the details." It is not merely the basic form of a leaf—the triune of linear, lacy, and blocky—but also the patterning of the leaf's edge. It might be entire (smooth), serrate (saw-toothed), crenulate (minutely scalloped), and so on. Even the patterning of veins can add to the overall effect. Some hostas— old-fashioned *Hosta ventricosa*, for example—have deeply incised veins that accent their plain green leaves.

Seeds germinate with either one or two seed leaves, called cotyledons. Those with one seed leaf are classified as monocots. Their true leaves always have parallel venation. Plants such as grasses, sedges, lilies, irises, hostas, bamboos, palms, and orchids are monocots. Many have straplike, linear leaves; none have compound leaves. The majority of monocots are herbaceous plants.

Those plants that germinate with two seed leaves are classified as dicots. Their leaves have reticulated or netlike venation. All broad-leaved trees and shrubs, and many herbaceous plants, are dicots. Dicotyledonous plants may have either simple or compound leaves.

As Brian Capon states in *Botany for Gardeners*, "Knowledge of such technicalities is not necessary to appreciate the fact that it is the unlimited diversity of leaf form and color that makes most houseplants and many garden plants so attractive." Perhaps not, but all too often we look but do not see, especially when it comes to the details. An awareness of the names for these differences may be just the encouragement needed to look again, and see more closely.

Focus on the three basic leaf shapes. Use blocky, bold, architectural shapes that contrast so well with lacy, intricate, fernlike shapes, and then balance the two with linear, straplike foliage. Remember that size in and of itself is not material: what is important is the relative size and, even more importantly, the contrasting shape of one leaf to another. Canadian ginger (*Asarum canadense*) would still be considered bold in form even though on average its reniform leaves are no more than 3 inches long by 6 inches wide, miniature when compared to those of butterbur (*Petasites japonicus*).

BOLD-LEAVED PLANTS

Gunnera manicata is a stoutly rhizomatous, giant perennial herb. At maturity the clumps can reach 10 to 12 feet across. Sturdy 6- to 7-foot-tall prickly stalks support palmately lobed, serrate, rounded to reniform leaves 7 feet across, sometimes even larger. Gunnera thrives in the moist, cool climate of the Pacific Northwest. Consider what this plant achieves at maturity and provide ample room, organic matter, and moisture. I would suggest a planting hole 6 feet long,

4 feet wide, and at least 2 feet deep, and abundant water in summer unless the plant is sited adjacent to a pond or other naturally moist site. Each spring, before growth begins, top-dress with a generous layer of aged manure. And, of course, choose a protected site where wind will not tatter the sail-like leaves. This stately plant is not for small gardens, or for those with hot summers, cold winters, or an arid climate. With effort, plants can be protected in marginal climates. I recall a specimen grown at Skylands in Ringwood State Park, New Jersey. This required a bottomless, topless wooden frame to cover the football-sized resting bud over winter, with the huge leaves folded over the crown, topped with a thick layer of straw, and finished off with stable manure. Remember, when attempting to grow marginally cold-hardy plants, it is prudent to plant in spring. This allows a full growing season before the plant is stressed by winter.

Whether you grow the culinary or the ornamental species, rhubarb is an elegant foliage plant. Garden rhubarb (*Rheum* ×*cultorum*), also known as pie plant, has ovate to cordate leaves. This is the plant for cold-climate gardeners, as it is hardy down to −30 to −40° Fahrenheit, zone 3. The ornamental rhubarbs include *R. australe*, which is relatively petite with dark green, rounded to broadly ovate leaves nearly 2 feet across, and *R. palmatum*, with apple-green, palmately lobed leaves 2.5 feet across. *Rheum palmatum* is also available as 'Atrosanguineum', whose scarlet buds unfurl into dark red leaves in spring. At maturity the color fades to green on the leaf surface, but the underside remains a rusty red, like old blood. Both species are hardy to zone 6.

By August the oldest leaves will be yellow, the others will have slug holes, and new leaves may be pushing forth if there has been ample rain. All rhubarbs may best be described as gross feeders. I find my rhubarb much appreciates a bucketful of fresh horse manure and urine-soaked straw dumped over the dormant crown in midwinter. The nutrients are washed into the soil by rain and snow, and the remains provide a summer mulch. Rhubarbs prefer an evenly moist yet free-draining soil; wet soil rots the crown. Both ornamental and culinary species do best with some midday shade.

Either a gardener likes cannas or abhors them, but rarely is anyone indifferent to these riotous, rhizomatous, stately plants for the summer garden. I appreciate them for their foliage but find the flowers on modern *Canna* cultivars blowsy and untidy. Such as these deserve not so much deadheading as disbudding. Available in any size required, from stately *C.* 'Omega' at 14 feet tall to *C.* 'Pink Beauty' at a scanty 28 inches, there are cannas for any garden scale. Their lanceolate leaves lend stature to the herbaceous border, where they may function as a backdrop or accent. While cannas I have placed in the open garden have died, I have had cannas survive and multiply for years in my zone 6 New Jersey garden when they are tucked up against the house foundation in a sheltered situation. In zone 8 (and perhaps zone 7) gardens, the rhizomes are reliably perennial in more open situations. Cannas are very easy to lift and store over the winter in a minimally frost-free place such as an attached but unheated garage. During the growing season cannas prefer a sunny site and moist, even wet, situations—standing water will not harm them. Better yet, they seem to be unpalatable to deer, woodchucks, and rabbits that like to dine in gardens.

With their lush growth, bananas often find a place in subtropical gardens and are the epitome of the tropical look for cold-climate gardeners. A sheltered site is generally a good idea, as their large oblong or elliptic leaves are readily shredded by wind, giving the plants a tattered, shabby appearance. Most bananas are hardy only in zone 10. However, they can be grown in any garden with warm to hot summers—even in zone 6, with its cold winters. While the *Index of Garden Plants* gives zone 9 as the limit of hardiness for *Musa basjoo*, Japanese fiber banana is far hardier than they suggest. My own plant easily survives New Jersey's zone 6 winters, though admittedly with the protection of a sheltering wall and deep mulch. Its fourth summer in the ground it shot up to 8½ feet tall with individual leaf blades over 4 feet long. Bananas, you see, are herbaceous plants. Provided the underground rootstock is not damaged, the plant will grow again when the top growth is killed back. While this tends to limit the height to one season's growth of 6 feet or so, rather than their full potential of 9 to 12 feet, diligent gardeners push the envelope. And after all, a Houston, Texas, cold snap will turn bananas to black slime, if not as thoroughly as a typical New Jersey winter. Bananas can be wrapped too, much like fig trees in New York City. For my own plant I have created a reusable banana shelter out of two inexpensive 30-gallon trashcans with their bottoms cut out, fastened smaller end to smaller end with silicone caulking and filled with dry wood shavings or fallen oak leaves. It has not been a completely satisfactory solution: some parts of the plant turned to mush the first winter. It did grow especially vigorously the following spring, but I don't know whether to attribute that to the style of winter protection or to the following growing season's weather (I was also burying any little "fertilizer packages" the cats brought me around the banana). Additionally, if I wrap it too early, before the weather has gotten chilly enough to induce dormancy, the silly plant continues to grow and even pushes the lid off its shelter.

Blood banana (*Musa acuminata* 'Sumatrana') has green leaves beautifully blotched wine red and solidly washed with burgundy beneath (see Plate 90). In zone 10 gardens it will reach 20 feet tall. I bring my 9-foot-tall plant, container and all, into the living room for the winter. This species can also be wintered over in a dormant state by cutting it back close to the ground in autumn, digging the root ball, and storing it in a cool dark place.

One year my local supermarket in New Jersey was selling potted dwarf bananas along with the usual assortment of summer bedding plants. While the *Musa acuminata* 'Dwarf Cavendish' I purchased could reach 6 feet tall under ideal conditions, it remained at about 3 feet tall in a container, producing numerous offsets. This is a convenient size for a balcony, rooftop, terrace, or patio plant.

The stateliest ornamental banana in wide distribution (relatively speaking) is *Ensete ventricosum* 'Maurelii', the Abyssinian banana. The red-flushed olive-green leaves have a red midrib. They grow about 9 feet long, clustered at the top of a trunklike pseudostem that grows about 12 feet tall in cultivation. The two magnificent plants I saw at Atlock Flower Farm, Ken Selody's display garden and nursery in Somerset, New Jersey, would have been ideal for dressing the stage for a production of *Aida* (see Plate 91). Winter cultivation in a greenhouse is necessary for Abyssinian banana if the plants are to achieve a stately size. Four to 5 feet is all that should be expected if it is cut back annually. All bananas prefer full sun, warm weather, and ample water during the growing season, and a rich soil that need not be especially deep.

Another bold presence for moist shady sites is *Astilboides tabularis*. Hardy to zone 4, this sizeable plant creates a majestic accent in cold-climate gardens. Pale green peltate leaves, broadly lobed with dentate margins, can easily reach 2 to 3 feet across. They balance on stalks 4 feet tall or more, looking like plates on a juggler's pole. While moisture is necessary, flooding is not, and inundated plants may rot.

You do not need an estate-sized property in the tropics to incorporate bold foliage plants into your garden. Pattern and shape are the important considerations, while scale is relative. Any hosta, from *Hosta sieboldiana* with its 18-inch-long parasol leaves to thumbnail-sized *H. venusta*, functions as a bold and blocky foliage plant. Another choice, *Brunnera macrophylla*, with modest leaves only 5 or 6 inches in length, is insignificant compared to a gunnera and petite compared to a banana. It is hardy down to zone 3, and the ovate to cordate dark green leaves make a handsome partner to ferns and astilbes that thrive in the same woodland conditions. Equally hardy, blue lungwort (*Pulmonaria angustifolia*) has hairy, bristly, fresh green leaves 7 inches long and a couple of inches wide. Both the species and its cultivars (selected for flowering characteristics) provide good contrast to the robust and glossy dark green foliage of *Euphorbia amygdaloides* var. *robbiae*. While references such as *Perennials for American Gardens* state that the euphorbia is hardy only to zone 8, I have seen it thriving in several zone 6 gardens in New Jersey. Prudence would suggest planting in a sheltered site, but I think this euphorbia is hardier than commonly suggested.

LACY-LEAVED PLANTS

A visit to Derreen in County Kerry, Ireland, in June 1998 felt like a trip back in time to the forest primeval. The moderating influence of the Gulf Stream provides the milder temperatures and high humidity that beguile tree ferns to lush and magnificent growth. *Dicksonia antarctica* would be superb as a companion to gunnera, for this tree fern from Australia and Tasmania, commonly called Tasmanian tree fern, has the size and heft for a large-scale partnership. It is hardy to zone 9, or even the warmer portion of zone 8 in a suitable microclimate. A passing snow shower will not kill it, though heavy wet snow can break the fronds. If you want to push the envelope by growing this plant in the cooler zone, consider protecting the trunk in winter. Japanese gardeners in Kyoto wrap their cycads in attractive straw coats, but a loose wrapping of burlap will serve the same purpose. Remember to include a cover at the top as well, to protect the inner crown (even more tender than the trunk), from which new fronds will emerge in spring. High humidity is a critical need. The stout trunk, up to 2 feet in diameter, is actually a much smaller stem thickly mantled with roots that should be protected and kept from drying out. Misting the trunk in dry weather is prudent. If planted in rich, moist soil, *D. antarctica* can tolerate full sun. It reaches 10 feet tall or higher, the arching evergreen fronds that crown the trunk growing 6 to 8 feet in length. The slow growth of this tree fern suggests a leisurely wait for small specimens to grow into large ones. Buy the largest available plant you can afford. Tasmanian tree fern is relatively easy to transplant, having a fairly small root ball. It is readily available and moderately easy to grow. Gardeners in British Columbia, Seattle, and San Francisco, where this plant is hardy, can sometimes find it offered for sale at their local DIY home store.

Gardeners in the frozen northern parts of zone 3 may not be able to grow tree ferns, but there are beautiful ferns capable of enhancing cold-winter gardens. And ferns are so variable—large or small, evergreen or deciduous, politely clump-forming or vigorously running—that you needn't feel restricted when making a selection. One of my favorites is the evergreen Christmas fern (*Polystichum acrostichoides*), a pretty thing with dark green fronds up to 2 feet long. Over time it forms multiple crowns closely tucked together. It is a simple matter to lift and separate the clump in early spring, while the new fronds are still tightly furled and coated with golden brown chaff.

Many ferns are suitable only for shady places, so you would think one that thrives in full sun would be popular. Somehow that doesn't seem to be the case with sensitive fern (*Onoclea sensibilis*), also known as bead fern. Perhaps it is so easy to grow that its very willingness becomes a negative. This isn't to say sensitive fern is a weedy plant; it is merely a good doer. Even so, it is often less favored than more temperamental ferns. To me the deciduous fronds, 2 feet long or more, have a tropical flair. With adequate moisture the rhizomes happily grow and spread in full sun, with new apple-green fronds produced throughout the growing season. Partial shade is better when soil moisture is only average. Sensitive fern shows its displeasure in dry conditions by turning limp and brown. Fronds turn an attractive straw-gold with the first frosts.

Felder Rushing's favorite, Japanese holly fern (*Cyrtomium falcatum*), also called evergreen holly fern, is indeed a beauty. It has a sprawling, vaselike form shaped by glossy dark green fronds whose leathery, serrate pinnae are like those of a holly leaf. This fern is popular in southern and southeastern states, happily naturalizing in New Orleans and like places. Though it is said to be hardy to zone 6, I think this would only be possible in a suitably protected microclimate. Zone 7 is a more realistic limit. However, because Japanese holly fern will accept low humidity, it adapts quite nicely to indoor conditions as a houseplant.

Black bugbane is hardly enticing as a common name for *Cimicifuga americana*, nor is goatsbeard for *Aruncus dioicus*. Both plants look rather like an astilbe on steroids, forming a vigorous mound of two- to five-pinnate lacey foliage. Provide humus-rich, moist yet free-draining soil in woodland shade and allow these self-sufficient plants to take care of themselves. Hardy down to zone 3, either would pair nicely with large hostas or *Astilboides tabularis*, but never with each other.

If palms are plants you associate only with Hawaii and Florida, think again. Palms are used with azaleas, camellias, and bamboo in traditional Japanese gardens. City gardeners in zone 6, where masonry, wind protection, and heat sources influence the climate, may have the opportunity to grow hardy palms as well. Remember that zone 6 is itself a variable. It makes a considerable difference if temperatures only plummet occasionally and not for long, or if they nosedive and stay there for a couple of weeks. Warm up to zone 7 in southeastern states and palms are definitely an option. In both zones the palms would be the lower-growing, clump-forming species rather than the tall tree-type palms lining a Miami boulevard. And keep in mind that palms are propagated by seed, not by grafting. Selection of seed from palms that survive the genetic sieving of a cold snap will result in a more cold-tolerant population.

Needle palm (*Rhapidophyllum hystrix*) is the most cold-tolerant palm: established plants can tolerate brief periods of −5° Fahrenheit. A smaller, clump-forming palm with deep green palmate leaves attractively silvered on the underside, this rare southeastern native gets its name from the numerous painfully sharp needles that protect its crown. You can expect slow-growing needle palms to reach about 5 feet tall and wide, although ultimately they can reach double that size. Site needle palm where it will be protected from cold winds, with adequate moisture and only very light shade. Adapted to warm, moist summers, this plant does poorly in the cool conditions of the Pacific Northwest.

Dwarf palmetto (*Sabal minor*) has a few, usually six or so, green to bluish green palmate leaves with a V-shaped split in the center (see Plate 21). It is native to the same region as needle palm but more prevalent. Plants grow best in regions with hot, humid summer weather, though in winter established plants can tolerate brief periods of 0° Fahrenheit or below. Dwarf palmetto's blue-green leaf color develops best in a sunny site—otherwise leaves will be green. Moist soil is also preferred. In the wild, plants may be exposed to flooding over the roots in winter. Due to their limited number of leaves, dwarf palmettos often look best when planted in groups. Extensive roots make older plants difficult to move.

Windmill palm (*Trachycarpus fortunei*) and its close relatives grow more treelike than *Rhapidophyllum hystrix* or *Sabal minor*. An occasional specimen is grown in zone 7b in New Jersey and on Long Island, proving hardy if planted in a sheltered site, and it is certainly hardy in zone 8. Windmill palm needs ample water but dislikes wet soils. Rich, fertile loam soil produces the best growth. Reliably cold weather results in hardier plants than alternate spells of warm and cold weather. Within five years a New Jersey specimen of *T. wagnerianus* grew more than 4 feet tall with only isolated protection from temperatures below 15° Fahrenheit and heavy wet snow. This species prefers full sun in zone 7, light shade in zone 8.

Very primitive plants, cycads existed when dinosaurs roamed the earth. Glossy, pinnate, evergreen leaves grow in a whorl. Cycads are slow growing and long lived—a specimen at the Huntington Gardens of San Marino, California, is edging up within a decade or so on the century mark. They are also durable, even seemingly indestructible. One winter Rhapsis Gardens in south Texas experienced a record-setting, century-mark low temperature of 11° Fahrenheit that froze a cycad into a leafless, rootless, centerless, donut-shaped lump; and yet the following spring this Jurassic survivor sprouted roots and offsets. Cycads are popular in Louisiana, Mississippi, and Texas, where they add dignity and interest in the shade of southern magnolias (*Magnolia grandiflora*). In cold-winter areas they are popular houseplants because of their slow growth and sturdy nature, which makes them tolerant of abuse and neglect.

Though it looks similar to a palm, sago palm (*Cycas revoluta*) is not actually a palm but a cycad. It is native to southern Japan, where at one time "pedigreed" specimens were trophies of war, triumphantly transplanted from the loser's garden to that of the victorious shogun. Sago palm is hardy in zones 9 through 11 and marginally hardy in zone 8. Since the species suckers very freely, over time an individual plant develops into a large colony with a compact clumping form. Very dark green, gracefully arching leaves reach 4 to 6 feet long. The individual pinnae are narrow and rather stiff. Since they neither wilt nor show other signs of stress, it can be difficult to tell when sago palms need watering. Though tolerant of a certain amount of drought, they do better if not suffering from dry conditions. On the other hand, they do not take well to being continuously wet. When grown in shady sites, or when winter temperatures are cooler, sago palms might need watering only every few weeks. When grown in full sun, or when summer temperatures are high, they will need more water.

STRAP-LEAVED PLANTS

Strap-leaved plants are monocots. They have parallel venation and a stronger superficial similarity to each other than plants with lacy or bold foliage. All grasses, from closely mown turf to stately ornamental grasses and woody bamboo, might be considered a paradigm for this category of foliage shape. Grasses have culms: rounded hollow stems with thickened nodes where the leaf blades attach. They differ from rushes, which are also rounded and hollow but lack nodes, and sedges, which have three-sided stems and also lack nodes.

One magical aspect of ornamental grasses is the amenity of sound they add to a garden, the susurrus of a breeze toying with their leaves. This aspect of our senses is often neglected in designing a garden. Visual impressions get first place and sound comes last. Nakamura-sensei, a teacher in my first intensive seminar on Japanese garden art (sponsored by Kyoto University School of Art and Design in 1997), spoke of the amenity garden, a garden that should appeal to all the senses.

Attractive appearance, ease of cultivation, and minimal maintenance all combine to make Siberian iris (*Iris sibirica*) a deservedly popular perennial. Narrow, medium green, grasslike leaves form a tidy clump far more graceful than the stiff, more swordlike leaves of bearded iris. Full sun and a moist yet free-draining soil high in organic matter suit them best, and zone 3 winters are acceptable. Partner Siberian irises with herbaceous peonies (*Paeonia*) for an attractive combination both in and out of flower. While the majority of these plants reach about 3 feet tall, *I. sibirica* 'Little White' only grows to a petite 12 inches.

Because their flowers last only a day, hemerocallis need repeated deadheading to keep them tidy. Their clump-forming linear leaves appear pinched into a V shape. The leaves of most species and cultivars grow about 18 inches long but appear shorter due to their arching habit. As summer progresses some leaves start yellowing, but a gentle tug is usually all that is needed to pull them loose. Charles Cresson, the third-generation caretaker of Hedgeleigh Springs, his family's garden in Swarthmore, Pennsylvania, refers to this process as "deadleafing." Siberian iris and hemerocallis would not be interesting side by side. The effect would be much more pleasing if they were separated by a peony (*Paeonia*) and a fern-leaved meadowsweet (*Filipendula ulmaria*).

LEAF TEXTURE

In *The Tropical Look*, Robert Lee Riffle refers to *Peperomia* as a genus that includes "some of the most deliciously beautiful leaves in the world, making them unexcelled as shady groundcovers or for low bedding plants in shady tropical and subtropical regions." P. J. Klinger of the Lake Brantley Plant Corporation in Longwood, Florida, certainly agrees. As we talked one August day, he extolled the virtues of *P. caperata* 'Emerald Ripple'. There was a bed of it outside his office window and not a single leaf was unsightly. *Peperomia caperata* is a clumping species, seldom over 12 inches tall, with shiny deep green leaves puckered like the pleats in an accordion. When you consider that the growing season in Florida stretches from February 1 to December 1, you can understand the appreciation P. J. has for plants that look good for ten months. Moreover, summers are steamy, hot, humid, and rainy. Under such conditions all sorts of fungi thrive—phytophthora, mildew, and other plant pathogens. In his search for alternatives to typical bedding plants, P. J. has found that many traditional foliage plants grown by the thousands for use in dish gardens, such as peperomias, provide superior performance as alternatives to forms of *Impatiens* for shady Florida gardens. He has found several other familiar foliage plants to be strong candidates as well. Aluminum plant (*Pilea cadierei*), for example, a species native to Vietnam, has glossy deep green to bluish green leaves beautifully marked with silver blotches between the midrib and two outer veins. I have a specimen of *Pilea involucrata* 'Silver Tree' whose leaves are entirely silver. In summer I keep it in an outdoor container with a silver and rose-pink rex begonia and two Victorian brake ferns (*Pteris cretica* var. *albolineata*), which have a distinctive broad white band in the middle of their ribbonlike fronds. The container is in an area so shady that the impatiens I had placed there could not flower. The foliage plants made a very satisfactory display indeed. Red ivy (*Hemigraphis alternata*) is another groundcover plant P. J. has been trying out. Native to Malaysia, it grows in partial shade to full sun and likes things moist. Three-inch-long oval leaves have a puckered surface like a bunched-up scatter rug. Green with a bronze-purple, somewhat metallic overlay, the leaf color is more intense with increased light. Persian shield (*Strobilanthes dyeriana*) is another contender.

Most plants have leaves that are papery, smooth, and supple. Have you ever picked a hosta leaf while it was still rolled up and gently uncurled it, amazed at the slick yet soft surface? The more you look, the more there is to see. The leaves of *Bergenia* species are coriaceous, meaning they are slick and leathery but also smooth and pliable. The leaves of lamb's ear (*Stachys byzantina*), coated with numerous wooly hairs, are soft and pettable as a flannel baby blanket. Some rhododendrons have leaves that are wooly underneath. *Rhododendron yakushimanum*, for example, has a dense coat of short, soft, chestnut-fawn-colored hairs completely coating the underside of its leaves. This indumentum appears to render such leaves less palatable to deer, too. *Farfugium japonicum* 'Crispatum' is a fantastic plant for containers, or in light woodland shade for fortunate zone 7 gardeners. Rounded green leaves appear gray thanks to a felted coating of short hairs. A ruffled edge accentuates its appeal. Lungworts (*Pulmonaria*) have a bristly surface more readily felt than seen. The green-striped golden leaves of yellow-stripe bamboo (*Pleioblastus auricomus*) feel velvety on the underside when gently slipped through your fingers. Canadian ginger (*Asarum canadense*) has more modestly sized, reniform, soft green leaves with a slightly downy appearance. European ginger (*A. europaeum*) is slightly smaller yet, with very lustrous dark green leaves. *Hosta plantaginea* has leaves with a very glossy, shiny surface underscored by deeply incised veins. And on and on.

Garden visitors may not consciously note such refinement of detail. Nonetheless, you—and they, on some level—will find plant combinations that take texture into consideration more appealing than those that do not.

LEAF COMBINATIONS

I do not want to give you the idea that any leafy plant is ipso facto better than a flowering plant, or that bunching a group of them together automatically creates a great garden. It is just as easy to mix and match foliage for a poor result as for a good one. But with just a little attention to detail it should be easy to avoid some very basic mistakes. Consider this: you most likely wouldn't create a flower garden all of daisies, even if some were pink, others yellow, and a few white. Similar leaf shapes placed side by side are just as boring. A green-leaved hosta planted next to another with glaucous blue leaves, adjacent to a third with crisp white edges, rubbing shoulders with one having yellow-centered leaves—a fine collection of hostas, perhaps, but definitely not a garden (see Plate 6).

That's not to say this style isn't used. The Victorians were quite fond of the fernery, a garden devoted to ferns, with dappled shade and moist but well-drained soil high in organic matter, often created in the form of a grotto. Roger Grounds, a contemporary British authority on grasses, invented the term *grassery* for a garden composed entirely of grasses. The PepsiCo Sculpture Gardens in Purchase, New York, includes just such a grassery, designed by Russell Page in the early 1980s (see Plates 11 and 12). There are approximately forty grasses and sedges on display—small ones, tall ones, even turf (that is to say grass paths). The garden includes a specimen of Indian bean tree (*Catalpa bignonioides*), with its large heart-shaped leaves, although this is a replacement for the first tree, which experienced several problems (perhaps the tree would have fared better if it had been more established and had been stooled). I found this grassery interesting the first time I saw it, but my interest quickly palled. For me it was just too much of a solo act. On the other hand, the small grassery grown by Jeff Tareila and Risa Sackman holds its own. This may be because there are proportionately more woody plants, fewer grasses, and the house itself functions as a backdrop. Edith Eddleman's design for the great perennial border at the J. C. Raulston Arboretum of the North Carolina State University in Raleigh, North Carolina, incorporates grasses and a diverse array of herbaceous plants and shrubs. Every time I visit, in any season, the grasses have a role to play as partners to the other plants. This example, for me, is the best of the lot. It uses herbaceous perennials, shrubs, and small trees for the pattern and texture of their foliage, in combination with colors other than green and the final fillip of flowers.

When you are designing a garden based on foliage, begin by selecting plants that allow you to use a diversity of shapes. Suppose the site you are thinking about is a patch of deciduous woodland with humus-rich, nicely moist soil. Astilbes would do well, as would cimicifugas. And ferns are the sine qua non of this kind of place. A fern planted by two similarly lacy (dare I say fernlike) plants is not very interesting. Start over, keeping the astilbe—let's say it's *Astilbe* 'Deutschland', whose lacy medium green leaves are accented with a froth of white flowers in July. Pair this with a hosta, one with medium leaves. Playing the tapered oval leaf shape of the hosta against the dissected astilbe leaf is definitely more interesting. On this basic level, shape against shape, an improvement has already been made. And there is room for other options, more possibilities. Will the hosta have a plain green leaf? Perhaps it will be *Hosta* 'Green Fountain' with its shiny green 10-inch-long leaves that form a dense mound. Or should it be a hosta with white flowers, such as *H. sieboldii* var. *alba* with its bright green leaves and a tallish scape of white flowers in August? It might help to remember that the astilbe flowers nearly a month earlier than this last hosta. For the greatest impact and longest span of effectiveness the best choice might be to pair the astilbe with a white-variegated hosta. While the two different foliage shapes remain the same, the variegated hosta leaves remain attractive for months and are further accentuated when the astilbe is in flower. Options include white-edged *H. crispula*, with lavender flowers appearing when the astilbe is also in flower, or *H. undulata* var. *univittata*, whose leaves are both yellowish green and blue-green, with a central white blotch and some white streaking. Gardens must have more diversity and complexity than can be created with only two types of plants: now we need the third basic shape, something linear and grasslike. Grasses, with only a couple of exceptions, are sun lovers. *Liriope muscari* is a readily available grasslike plant for leafy soil in shade. Narrow, dark green, evergreen leaves gracefully arch over for a moundlike habit.

> When you are designing a garden based on foliage, begin by selecting plants that allow you to use a diversity of shapes.

Now that the plants have been selected, there is one more step. How many of each kind of plant do you need to create the proper balance? The primary factor is how much space you have to fill. A city lot with a small back garden measured in square feet is a different situation than a sweeping suburban site of an acre or more. Clearly, the larger the site the more plants it requires. You cannot create a drift of one kind of plant, nor is it as simple as using equal numbers of each kind of plant. Since the plants are not equal in size, volume, or scale, using equal numbers would not be the most attractive solution. Always plan on using more finely textured, smaller plants to aesthetically balance the bolder, more coarsely textured ones. And keep in mind that in groups of less than a dozen plants, odd numbers are generally more visually pleasing than even. Visually, over a dozen items are not "counted" as readily at a glance.

For the sake of discussion let's say you need about thirteen plants. If you choose three hostas and three astilbes, that leaves room for seven liriopes. Plant the astilbes in a scalene triangle, two at the front of the bed and one in back. Plant the hostas in a similar triangle but with two in back and one in front. Now weave the liriopes along in front, but avoid planting them all in a single lollipop row. This simple design will be quietly pleasing from spring through early autumn. If space allows and you must have flowers, use white impatiens for additional summer interest.

Foliage is simple and easy to use as a foundation for good garden design, but there are a couple of points to keep in mind. First, make sure all the plants grow with the same conditions of soil, moisture, and light. I remember a display garden at the 1992 Floriade in Holland. There was an exquisite combination of red-leaved coleus (*Solenostemon scutellarioides*) and *Gazania rigens*, with warm orange-red flowers. "Aha!" I thought to myself. "The coleus wants a moist soil, and gazania needs good drainage. This must be some new cutting-edge horticultural technique." Upon inquiring how they did that, I got my answer: the coleus were replaced every three weeks or so. Not my style of gardening, nor, I imagine, one that most gardeners have the time, energy, or budget to allow for. Secondly, look for sturdy plants with few problems—mildew-resistant cultivars of *Phlox paniculata* such as 'David' and *Monarda* 'Jacob Cline', for example. This is basic for any sensible gardening. Focusing now on foliage: look first at the shapes of leaves before playing around with color. Form follows function. Good black-and-white photography has a certain elegance and clarity without the need for color. In the same way, overlaying color on poor leaf combinations will not create a well-designed garden. Consider a pairing of Canadian ginger (*Asarum canadense*) and maidenhair fern (*Adiantum pedatum*), two easy, shade-tolerant plants (see Plate 4). The ginger has a medium green reniform leaf; the maidenhair fern has apple-green fronds that are pedatisect (palmately divided with the outermost lobe at each side, the lobes themselves divided, in a horseshoelike arrangement). These two plants complement each other, creating the graceful pattern of a strong blocky shape against a finely textured lacelike form. Contrast this to a pairing of *Hosta* 'Thomas Hogg' and *Polygonatum* ×*hybridum* 'Variegatum'. Both have oval leaves and a white margin. One is taller and arching; the other is more low growing and forms a clump. It requires a second look, a closer inspection, to appreciate that there are two different plants. Variegated foliage is not sufficient to carry a design lacking appropriate combination of form. Before moving on to colors other than green, begin with shape and texture.

CHAPTER 2

❧

Considerations of Color

If you live in a temperate region, your expectation—your default mechanism, if you will—is that plants have green leaves. Green as grass—green trees, green shrubs, green perennials, green groundcovers. Some trees, shrubs, and perennials native to temperate climates have a copper to red color when they first emerge from winter's protective bud, turning green as they mature. Many more trees and shrubs, as well as a few perennials, have orange to red or purple color in fall. Tropical regions have a greater proportion of colorful foliage plants.

Sometimes plants sport, spontaneously mutating in either flower or leaf. A normally green-leaved shrub might suddenly have a variegated shoot, for example. Gardeners can isolate and propagate such aberrant offspring through tissue culture or by grafting. Some plants are very stable; others, such as hostas, are extremely changeable. Novelty may have a fascination all its own, but keep in mind that there is a major difference between a well-designed garden and a collection of plants.

HEALTHY PLANTS

It is important to develop an understanding of fertilizers and how to use them, and your starting place should always be with a soil test. Your local cooperative extension agency can sell you a test kit with instructions on how to take a sample and where to send it for analysis. At minimum the results will provide figures for the soil's nitrogen, phosphorus, and potash levels, as well as the pH, and suggest how much of what nutrients are necessary to grow a lawn, shrubs, perennials, vegetables, or whatever else it is you want to grow.

Nitrogen, phosphorus, and potash, often referred to as macronutrients, are the three essential elements of fertilizer. All fertilizer labels are required to list the content's proportion of nitrogen, phosphorus, and potash, sometimes using the acronyms of N, P, and K. Adequate nitrogen is fundamental for leaf growth. Healthy plants are characterized by good green leaves, though different plants have different needs. A lawn needs more nitrogen to grow well than do trees and shrubs, just as spinach and other leafy vegetables need more nitrogen than do carrots, for example. New leaves opening from buds on the tips of shoots require relatively more nitrogen than do older leaves, and they are given priority. A plant will move nitrogen from old growth to young growth if the plant is not receiving an adequate supply. Unable to maintain chlorophyll production, older leaves will then turn yellow and the overall growth rate of the plant will slow down. This should not be confused, however, with the normal decline of growth in autumn.

Too much nitrogen also has negative results. Leaves become softer, more appealing to pests, and more prone to diseases such as mildew and rust. Stems grow weaker and plants must be staked to keep them from falling over. Excessive nitrogen applied too late in the season promotes lush growth that has no time to mature before cold weather arrives—a wasted effort for the plants. I usually reduce nitrogen application in my garden in early to mid July, certainly by the time cicadas are shrilling in the treetops. Excessive nitrogen can also affect some variegated plants, overstimulating the leaves so that they produce more chlorophyll and turn green.

Magnesium, a secondary nutrient, is also important for good green leaves as it too is necessary for chlorophyll production. When soil pH is neutral to alkaline there is usually sufficient magnesium available for plants, but when soils have an acid, low pH there may be a magnesium deficiency. Older leaves turn yellow and their edges may curl up, or they may turn yellow with only the veins remaining green. Application of dolomitic lime, which contains magnesium as well as calcium, is a simple treatment for lawns and vegetable or flower gardens. Too much lime can harm ericaceous, acid-loving plants such as rhododendrons and azaleas, which are unable to utilize iron if the pH is higher than they favor (iron is another necessary element in chlorophyll molecules). Magnesium sulfate is readily available as Epsom salts. After dissolving Epsom salts in water (a tablespoon to a quart) you can apply the solution to plants that need magnesium to green up their leaves. Moreover, a pleasant, relaxing soak in a tub of hot water treated with Epsom salts is a good end to a hard day of gardening.

Iron is most available to plants if the pH is slightly to extremely acid. The influence of a high pH may keep plants from assimilating the iron they need, resulting in anemic leaves poor in chlorophyll. This physiological problem is called chlorosis. If the soil pH level for acid-loving plants such as *Pachysandra terminalis*, rhododendrons, and hollies is too high, the plants will have difficulty assimilating magnesium and iron. Chlorotic plants exhibit yellow leaves with green veins. A quick, temporary fix can be achieved with chelated iron. Chelating agents have the ability to maintain iron and other necessary metals in a non-ionized form that is soluble in water, allowing these micronutrients to be easily absorbed by the plants. Dissolve the dull yellow crystals in water following the directions on the package and apply to the leaves and surrounding soil. The long-term solution is to lower the pH to the appropriate level.

On the whole it is better to feed your plants a balanced diet with complete nutrients rather than a single-element fertilizer. Phosphorus is essential in all phases of plant growth but is especially associated with vigorous root growth and increased resistance to disease, as well as plant maturation. Potash is another name for potassium. It too is essential for healthy plant growth. The role played by potash is less well understood than those played by nitrogen and phosphorus, but we do know that potash helps plants survive the effects of adverse soil or weather conditions, contributes to the production of sturdy stems, and, for some plants, improves resistance to disease.

Regardless of whether you choose to use organic or inorganic fertilizers, which is a personal choice, it is true that having organic matter in the soil is critical for healthy plants. Humus, compost, and other organic "roughage" improve soil structure, holding moisture and nutrients in sandy soil and opening airways in heavy clay soils. Soil microorganisms that live in the organic matter also increase the availability of nutrients. Unlike money in the bank, organic matter does not remain and increase. Supplies need constant renewal. When you comprehend that one acre of deciduous woodland drops 1 to 1½ tons of leaves and litter every single year, you will have some idea of the substantial scale of cycling biomass in the natural scheme of things in temperate zones.

Watering is also important—lovely if it arrives as needed from the heavens above, but sooner or later, more often than not, we need to supplement with a hose. Water thoroughly when necessary, and then wait until more water is needed before again turning on the hose. Don't guess: use a rain gauge to keep track of how much fell and when, in order to provide an accurate record of precipitation. When you do irrigate it also helps to know how long to turn the water on for. Hose diameter, the spray pattern of the sprinkler head, and water pressure all influence the delivery. While you cannot calibrate a sprinkler, it is possible to determine how best to utilize it. Place several clean tuna cans in a grid, especially at the edges and center of the sprinkler's delivery pattern. Use a ruler to measure how much water has collected in each can after the hose has been in use for thirty minutes, and check again after an hour. You'll want to know how much water is delivered in what portion of the spray when the hose is run for how long.

The type of soil you are watering should also influence irrigation methods. After a few dry days dig a hole and place inside it, about an inch or so into the soil, a coffee can with both ends removed. Fill the can to its top with water and see how quickly the water sinks into the soil. This is your infiltration rate. As soon as the can is empty, promptly fill it with water a second time and watch how soon it empties. This is your retention rate. Ideally the water should sink in at a quick to moderate speed the first time but more slowly the second time, an indication that the water is percolating freely into the soil but hanging on once it gets there. If it drains quickly both times, the soil is sandy. Sandy soil is low in loam and organic matter, usually poor in nutrients, and quick to dry out, warming up faster in spring. It will need to be watered more frequently. If the water drains slowly both times, the soil is probably high in clay. Heavy clay soil is usually fertile and high in nutrients; but it is also composed of tightly packed particles that are difficult for roots to penetrate, and it lacks air, which can lead to root rot in susceptible plants. Such soil is cold and slow to warm up at winter's end. Watering is needed less frequently and must be applied with care so that water does not puddle on the surface or run off without penetrating.

Try to add organic matter to the soil whenever you dig up the ground, whether you're planting something new or lifting and replanting an existing plant.

Organic matter, as the oft repeated (and always valid) statement goes, will improve difficult sandy and clayey soil types and help to maintain healthy ones. Simply mulching with shredded autumn leaves will be helpful. Try to add organic matter to the soil whenever you dig up the ground, whether you're planting something new or lifting and replanting an existing plant. Compost is the easiest organic matter to come by since every garden—even a tiny garden such as the one kept by my sister, Haya Meyerowitz, on a balcony in a suburb of Jerusalem—produces plant waste, and since every kitchen produces waste in the form of potato peels, coffee grounds, old lettuce leaves, and such. Mixing a quantity of greens (weeds, grass clippings, manure from vegetarian animals) with a greater quantity of browns (autumn leaves, mulch hay, straw, shredded newspaper) will provide a quicker decomposition than could be produced by either type on its own. Turn the pile frequently to speed up the process, or let it sit for a more leisurely approach and a compost that will rot in its own time. Compost is ready to use as a soil amendment when the material is an earthy brown, uniform in appearance rather than recognizable as various different ingredients, and when it gives off a pleasant mushroom smell.

No matter the potential of any plant, if it is not well grown the results are bound to be disappointing. Imagine a drooping coleus (*Solenostemon scutellarioides*) in need of a drink, or a pachysandra with green-veined yellow leaves trying to grow next to a new concrete sidewalk—not a pretty sight. Random applications of fertilizer are unlikely to provide the balance of nutrients your plants need, and applying fertilizer without water can actually harm them. Understanding how plants work is the first step in learning how to keep them healthy.

GREEN LEAVES

I'm like Rudyard Kipling's insatiable elephant's child, always asking why: why is the sky blue, why is the grass green, why can't a cow have kittens? For the purposes of our discussion I'll limit myself to answering the second question. While to our eyes sunlight appears white, if you have ever played with a prism you know that it contains all the colors of the rainbow, from red through violet. Grass, like most other plants, is green because its leaves absorb all colors except yellows, oranges, and some blues; and these reflected colors are perceived as green.

Chlorophyll—named from the Greek *chloros* (green) and *phyll* (leaf)—is a green pigment that absorbs most reds and some blues (there are actually two forms of chlorophyll, but since they're both green let's not worry about more details). Chlorophyll uses this absorbed light energy to convert atmospheric carbon dioxide into sugar, a process we call photosynthesis. Since there is more energy in sunlight than in the portion of the spectrum absorbed by chlorophyll, accessory pigments help the leaves make use of other wavelengths. Carotenoids, which are yellow to orange in color (they also provide the color for egg yolks and carrots), are able to absorb some of the blue and green wavelengths that chlorophyll is unable to absorb and pass that energy on to the chlorophyll molecules. Xanthophylls are another group of pale yellow pigments that also absorb some blues and greens, colors not available to chlorophyll.

NON-GREEN LEAVES

Foliage gardens can be as colorful, sometimes even more colorful, than a garden based on flowers. *Canna* 'Tropicanna' has leaves of peach, orange, red, purple, and dark green (see Plates 42 and 43). It is a colorful accent for my hot, tropical border from the time a 22-inch-diameter pot of it goes outdoors in late May until I haul it under cover at the end of September, sometimes even later. That's a four-month return for watering and occasional fertilizing, as opposed to the couple of weeks of bloom featured by *Liatris spicata* 'Kobold' and *Monarda* 'Jacob Cline'. Both plants are attractive while in flower, but the effect lasts only a brief part of the summer, and they require tedious deadheading afterwards.

Eric Shalit, as previously mentioned, features big, bold foliage in his Seattle garden. As it turns out, Eric also has a thing for plants with burgundy to purple or silver leaves, and for those with patterning and variegation, striation, or spots. He makes use of color but not at the expense of texture. There are lots of cannas in Eric's garden—some 10 feet tall with purple leaves, others with stripes. He cares little about their flowers. His gray, thistlelike cardoons (*Cynara cardunculus*) used to be the big plants but are now, reports Eric, dwarfed by the real giants. Finely textured, gold-leaved *Robinia pseudoacacia* 'Frisia', gray, spikey South African honeybush (*Melianthus major*), and orange-, red-, and umber-striped *Phormium* 'Maori Sunset' are colorful, but note the underlying leaf shapes. Think first of form and outline, then color.

YELLOW

No doubt you are well aware that not all leaves are green. Some, for example, are yellow. Yellow-leaved plants are able to grow nearly as vigorously as plants whose leaves are entirely green because they possess carotenoids and xanthophylls. While plants with yellow leaves lacks chlorophyll, such plants are still quite capable of photosynthesis and growth.

Healthy green leaves produce chlorophyll throughout the growing season. Aging leaves lose their ability to produce chlorophyll and turn yellow before falling off the plant. Additionally, as summer wanes and the days become shorter, chlorophyll production ceases in deciduous plants. As the chlorophyll disappears from the leaf, the yellow pigments that were masked by its presence are revealed. This is why many autumn leaves turn yellow.

Would you have any idea what shade of yellow "gamboge" might be without checking a dictionary first? Not me. Yellow-leaved plants range from appealing to sickly. They are often called "golden." You will not find "yellow

A well-considered combination of leaf shapes, including the plain green leaves of *Pulmonaria rubra*, the grasslike blades of *Liriope muscari,* and the sturdy, whorled leaves of *Pachysandra terminalis*. This foliage requires minimal maintenance and provides long-term interest in a shady garden. Illustration by Redenta Soprano.

Using the same leaf shapes—indeed, the same plants—this combination features variegated cultivars instead of entirely green species. The attractively silver-spotted leaves of *Pulmonaria saccharata* 'Mrs. Moon', the gold-edged linear leaves of *Liriope muscari* 'Gold Band', and the crisp white-margined leaves of *Pachysandra terminalis* 'Silver Edge' create a lively planting. Illustration by Redenta Soprano.

hinoki cypress" in a catalog, though "golden hinoki cypress" is readily available. The word "golden" may sound richer and more exciting than plain "yellow," but it is not especially accurate. Gold is warm, heavy, and massive, while yellow is light, lively, and fresh. Yellow-leaved cultivars, and those with yellow flowers, often have names that suggest their golden character, names such as 'Aurea' or 'Aureus' for warm golden hues, 'Citrinus' for clear yellow, 'Luteus' for yellow with a hint of orange, 'Flavus' or 'Lutescens' for a paler yellow, and 'Ochroleucus' for a yellow with a hint of brown made pale with a tinting of white. These may be subtle nuances, but they are differences: yellow versus gold, bright versus pale.

RED AND PURPLE

Compared to green, yellow, or silver, purple is a dark color. Photographers are well aware of this, since focusing on somber-leaved plants means opening the lens aperture to let in more light than when taking a picture of adjacent green-leaved plants. When using these dark-leaved plants, add a brighter companion to lighten things up. Perhaps you have chosen *Canna* 'Tropicanna' for your starting point, with its vividly colored leaves, and in looking for a linear companion you decide upon purple fountain grass (*Pennisetum setaceum* 'Ruby Giant'). Now select a plant with chartreuse, lemon-lime leaves to add a lighter accent. A couple of ornamental sweet potatoes fit the bill: *Ipomoea batatas* 'Margarita' with its spade-shaped yellow-green leaves and *I. batatas* 'Ivory Jewel' with its white-splashed green to chartreuse leaves.

Similarly, I've planted *Canna* 'Intrigue' in the bed beneath my study window, in a sheltered spot right next to the house so that the rhizomes winter over from year to year. Their tall stems with narrow, dark copper-purple leaves form the background. The next layer out includes *Dahlia* 'Bishop of Llandaff', with dark, serrate foliage and scarlet-red flowers, and *Hemerocallis* 'Heart of Africa', with fountains of narrow, grasslike green leaves and, in July and August, flowers of the deepest plum color with a warm tangerine throat. Annual flowers fill in the next row, since tulip bulbs are planted each fall and discarded after blooming in spring—a sequence that does not permit the use of perennials. I may plant, for example, *Zinnia* 'Envy', which has light green flowers, *Nicotiana langsdorffii*, and edge the very front of the border with silver lamb's ear (*Stachys byzantina*). I just love this set of foliage combinations accented with flowers: silver to soft green, soft green to dark purple.

Anthocyanins are water-soluble pigments that color leaves, fruits, and flowers. The color might be spread throughout the leaf, as with *Tradescantia pallida*

'Purple Heart' or *Canna* 'Intrigue', or it may be located just along the petiole and major veins, as with bloody dock (*Rumex sanguineus*). In springtime, emerging shoots of some temperate-climate plants such as herbaceous peonies (*Paeonia*) and young leaves of red-flowered astilbes and andromedas such as *Pieris formosa* var. *forrestii* contain anthocyanins and display attractive reddish color (see Plate 110). It is a mystery, though, why certain plants have this response to short day length, when sunlight is weaker than in summer.

Considering that day length is more constant towards the equator, why do plants such as mango (a fun houseplant to raise from a pit in the same way as an avocado) have red leaves when they first grow? Tropical plants that experience a rapid growth spurt often show red color in young leaves. One theory suggests that such leaves are more "cost-effective" for plants to produce than chlorophyll-rich green leaves. Since grazing and browsing animals have a predilection for tender new growth, it makes more sense for plants to produce new leaves that are red to purple, rather than investing energy in the manufacture of chlorophyll. The color could also function as a screen for ultraviolet radiation, though it is more often the colorless flavonoids, abundant in leaf surfaces, that serve this purpose.

Many plants growing in shady tropical forests have leaves that are either entirely red-purple or green above and bright purple underneath. *Calathea lancifolia* is a Brazilian native with olive-green leaves marked with a darker midrib and many dark green spots on top, and a beautiful purplish red on the underside. *Maranta bicolor*, from northeastern South America, produces leaves that are olive-green on the surface, with feathery gray markings and darker green blotches, and a deep wine color beneath. Some hypothesize that these additional pigments provide a way to bounce light back to the photosynthetic chlorophyll, something that would be quite useful in the very low light conditions of the jungle floor, but this has not been reliably proven.

There are a few cultivars of beet (*Beta vulgaris*) grown for their deep rich red-purple leaf color, including *B. vulgaris* 'MacGregor's Favourite' and *B. vulgaris* 'Bull's Blood'. As anyone who has peeled and cooked raw beets is aware, they also contain water-soluble red pigment. This pigment, however, is not anthocyanin but betalain. Betalains are found in a small number of plants, including pokeberries, celosia, amaranthus, and spinach, most commonly in their flowers.

Some plants have hairy leaves. These hairs are nonliving epidermal outgrowths called trichomes, and they can modify or influence leaf color. The large, soft, jagged-toothed leaves and trailing stems of velvet plant (*Gynura aurantiaca*), also known as purple passion plant, look purple because they are densely clothed with violet-purple trichomes. But if you shaved off these trichomes the plant would be green. The young leaves of naranjilla (*Solanum quitoense*) are a lovely soft purple and white just as they unfold. As they grow, the leaves retain purple hairs on the underside, and at maturity have only a short fuzz of purple hairs on the midrib and larger veins on the large green leaves.

GRAY, SILVER, AND BLUE

I love the look of gray (or silver, or glaucous blue) foliage. It blends with any flower color, lightens shady places, and looks so cool on a hot summer day. I have another planting of *Canna* 'Intrigue', this time placed in a very narrow bed along the deck, with *Perilla frutescens* adding its dark purple leaves. Alleviating this black hole of foliage is *Plectranthus argentatus*, with its barely fuzzy silver leaves. This is especially attractive early in the morning when tiny water droplets glitter at the edges of its leaves. This overflow relief mechanism, which causes leaves to secrete water, is known as guttation. It also occurs in lady's mantle (*Alchemilla mollis*), among other plants.

Why do some plants have gray leaves? A couple of different mechanisms give leaves this look. Each serves a specific purpose, increasing survival under difficult conditions.

Consider the hot, dry conditions of a desert in western North America or the Mediterranean maquis. Some plants that grow in these places have hairy leaves. Lamb's ear (*Stachys byzantina*) is a popular garden perennial with fuzzy leaves. It used to be thought that hairy leaves reduced transpiration to protect these plants from water loss. The process is more sophisticated than that, however. The silver or white trichomes that make *Stachys byzantina* so pettable actually keep the leaf cooler by reflecting infrared radiation. The leaf thereby avoids potentially lethal high temperatures and, since it is cooler, water loss through transpiration is also reduced.

Interestingly enough, trichomes can serve the opposite purpose and keep leaves warmer. Leaves densely coated with trichomes, such as those of high mountain plants like edelweiss (*Leontopodium alpinum*), have extra protection against cold nights, the trichomes keeping them a few degrees warmer than they would be otherwise. This explains too why many edelweiss grown in nonalpine rock gardens are green rather than gray. They do not need the same degree of protection in the more benign conditions found at lower elevations.

An interesting adaptation to xeric conditions can be found in eastern red-bud (*Cercis canadensis*). Native from Massachusetts to northern Florida, west to Missouri, Texas, and even down into northern Mexico, eastern redbud includes several botanical varieties that are environmentally induced morphologies. Where it grows in eastern woodlands the minimum rainfall is 35 inches per year. In the more arid regions of southeastern New Mexico and north central Texas, into the Texas panhandle and Oklahoma, precipitation ranges from 30 down to 20 inches of rain per year. Eastern redbuds growing here are found as *C. canadensis* var. *texensis*. They have a waxy coating on their leathery, dark green, reniform leaves. Though this variety is less cold hardy, only to zone 8, 'Oklahoma' is said to be hardy to the warmer portion of zone 6. In the far western regions of its range, in the Trans-Pecos region and into mountain canyons of the Chihuahuan Desert, annual precipitation may be as little as 12 inches per year. *Cercis canadensis* var. *mexicana* protects its foliage with a leaf covering of pubescent fuzz. These adaptations are expressed where rainfall is limited. When either variety is grown in wetter regions or with supplemental irrigation, the waxy or fuzzy nature of the leaf is reduced or suppressed.

Trichomes seem to have the added benefit of protecting plants from pests. Hairy leaves are not as popular with chewing and sucking insects or leaf-cutter bees. In fact, I have noticed that even white-tailed deer tend to leave fuzzy-leaved plants alone.

There is a downside to these plants, however. Plants with a dense coat of trichomes do not photosynthesize as well as plants lacking the hairs, since they reflect more light than just the infrared wavelengths. Hairy-leaved plants need to grow in conditions of full sunlight and often require well-drained soils as well. Otherwise they become subject to various rots and molds.

Other dryland plants use epicuticular wax (a fancy way of naming a loose reflective surface wax on the leaf surface). This wax is easily removed. Picking fresh, ripe blueberries in June, however gently, leaves a blue-black smudge on their silver-blue surface. Similarly, just touch a succulent specimen of *Echeveria elegans* 'Kesselringii' with its blue-gray leaves in a ball-like rosette and see the bluish bloom wipe off. The fact that even the lowly cabbage coats its glaucous leaves with epicuticular wax may be confirmed by rubbing the older leaf's surface to remove the wax and expose the green beneath. What's the use of this wax? No doubt it reduces water loss. But it also keeps the leaf surface drier, thereby reducing the possibility of fungal disease or algae growth; reflects away infrared radiation to keep the leaf cooler; and contains colorless flavonoids that filter out harmful ultraviolet radiation.

VARIEGATION

Variegation is the term used to describe leaves that are blotched, streaked, striped, freckled, or otherwise spattered with some color other than green. While any of the Latin terms for color that appear as cultivar names—'Aureus', for example—may refer to flowers as well as leaves, the names for variegation are certain to apply to foliage. The secondary color in variegated leaves is most often yellow or white. Linear-leaved monocots almost always exhibit lengthwise stripes following the pattern of venation, as is true of *Iris pallida* 'Argenteovariegata' with its crisp white markings and *I. pallida* 'Aureomarginata', which is brushed with buttery yellow. A number of ornamental maiden grasses (*Miscanthus sinensis*) display conspicuous stripes: 'Cabaret' has 1-inch-wide, ribbonlike leaves with a creamy white center and narrow dark green margins, while 'Cosmopolitan' reverses the effect with its dark green center and creamy white margins. Of course there's always one that needs to be different—*M. sinensis* 'Strictus' has transverse, horizontal bands of creamy yellow that appear with warm weather.

Hostas are monocots as well but have blocky leaves, in contrast to the narrow, linear blades of various grasses. Because hostas feature bolder shapes, and because they can be genetically unstable when it comes to variegation, there are many options to choose from—from something subtle and simple to something quite striking. Hostas present this tremendous diversity on a couple of basic patterns of variegation. There are marginata types: green-leaved hostas with a white or yellow edge. Picta or mediovariegata types have a central blotch that may also be either white or yellow. Some have yellow centers that fade to white. Other, primarily older, cultivars start the season as yellow-variegated plants but mature to all-green. A few cultivars are prone to change: I've had *Hosta* 'Frances Williams' throw an all-yellow shoot on a crown otherwise producing normally yellow-margined leaves. Streaky, splotchy hostas with irregular patterning are the most unstable and may turn solid green, solid yellow, or revert to a more stable edge- or center-patterned variegation.

The patterning in some variegated plants can be an irregular overall mottling caused by a viral infection, as with the prettily yellow-marbled foliage of *Abutilon pictum* 'Thompsonii', a nice stable form of flowering maple that will

> One reason why it is important to figure out what causes variegation is that the different mechanisms involved will influence a plant's propagation.

Plate 1. The lacy fronds of maidenhair fern (*Adiantum pedatum*) create a waterfall-like effect as they tumble down the face of a wall.

Plate 2. The slim leaves of moisture-loving blue flag (*Iris versicolor*) delicately weave through the fronds of a *Dryopteris* species for a pleasing partnership of linear and lacy.

Plate 3. The substantial *Hosta sieboldiana* var. *elegans* anchors the ribbonlike, linear leaves of sweet flag (*Acorus calamus*).

Plate 4. Pattern play on a more refined scale: the apple-green fingerlike fronds of maidenhair fern (*Adiantum pedatum*) arch protectively over the rounded forest-green leaves of Canadian ginger (*Asarum canadense*).

Plate 5. Good plants cannot salvage poor design. The messy haystack effect of daylilies (*Hemerocallis*) backed by a grass and fronted by *Liriope muscari* 'Gold Band' has little if anything to recommend it.

Plate 6. Contrast of shape is necessary for good design. The identical leaf shape of different hostas grouped together provides no focal point.

Plate 7. Old-fashioned *Hosta ventricosa* grows in a groundcover of English ivy (*Hedera helix*). The two plants contrast pleasingly in shape, scale, and shades of green, proving that simple, familiar plants with dissimilar leaf shapes can create just the sort of effective combinations that result in attractive gardens.

Plate 8. *Hosta sieboldiana* emerges from a mass of sweet woodruff (*Galium odoratum*).

Plate 9. Never overlook the serendipitous effect of happenstance: *Hosta sieboldiana* var. *elegans* acquired *Geranium macrorrhizum* as a partner when the hardy geranium spread beyond its original planting site. The combination is charming while the geranium is in flower and will endure even after the flowers fade.

Plate 10. Plants can solve landscape problems in addition to merely looking good. This clever planting of ornamental grasses—a taller *Miscanthus* species, a softly mounding *Pennisetum* species, red-tipped *Imperata cylindrica* 'Rubra', steely blue *Festuca ovina* 'Glauca', and more— so thickly fills this small front garden that children can no longer cut across the corner.

Plates 11 (opposite) and 12 (above). The grassery designed by Russell Page for the PepsiCo Sculpture Gardens, seen here at its peak in early autumn when subtle colors have shifted and flowers and seed heads have added to the display.

Plate 13. New buds appear just a few days after this purple-leaved smokebush (*Cotinus coggygria* 'Royal Purple') has been given its regular springtime cutting back. Stooling encourages the production of long, straight shoots and larger-than-usual leaves.

Plate 14. Similar colors neither conceal the situation nor improve the design when leaves are too similar in shape, as with this pairing of coleus and hosta.

Plate 15. A golden hosta and purple perilla (*Perilla frutescens*) remain a poor combination despite contrasting colors. Notice too how the purple leaves recede and are less visible than the yellow leaves.

Plate 16. Attention to detail is important: the silver foliage of lavender cotton (*Santolina chamaecyparissus*) accentuates the dark green needles of dwarf mugo pine (*Pinus mugo* var. *pumilio*).

Plate 17. A summer border at Longwood Gardens in Kennett Square, Pennsylvania, relies on foliage color to create a superb display. Seen at a distance, the somber purple-black of *Hibiscus acetosella* 'Red Shield', rich violet of *Tradescantia pallida* 'Purple Heart', and soft silver of *Senecio cineraria* 'Cirrus' create a lively combination, accented by the blue flowers of *Salvia farinacea*.

Plate 18. The combination holds up even with a more detailed inspection of the border, since leaf shape and surface texture continue to engage our attention.

Plate 19. Shape, texture, and color work well together in this interesting combination of two familiar plants: lamb's ear (*Stachys byzantina*) and yucca (*Yucca filamentosa*). The swordlike green leaves of the yucca are gentled by the furry gray foliage of the lamb's ear.

Plate 20. At first glance one might mistake this summer phlox for some exciting new gray-leaved cultivar instead of realizing it is suffering from serious mildew problems.

Plate 21. The sturdy foliage of dwarf palmetto (*Sabal minor*) creates a lush display in the dense shady woodland of this Louisiana garden.

Plate 22. Foliage color enlivens a shady garden. Tom Mannion combines *Aucuba japonica* 'Gold Dust', *Liriope spicata*, and a lacy fern in his Alexandria, Virginia, garden.

Plate 23. The dark evergreen background provided by an azalea allows *Pittosporum tobira* 'Variegatum' to better display its white-edged gray-green leaves.

Plate 24. A subtle, pleasing display is created when the ubiquitous *Pachysandra terminalis* is partnered with *Ophiopogon jaburan*. In combination these two evergreen plants gain an attraction neither would have on its own.

Plate 25. The blocky rounded leaves of coltsfoot (*Tussilago farfara*), which is frequently considered a weed, in partnership with the thin evergreen ribbonlike leaves of *Liriope spicata*. Designer Wolfgang Oehme included this attractive carpet of foliage in the shade at the Towson Courthouse Garden in Towson, Maryland.

Plate 26. Cut-leaf Japanese maple (*Acer palmatum* f. *dissectum*) trails its filigree burgundy foliage over the tidy groundcover created by the blunt purple-flushed leaves of *Ajuga reptans* 'Atropurpurea'. Red-flowered, copper-leaved *Begonia semperflorens* serves as an attractive summer accent. This simple bijou combination works as well in city shade as in a suburban locale.

Plate 27. Drought-tolerant, shade-tolerant, deer-proof lungworts (*Pulmonaria*) are invaluable for the shady garden, featuring silver to silver-spotted leaves.

not cause problems for either other plants or the gardener (see Plate 70). The other possibility is that the plant is a chimera, named for a mythological monster with a lion's head, goat's body, and serpent's tail. A chimera is a plant made up of genetically different tissues. A red apple with a tidy yellow-speckled skin segment is a chimera. So are lots of variegated plants.

One reason why it is important to figure out what causes variegation is that the different mechanisms involved will influence a plant's propagation (and I am indebted to Bob Brown of Cotswold Garden Flowers in Worcestershire, England, for his explanation of this). For instance, some variegated plants can be raised from seed. With both *Lunaria annua* 'Variegata', an honesty (also called money plant) with white-speckled leaves, and *Aquilegia vulgaris* 'Woodside' (Vervaeneana Group), a columbine with yellow-speckled leaves, speckling is inherited and carried by the seed. In general, plants exhibiting finely dispersed speckled variegation over their entire leaf surface will produce variegated offspring from seed. When the entire leaf displays this patterning, as with the columbine and honesty, 100 percent of the seedlings will be variegated. (Keep in mind, though, that all columbines, including *A. vulgaris* 'Woodside', are promiscuous to an amazing degree. Should there be green-leaved columbines within 30 feet or so, the 'Woodside' seed will be of mixed parentage and some seedlings will have green leaves. Keep the columbines chastely separated, though, and the 'Woodside' offspring will display the yellow-speckled leaves.) If the variegation randomly covers only a portion of the leaves, a matching portion of seedlings will be variegated.

When variegation is chimeric it is clearly organized at the edges or middles of leaves. Plants have two distinct layers: an inside layer and an outside layer. When the outside layer is devoid, or mostly devoid, of chlorophyll, the expression of this shows most strongly at the edges of the leaves, where the outside layer is the only layer visible. (Chlorophyll is not produced in the epidermal ["skin"] cells of a leaf.) The middle of the leaf may exhibit a subtle graying, as the chlorophyll-free outside layer influences the appearance of the green inside layer (*Cornus alba* 'Elegantissima', for example, a lovely shrubby Tartarian dogwood, has white margins to its gray-green leaves). This outside layer extends only to the hypocotyl, where the root tissue begins, and the inside layer extends only as far as the flower. Therefore seed will lack the genetic information for chlorophyll production. Seedlings will germinate with white leaves and die as soon as the food stored in the cotyledon is used up. Organized chimeric variegation in the outside layer, where seedlings germinate with white leaves and die, can be a very useful thing. Otherwise an invasive plant in its green-leaved form such as codlins and cream

(*Epilobium hirsutum*) will be effectively sterile in its variegated cultivar, *E. hirsutum* 'Well Creek'.

Likewise, root cuttings of variegated plants—for example, *Phlox paniculata* 'Norah Leigh' and *P. paniculata* 'Harlequin'—will produce only green-leaved plants. (*Phlox paniculata* is traditionally produced by root cuttings so that plants are free of stem nematodes.) This is because the variegation is a cell defect and not a genetic one. As long as the flaw persists through cell division, portions of the leaves will remain white or cream. The roots, however, contain the correct genetic code, and the shoots they produce will have green leaves. When plants are divided, as an alternate means of propagation, the resulting root disturbance occasions the production of sucker shoots with green leaves. This leaves propagation by shoot cuttings as the only option. Production of *Phlox paniculata* is slow from such cuttings, which explains why 'Norah Leigh' was scarce and expensive for a long period of time.

When the inside layer of a plant is devoid, or mostly devoid, of chlorophyll, this manifests itself in a leaf with a variegated center, masked at its edge by the chlorophyll in the outside layer. Seed from plants variegated in this manner will be predictably all-green.

An article in the August 1997 issue of *HortScience*, volume 32 (5), describes yet another type of chimera, in which a wedge of genetically unique tissue is present through all the cell layers. Neat and tidy sectors generally do not persist, since, as cell division proceeds, cells are shoved out of line relative to each other. Additionally, this type of chimera tends to be unstable, as axillary buds tend to give rise to either entirely green or the more typical inside-edge variegation. This may explain the frequent reversions of irregularly patterned hostas to all-green, all-yellow, or more stable edge- or center-patterned variegation.

Keep in mind too that certain gray plants—Japanese painted fern (*Athyrium nipponicum* 'Pictum') and gray-spotted lungworts such as *Pulmonaria saccharata* cultivars, for example—are not really variegated. Their gray color is the result of an air gap just under the leaf surface that reflects light.

Japanese gardeners are especially captivated with variant plant forms, including those that are variegated. *Variegated Plants in Color* by Yoshimichi Hirose and Masato Yokoi includes almost three hundred pages, each filled with photographs of variegated perennials, trees, shrubs, cacti, and succulents, arranged alphabetically. There is some text, in both English and Japanese, but the book is basically a catalog. Timber Press has reissued Susan Conder's *Variegated Plants*, and though fewer plants are listed here than in *Variegated Plants in Color*, the book is more useful to gardeners for its helpful discussion of cultivation and garden uses.

❧

CHAPTER 3

Into the Shade

WOODLAND GARDENS

Spring yammers in the woodlands. Trees are barely laced with the delicate green of unfolding leaves when the forest floor leaps into active growth. From day to day herbaceous plants erupt from the soil and race to bloom before the tree canopy closes over, reducing sunlight and energy for flowering and seed production. Assorted bulbs, from snowdrops (*Galanthus*) to daffodils (*Narcissus*) and wood hyacinths (*Hyacinthoides*), parade their gay flowers, to be followed by fading foliage. Their aging greenery requires some disguise as it should not be braided, folded, or knotted. Native plants such as Dutchman's breeches (*Dicentra cucullaria*) and Virginia bluebells (*Mertensia virginica*) may wait more patiently until spring has well taken hold, but have the same fugacious pattern of growth: they flower and then fade away just like the bulbs. The resulting gap must be camouflaged. Gardeners regard bare places as potential planting sites, often to the detriment of plants in estivation (the summertime equivalent of hibernation). Mother Nature also abhors a vacuum, but sometimes what she plants are weeds to a gardener.

By late spring the trees are in full leaf. Sunlight dims to dappled brightness, partial shade, or stygian gloom. Enticed by the cooling shade of canopy trees, you stroll into the summer woodland. There are few flowers to see now. Once the spring fling is over, shady gardens depend on foliage for their display. Bloodroot (*Sanguinaria canadensis*) is an excellent example: flowers last less than a week before their fragile white petals fade away, but attractive foliage remains throughout the summer. The orbicular leaves may vary from barely dimpled to more deeply lobed. For a pleasing display, pair bloodroot with a fern or astilbe.

Another creative combination matches *Hosta* 'Krossa Regal' with sweet cicely (*Myrrhis odorata*). Long-stalked gray-green leaves give the hosta a tall vase-like form. Plant the sweet cicely so its grayish fernlike leaves arise between the hostas, using about half a dozen sweet cicely for every three hostas. Sweet cicely is also well-matched with false Solomon's seal (*Smilacina racemosa*), alternatively known as false spikenard or Solomon's plume. The arching stems and oval, somewhat ridged or pleated leaves of false Solomon's seal provide a good contrariety of form. Another simple and charming alliance places the downy, plump, kidney-shaped leaves of Canadian ginger (*Asarum canadense*) adjacent to the black stems and apple-green fronds of maidenhair fern (*Adiantum pedatum*). The color and surface texture of Canadian ginger are closer to those of the maidenhair fern than to the very polished, glossy, deep green, reniform leaves of European ginger (*Asarum europaeum*). Combine European ginger with Japanese forest grass (*Hakonechloa macra* 'Aureola') if you want even more of a flourish (see Plate 32). The grass features gracefully arching yellow blades thinly penciled with dark green—an excellent foil for the ginger. Or match the grass with a bold, gold-edged hosta such as *Hosta* 'Frances Williams' (see Plate 31). Mix and match foliage shapes, then layer on color. The quiet beauty of a woodland garden invites meditation as you stroll, contemplating the benefits of attractive, low-maintenance foliage. No deadheading, no staking: only great enjoyment.

Summer heat and humidity come quickly to the heart of the South. Louisiana and Mississippi gardens display a glory of azaleas and camellias in March, but blooms are gone by April. Tremendously diverse broad-leaved evergreen trees and shrubs create year-round foliage display. Trees create welcome shade, forming umbrellas to block the torrid sun. The walls of garden rooms are formed with shrubs rather than lath and plaster, perhaps utilizing the bold, glossy, palmate foliage of *Fatsia japonica*, whose tender young green leaves form a lively display against the darker green of those already mature. At Monmouth, an old plantation home in Natchez, Mississippi, the dry shade beneath an evergreen live oak (*Quercus virginiana*) is enlivened by the pinnate foliage of *Indigofera kirilowii*, which persists after the pea-like flowers have faded. Tropical plants seen elsewhere struggling in pots become lush and verdant when released from living room captivity. *Monstera deliciosa* boldly rambles as a tropical perennial in many a garden in the Garden District of New Orleans.

Seasons turn in their cyclical dance, most obviously when winter grips the land in ice and bleaches garden colors. Summer woodlands become a tranquil green retreat. A lofty, leafy roof upheld on columnar trunks of oak (*Quercus*), maple (*Acer*), tulip poplar (*Liriodendron tulipifera*), or beech (*Fagus*) filters the light and cools the air. The contrast between deciduous and evergreen creates a pleasing textural balance. Broad-leaved evergreens are far fewer in number outside the South and Southeast, and they are mainly shrubs at that: rhododendrons, mountain laurels (*Kalmia latifolia*), *Pieris japonica*, *Leucothoe fontanesiana*. Perennials with good-looking summer foliage carry the display forward beyond the flowers of spring.

CITY GARDENS

Gardeners who live outside metropolitan areas often forget what urban life is like for those growing plants in the big city. Sure there is shade, but it is created by buildings rather than by trees. Because masses of masonry, skyscrapers, pavement, and roadways soak up daytime heat and return it at night, many city gardens don't experience the beneficial cooling that suburban and rural properties enjoy. City canyons reveal a narrow slit of sky, and a window box with ivy becomes a green oasis.

Seattle gardener Eric Shalit grew up in Brooklyn, New York, where, as he remembers, there were three kinds of plants: trees, bushes, and lawns. I too spent my childhood in Brooklyn. Most, though not all, of the mature trees shading the summer streets of our relatively verdant Midwood neighborhood were welcome. One, a female ginkgo, had everyone walking on the other side of the street when its attractive but vomit-scented fruit splattered the sidewalk every autumn. My parents' property included two large maples. Regular attempts to grow grass in their heavy shade were doomed to failure on a yearly basis. Eventually a more satisfactory solution was found by planting periwinkle (*Vinca minor*), also called running myrtle. There were two kinds of hosta (commonly called funkia at the time). A row of one type with all-green leaves bordered the garage. In retrospect, thinking of the deeply incised veins and pointed midsized leaves, I think it must have been *Hosta ventricosa*. Along the side of the house were two circular, raised rose beds. The soil was held in place by a green-and-white-leaved hosta, most likely *H. undulata* var. *univittata*. My sister, my brother, and I each had a small garden plot. One morning my mother said she'd dreamt that everything I had ever planted had grown, and my little piece of ground had turned into a jungle (perhaps it was more of a nightmare than a dream). I do remember growing, among other things, castor bean (*Ricinus communis*). Our cat used to lie in the shade of the huge palmate leaves and I would pretend she was a leopard in a jungle.

If I were back on Seventeenth Street today I'd put more effort into improving the soil. Back then we'd just dig holes and stuff plants in them, wondering later why they did so poorly. I cannot recall compost, peat moss, or any organic matter being added to the hard-packed soil, other than the coffee grounds my mother threw on the roses by the back door. That was the only place I ever saw earthworms, and the roses, some old-fashioned variety with beautiful buds and full, fat, pink flowers with marvelous fragrance, thrived. "Mulch" was a word—and a concept—absent from our vocabulary.

Cindy Goulder, a landscape designer based in New York City, calls her occupation "ecological landscape design," as it has both ecological and aesthetic dimensions. She has been employed on public landscape restoration projects and has worked with the Parks Department on a native plant education garden. Because nature, as she points out, is otherwise lacking and oversimplified in New York, Cindy looks for plants that let the beauty and complexity of ecological processes be clearly expressed and discovered. Plants must be tough enough to withstand polluted air and water, toxic soils, and the urban conditions of shade and heat. She uses plants and plant communities to restore the lost sense of nature common to so many urbanites. As a landscape designer Cindy seeks first to establish a matrix that is solidly green and natural, and then overlays subtle details (foliage texture) and more obvious effects (high ornamentation with lots of colorful foliage). Plants are always selected for foliage, as well as for plant habitat, various ecological characteristics, and maintenance requirements. Cindy points out too that good-looking foliage is a reliable indicator of plant health.

Strong doses of green are necessary, says Cindy, in city places that have little of it. Many coniferous evergreens have bright new growth in strong contrast to mature foliage. *Acer palmatum* 'Bloodgood' is a special favorite of hers, with its reddish leaves that unfold in spring, changing to green between seasons. In autumn the leaves of this cultivar transform to a clear, bright red and, when backlit by the sun, have the lambent glow of stained glass.

"So who needs forsythia?" notes Cindy, when there is *Spiraea japonica* 'Gold Mound' with new yellow growth in spring that turns to mixed yellow-chartreuse and deeper shades of green in summer. She appreciates Japanese forest grass (*Hakonechloa macra* 'Aureola') for its lovely, arching, linear form that looks as if it were combed by the wind and for its golden leaves thinly penciled in green (see Plate 30). Lady's mantle (*Alchemilla mollis*) is especially nice after a rain, water droplets collecting on its leaves like moonstones. Ferns are an important part of her plant palette: cinnamon fern (*Osmunda cinnamomea*), for example, which shoots straight up in spring and then softens as it opens.

Lady fern (*Athyrium filix-femina*), ostrich fern (*Matteuccia struthiopteris*), and royal fern (*Osmunda regalis*) are other tall-growing, deciduous favorites. Christmas fern (*Polystichum acrostichoides*) is especially useful, as it is evergreen. Cindy finds "the shape of foliage, particularly of perennials and grasses, critical in design. For example, the straplike foliage, such as that of irises and daylilies, has entirely different emotional as well as structural effects from, say, the large rounded flat leaves of forms of heuchera and alchemilla. The upstretched arms of the former are joy-evokers to me, while the latter are more grounding."

City dwellers who would be gardeners may not even have a ground-based garden. Rooftop and balcony gardens on high-rise buildings require decisions not faced by gardeners who "do it in the dirt." Soil is heavy, so weight is a necessary concern to be factored in with the structural strength of the load-bearing area. Everything—soil, pots, plants—either comes up in the elevator or, for major projects, over the rooftop with the aid of a crane. Watered plants should not sprinkle neighbors on lower floors. Plants must be good tenants, paying rent for an extended period, just as with plants in the tiny Japanese *tsubo-niwa* courtyard gardens of the Edo period. Foliage has extended aesthetic value, unlike flowers, which come and go. Keep in mind that rooftop gardens are akin to seaside gardens: both are windy, exposed, and subject to harsh conditions. Drought-tolerant plants are a sine qua non.

TREES

A spacious property provides the space for large canopy trees, smaller understory trees, shrubs, perennials, and groundcovers. Urban gardeners have fewer options—an oak or tulip poplar is out of the question. The choice falls between a smaller-growing, shade-tolerant understory tree and a large shrub. Planting a single large tree where space is limited reduces further planting options. The big maples at my childhood home meant that smaller trees and shrubs were removed from consideration, and not even perennials were a viable option— groundcovers were about the only category of landscape plants left open to us. Since there were large trees on the planted median, additional large trees were not even needed for shade on site; and besides, there was a porch across the front of the house. The notion of cutting down healthy mature trees is anathema to most gardeners, who prefer to work around whatever limitations trees impose. One option in this kind of circumstance is to create summer containers of colorful, shade-tolerant, tender plants such as coleus (*Solenostemon scutellarioides*) and caladiums. Houseplants such as cast iron plant (*Aspidistra elatior*) can also take a summer vacation outdoors, to return indoors in fall, rejuvenated. In places where cast iron plant is hardy, it can even be planted in the garden. It is tolerant of heavy shade, though supplemental watering is usually required to keep it from becoming a tattered, shabby, browning mess.

Smaller trees that cast lighter shade are more suitable for restricted spaces. Small maples such as *Acer palmatum*, *A. shirasawanum*, *A. griseum*, or *A. pensylvanicum* are elegant choices. *Amelanchier laevis*, a shadbush, has a lovely vase-like form, attractive spring flowers, delicious berries that birds love to eat, and striking orange-russet fall color (see Plate 109). Flowering dogwood (*Cornus florida*) has matching characteristics of flower, fruit, and excellent fall foliage. In cold climates consider using crab apples (*Malus*), which include a diverse array of cultivars: small lollipop trees only 5 feet tall, some with a weeping habit, others with purple foliage.

Scale should also influence plant choice: what might pass as a large shrub in an expansive landscape serves equally well as a tree in a smaller garden. The visual clues that say "tree" to us include an absence of lower branches and a single trunk (though in some cases it may be a few trunks). Pruning away lower branches on plants such as *Magnolia stellata* or *Vaccinium angustifolium* will help to convey the template for a tree in the mind's eye.

SHRUBS

Diversity is more aesthetically interesting than uniformity. Where deciduous trees provide the shade, adding at least a few evergreen shrubs will provide a strong visual contrast, most striking in winter when all else is bare. Most conifers are sun lovers, but there are a few options for shady sites. Yew (*Taxus*) is perhaps the most readily available coniferous shrub. Traditionally it is used for short or tall hedges, geometric or figurative topiary, or foundation plantings, all as a result of its tolerance for regular, repeated clipping into solid forms. Yew can also be left to grow in an informal manner for a softer, more irregular outline. Careful hand pruning will allow control of height and width without suggesting regimented control. Consider planting a line of yew to define a boundary of a garden room, to create a wall behind a bench in the shade, or as a dark forest-green accent in contrast to the white trunks of birches (*Betula*). The prostrate form of English yew (*T. baccata* 'Repandens') is an elegant cultivar that creates a lovely low carpet to skirt the ground beneath an understory tree. Unfortunately, yew is very popular with deer as a salad bar special.

Japanese plum yew (*Cephalotaxus harringtonia*) has longer, looser, dark green needles, which makes it less suitable for pruned effects. It is, however, impervious to deer attacks, even in Japan at the deer park in Nara. 'Duke Gardens' is a spreading form that takes its time to reach 2 to 3 feet high and 4 to 5 feet wide. Shade is needed for the best dark green color, as needles turn yellow with more sun. 'Fastigiata' is an upright form that slowly creates a broad pillar— 7 feet wide and 10 feet tall—of steeply upright branches.

Russian cypress (*Microbiota decussata*) resembles one of the flatter-growing junipers, but, unlike those sun lovers, it will accept light shade. Growing as a flat, spreading, finely textured shrub, it has a charming and elegant appearance. The small scalelike needles turn an attractive bronze in winter. Over time they spread widely, forming an evergreen ground-hugging pancake of foliage.

Japanese plum yew and Russian cypress are slow to propagate and conse-quently less available and more expensive than yew. You won't find either one at roadside garden centers, which offer only the most familiar plants. This does not make them any better or worse, of course: they are excellent accent plants but are unsuitable for hedges or topiary.

Broad-leaved evergreens are a possibility, more or less, depending on how severe winter conditions might be. Go north to zone 3 and they are simply not much of an option. At about 18 inches tall, Lapland rhododendron (*Rhododendron lapponicum*) is rather on the short side. It is also hardy right to zone 1 and suffers in hot summers, just about anywhere above zone 6 unless at a cooling elevation. The small deep green leaves provide fine texture.

In zone 6 there are more plants to choose from: mountain laurel (*Kalmia latifolia*), any number of rhododendrons, lily-of-the-valley shrub (*Pieris flori-bunda*), also called andromeda, and *Leucothoe axillaris*. Growth habit varies from upright, as for the mountain laurel, rhododendrons, and lily-of-the-valley shrub, to the low and arching leucothoe, with ovate glossy green foliage the norm. Remember that large rhododendron leaves curl into cigarlike tubes in cold weather. The members of *Pieris* and *Leucothoe* are deer resistant.

Sweet box (*Sarcococca hookeriana* var. *humilis*), which reaches 12 to 18 inches tall, grows low enough to render it a more subtle accent in the landscape. It is an excellent plant to face down taller shrubs, integrating them into the landscape without an abrupt transition, as would be provided by something like periwinkle (*Vinca minor*). Sweet box is a good-looking choice for shrubs with bare shanks, such as some of the *Viburnum* species that arch outward as they grow upward.

Inkberry (*Ilex glabra*) is an evergreen native holly suitable for damp, shaded places or drier, sunnier places, and will even tolerate deicing salt. Hardy from zones 5 to 9, it generally grows from 4 to 6 feet tall, though it may reach up to 10 feet tall, and spreads as widely. Inkberry responds well to pruning and may be clipped into hedges. It provides a relatively fine texture, since leaves are ¾ to 2 inches long. 'Compacta' is an older cultivar that tends to get leggy and open at the base with age. 'Shamrock' is a selection with denser growth and shiny dark green leaves. 'Nigra' retains its leaves right to the base, even on older plants.

Mountain laurel (*Kalmia latifolia*) is the state shrub of Connecticut and epitomizes spring in the region. Pink buds open to a froth of white flowers that billow along roadsides, power line right-of-ways, and woodland edges. This shrub was brought into cultivation, and the fashion is to keep it juvenile, constantly clipping it back into a fat round dumpling clothed with foliage to the ground. The wild shrubs are 10 feet tall with sinuous black trunks that arch overhead and glossy, dark green, lanceolate leaves in clusters at the tips of the branches, and I find these much more powerful in the landscape. A mountain laurel placed in some cramped foundation planting under the living room window will need constant shearing if the interior is not to turn dim and gloomy. The best option is to move it out from such positions. When allowed room to stretch and spread, a mature mountain laurel can shelter a tapestry of ferns and other shade-tolerant perennials in homage to its woodland origins. However, if it must be wedged up against the house, make an appropriate selection so as to reduce maintenance chores. 'Elf' is a miniature form, with a growth rate and leaf size scarcely half that of its wild ancestors. Flowers are just a bit smaller than on full-size shrubs. 'Little Linda' is lower growing than 'Elf' and spreads more widely. Flower buds are red, softening to a medium pink as the flowers open. 'Minuet' is another dwarf form, with especially dark glossy foliage and white flowers banded with cinnamon red on the inside. These cultivars display compact growth resulting from closely spaced growth points, so leaf clusters are more closely bunched together. Young plants require some pruning to coax them into a multi-stemmed habit that will display elegance and charm at maturity.

Leucothoe is another genus of American shrubs with Japanese and Chinese cousins. In this case, however, the native species are more popular in gardens than their exotic relatives imported from abroad. I appreciate the arching, mounded habit of leucothoe, as well as its branches, which are well dressed with leathery, ovate, lustrous dark green leaves narrowing abruptly to a point. Small, white, bell-like flowers arranged in trailing strings adorn the last foot or so of the shoots in late spring, emerging from the leaf axils. Interior shoots buried under the mound of growth eventually die, concealed from view. An occasional rooting around at the base of the shrub—clipping out the dead shoots right at ground level and dragging them out for disposal—is the minimal maintenance required.

Most of the popular species are hardy to zone 5 or 6 and prefer a shaded site with soil high in organic matter, moist yet freely draining conditions, and low pH. Another plus: deer ignore them.

At 2 to 4 feet tall and half again as wide, *Leucothoe axillaris* is a relatively small-growing shrub, and is frequently offered as *L. axillaris* 'Compacta', an even smaller clone. A pleasing partnership results when a small upright deciduous tree such as Japanese maple (*Acer palmatum*) displays its finely textured small leaves on spreading branches above the lustrous darker green of the shrub. During winter the maple's smooth gray bark stands in contrast to the evergreen leaves, which often turn burgundy in cold weather. Though hardy from zones 6 to 9, *L. axillaris* will grow in a protected zone 5 site. *Leucothoe catesbaei* is larger, reaching 5 feet tall, and hardy to zone 5. The two species are sometimes listed as synonyms, and both are often confused with dog hobble (*L. fontanesiana*) as well, as the three differ only in those small details that delight taxonomists but are easily overlooked by home gardeners. The only practical reason to be concerned by this is that if you live in zone 5 *L. fontanesiana* will be the most reliably hardy. This species is larger than the other two, growing 6 feet tall or more. I confess to a preference for the less readily available straight species, which may be used to conceal a view at a turn in the garden path and to coax garden visitors to explore around the corner—but only in woodland shade, as *L. fontanesiana* suffers badly when exposed to direct sunlight or drying winds. Nurseries are more prone to offer 'Nana', the dwarf form of the species, which only reaches 2 feet tall but is still capable of spreading 6 feet wide. In spring the young leaves of 'Scarletta' are glossy scarlet, barely tinged with purple. They mature to a dark green in summer, before turning glossy burgundy in autumn and winter. And then there is 'Rainbow', which looks like some spumoni ice cream swirl, its new growth changing from red to pink and cream and later to green and white. *Leucothoe keiskei* is a dainty Japanese cousin.

Common box (*Buxus sempervirens*), often just called boxwood, is thought of as a quintessentially southern shrub, planted in pairs by the entries of stately Virginia homes in Thomas Jefferson country, manicured into green garden walls from knee-high to 12 feet tall. It is hardier than it is usually given credit for, from zones 6 to 8, with some cultivars hardy even in the colder portion of zone 5. In zone 5, protection from winter sun is important so as to prevent the plant from burning. Also avoid planting common box near roadways that might be salted for winter snow removal, as it is very susceptible to salt damage. Plants appear to be deer resistant as well, for I have seen the varmints stroll right past them on their way to a tastier snack. There is a drawback to common box, and that is its pungent aroma, which is best likened to that of a dirty litter box.

However, the scent is strongest right after pruning and is not a day-to-day disadvantage.

'Vardar Valley' is one of the most cold-hardy *Buxus sempervirens* cultivars. It grows 1 to 4 inches a year, reaching 6 feet tall and 10 feet wide after eighty years or so, a flattened, compact mound of dark green to bluish green foliage. 'Pullman' is another choice, more cold tolerant than the usual run of boxwood cultivars and able to grow in zone 5 if given winter protection. Careful siting will be important in these conditions, and it may also help to use an anti-desiccant spray, which coats the surface of the leaves to reduce water loss. A deep mulch where necessary, a discreet bushel basket filled with oak leaves and upended over the delicate plant, even pots of tender plants snoozing in the garage—I can live with these options. Swaddling a marginally hardy shrub in burlap certainly works, but I find such vegetable mummies unattractive additions to the winter landscape.

> Swaddling a marginally hardy shrub in burlap certainly works, but I find such vegetable mummies unattractive additions to the winter landscape.

The popular *Buxus sempervirens* 'Graham Blandy' looks like a narrow green finger pointing skyward. Though only 1 foot wide, it grows 10 feet tall, having a very narrow, columnar habit of growth with no side-branching, an effect created by the strong, straight shoots that rise directly vertical from the base. 'Graham Blandy' grows in sun or partial shade, loamy or clay soil, and tolerates air pollution, windy sites, even some drought. It will not, however, tolerate wet soil or salt.

Variegated common box is usually suggested for zones 7 and 8. However, white-variegated *Buxus sempervirens* 'Elegantissima' grows quite nicely at Willowwood Arboretum in Far Hills, New Jersey, showing only a modest amount of yellowing in the worst winter weather. A compact pyramidal form, densely clothed in dark green foliage irregularly edged in creamy white, makes this 5-foot-tall, 3½-foot-wide common box look like stage dressing for a performance of *The Nutcracker*. There are several other white-variegated cultivars, each looking very much the same as 'Elegantissima', including 'Albomarginata', 'Argentea', 'Argenteovariegata', 'Elegans', and 'Variegata'. Two others, 'Aureovariegata' and 'Marginata', differ only in having a yellow margin to their dark green leaves.

Dwarf box (*Buxus microphylla*) is native to Japan, Korea, and China. A highly variable species, its leaves are usually a paler green than those of common box, sometimes turning bronze in winter, though this is simply a color shift and not a sign of damage. There are several varieties. Dwarf Japanese box (*B. microphylla* var. *japonica*) is hardy from the warmer portion of zone 6 through zone 9 and has relatively large leaves, over 1 inch long. This variety includes the cultivars 'Morris Midget' and 'Rotundifolia'. 'Morris Midget' is hardy down to zone 5 and grows less than 1 inch a year until it reaches 18 inches high by 36 inches wide. Should even this dainty mounded habit be too much for your site, remember that boxwood can be cut back rather harshly. Late winter or early spring is the best time for any severe pruning, which should be followed by fertilizing, watering, and mulching. Korean box (*B. microphylla* var. *koreana*), one of the hardiest boxwoods, is suitable for use from the colder part of zone 5 to zone 8. In winter the dull green leaves turn a golden brownish green.

Some lovely cultivars of *Buxus sempervirens* × *B. microphylla* var. *koreana* have been selected at Sheridan Nurseries in Ontario, Canada. *Buxus* 'Green Gem' has deep green leaves and a pleasingly plump, globose form. Slow growing, it needs little pruning. *Buxus* 'Green Mountain' has similarly deep green leaves but is more upright and pyramidal in habit. *Buxus* 'Green Velvet' has a full, rounded form and this, coupled with its vigorous habit of growth, makes it especially useful for parterres or low hedges.

Rather different in appearance, Oregon holly grape (*Mahonia aquifolium*) has pinnate foliage nicely serrate along the edges (see Plate 108). The surface texture is dull to glossy, depending on which clone is obtained. Winter color may be a rich red-purple if there is sufficient sunlight to encourage the color shift without causing winter burn, a desiccation and browning of leaf edges. Though Japanese mahonia (*M. bealei*) is often said to be hardy only to zone 7, I have grown it for many years, through an assortment of winters, in both my Connecticut and New Jersey gardens. I appreciate its ability to grow in dry shade while still maintaining elegant hollylike foliage. Since zone 6 gardens approach its limits of hardiness, this shrub thrives but does not self-sow. In my friend Bobby Wilder's garden in Raleigh, North Carolina, Japanese mahonia seeds with happy abandon. In fact, some of my own plants have come from his garden, where on a visit I helped him remove a few of the "weeds" (one person's weeds are another person's treasures). One June I visited a New Jersey garden center and noticed a specimen of Japanese mahonia that was loaded with bloomy blue berries. I collected a generous amount of seed, removed the pulp as best I could, and soaked it for a couple of days to rot off what remained. Rubbing the seed clean and sowing it in a deep flat resulted in bountiful germination just three weeks later. Another spring I pricked out over 175 seedlings and, running out of pots and patience, gave the remaining 40 or so to a couple of friends.

The milder the winters in your region, the wider the palette of broad-leaved evergreen shrubs you will be able to explore. Camellias are commonplace in southern and southeastern gardens. The glossy green leaves on these elegant small trees are outstanding in bare winter woodlands. A single specimen can be used to accent and anchor a foundation planting. Japanese fatsia (*Fatsia japonica*), native to southeastern Asia, is a popular broad-leaved evergreen shrub in Louisiana and Mississippi, where it is sometimes used to fill in beneath evergreen live oaks. Large, glossy, palmately lobed evergreen leaves can easily reach 14 inches long and wide. While Japanese fatsia will effortlessly reach more than 10 feet tall, forming a scraggly small tree, it is commonly cut back to about 6 feet high. Spring pruning, coupled with a light fertilization, will encourage vigorous new growth. Japanese fatsia is hardy from the warmer part of zone 7 into zone 9. In zone 7 and the cooler portion of zone 8, it requires winter protection in the form of shade and shelter from wind. While Japanese fatsia can be used as an espalier, its intergeneric hybrid offspring ×*Fatshedera lizei* is more popular for this purpose. English ivy (*Hedera helix*), the other parent, gives ×*Fatshedera lizei* a more vining habit. The leaves are equally lustrous but smaller, only about 10 inches long. Support is needed, as ×*Fatshedera lizei* is more of a sprawler than a scrambler. After it gets about 5 feet tall it falls over, only to gamely attempt another ascent. Tied in to a trellis or other support, it creates a lovely espalier, or a fence or hedge ("fedge," see chapter 9). Alternatively, use regular pruning to keep it maintained as a shrub.

Japanese aucuba (*Aucuba japonica*), also called Japanese laurel, is one of those tolerant plants that accepts abuse, a trait for which it is denigrated. It grows for know-nothing homeowners in the heart of southern cities, asking only for some winter shade and a reasonably moist soil. Japanese aucuba is hardy from zones 7 to 9, but it will grow as an herbaceous perennial in zone 6, dying to the ground in winter and shooting up again in spring. Dark, leathery olive-green leaves, 3 to 7 inches long and half as wide, are evergreen. Japanese aucuba is most frequently seen in one of its numerous variegated forms: options range from gold-speckled 'Variegata', so flecked and blotched that it is commonly called gold dust plant, to 'Picturata', which features a large gold blotch in the center of each dark green leaf, and 'Sulphurea' with its pale yellow leaf margins. These cultivars add brightness to dark woodland settings. All-green forms are more rarely seen: lanceolate 'Lance Leaf', serrate 'Dentata' and 'Serratifolia', and narrow 'Longifolia', all excellent shrubs that require little maintenance and are best used as backdrops for showier perennials, as evergreen partners with deciduous shrubs, or massed to screen out an unwanted view. The variegated forms are most likely to burn, summer or winter, and even the all-green cultivars do better with shade—deep shade is acceptable. Handsome red berries are a possibility, but only if you keep in mind that some cultivars are female, others male, and both sexes are needed for fruitfulness. As I discovered myself, Japanese aucuba is easy to propagate: all ten tip cuttings of current growth taken in September rooted in a closed plastic box under grow lights, without bottom heat or mist.

The unusually trouble-free Japanese pittosporum (*Pittosporum tobira*) shows up in malls and upmarket offices in my part of the country. This is another fascinating shrub I wish I could grow. Its limited range finds it hardy in the warmer part of zone 8 to the cooler part of zone 9, and, when planted in a sheltered, protected microclimate, in the warmer part of zone 7 and the cooler part of zone 8. Japanese pittosporum is commonplace in southeastern states. The species, which has bright to deep green, rounded, evergreen leaves, does not show up in gardens as much as *P. tobira* 'Variegatum', which has cool gray-green leaves irregularly margined in creamy white (see Plates 23 and 58). A slow-growing cultivar, 'Variegatum' reaches about 5 feet tall and spreads even wider. It makes a lovely accent in the piney woods at Louisiana State University's Rural Life Museum and Windrush Gardens in Baton Rouge, where the regular layering, branching pattern (similar to that of flowering dogwoods and azaleas) creates a delicacy of form that looks magnificent under the high canopy. The effect is further enhanced by its subtle color and fine foliage texture. 'Variegatum' is salt tolerant and popularly used for gardens along the shore. It is excellent planted in large containers, left unpruned as a soft billowy hedge, or clipped into more formal outlines.

When deciduous shrubs are added to a chorus of woody plants, it should be because they provide some special attribute, whether it be foliage texture or shape, unusual color or variegation, or seasonal color. The bold, coarse, lobed leaves of oak leaf hydrangea (*Hydrangea quercifolia*) are shaped like magnified oak leaves. Their dull surface contrasts nicely with glossy foliage, while their coarse texture plays well against smaller leaves. In addition, fall color is a strong purple-red, even under moderate to rather heavy shade. Dogwoods come in shrubby versions, some with variegated foliage. *Cornus alba* 'Elegantissima', for example, has oval medium green leaves crisply edged in white, and adds a bright note to sites with light to dappled shade. Another good choice is *Kerria japonica* 'Picta', whose small serrate leaves are also nicely edged in white. Spicebush (*Lindera benzoin*) is a common native shrub found in wet woodlands from the Northeast to the Southeast. The only hardy member of the olive family (Lauraceae), spicebush has large oval leaves that appear after its small yellowish green flowers open in early spring. The leaves are light green, turning a glowing clear yellow in autumn, and are fed upon by spicebush swallowtail butterfly larvae. The naturally occurring combination of spicebush and skunk cabbage (*Symplocarpus foetidus*) is worth replicating in an informal, naturalistically designed shade garden with damp to wet soil. The bold leaves of skunk cabbage are easily mistaken for a green hosta and only smell when stepped upon (something I try to avoid with anything other than groundcovers). The inclusion of cinnamon fern (*Osmunda cinnamomea*) would improve the display, with the large fern's lacy texture playing against the coarse bold shape of the skunk cabbage, changing a conceivably difficult, swampy, shaded site into an attractive feature. Additionally, cinnamon fern turns a nice straw-gold in autumn, a complement to the clear yellow of spicebush.

Fever tree (*Pinckneya bracteata*) is an odd—odd as in fantastic, unusual, extraordinary—large shrub (some would call it a small tree) from the extreme southeastern states of Georgia, South Carolina, and Florida, where it is found growing along the edges of wet, coastal plain forests and swamps. It has oval, elliptic, or ovate leaves up to 8 inches long, of a pleasing medium green, with some gloss to the surface. What makes fever tree exceptional is its enlarged, leaflike calyx segment, reminiscent of a poinsettia's colorful bracts, but of a soft dusty pink. And like a poinsettia's bracts, fever tree's showy pink bracts last for months. I succumbed to the charms of this plant to become the successful (and only) bidder when one was donated to a silent auction plant sale at my local chapter, the Watnong Chapter, of the North American Rock Garden Society. Honest horticultural lust strikes again. The donor told me her New Jersey garden was in zone 7 and she had mulched deeply to bring the parent plant through the winter.

Pinckneya bracteata is generally reported as being hardy from the cooler part of zone 8 to the cooler part of zone 9, southward of the upper Piedmont region. Rob Gardner, curator of native plants at the North Carolina Botanical Garden, Chapel Hill, tells me that fever tree is hardy in his zone 7 region, barring the most extreme winters. The botanical garden has several specimens, which have been growing there for at least a decade, more than long enough to encompass yearly seasonal variations. Rob's own garden includes half a dozen fever trees, which I take as a good indication of their attractiveness: even though he can enjoy them at work, he still wants them at home. The shrubs are planted in loamy clay soil and, he says, seem to be very happy: "This is a species often seen growing in wetter soils in the wild, but in my experience it does much better in cultivation when sited in average soils that are well drained (or at least moderately so). Under the conditions around Raleigh, pinckneya is fairly fast growing and early blooming." Richard Bir, author of *Growing and Propagating*

Showy Native Woody Plants, notes that fresh *P. bracteata* seed germinates in ten days at 75° Fahrenheit under mist. Rob Gardner confirms this, adding that fever tree does not require any special pregermination treatment.

My garden, however, is firmly zone 6, and I doubt I could push my little fever tree into surviving anyplace colder. In *Native Shrubs and Woody Vines of the Southeast*, Leonard E. Foote and Samuel B. Jones, Jr., recommend *Pinckneya bracteata* as a specimen or accent plant. My young plant is a modest 2½ feet tall in its container and appears to be setting a nice crop of seeds. It has attractive foliage and colorful bracts that made a good show its first summer. In winter I will bring it into our attached, unheated garage, where temperatures descend to 38° Fahrenheit along the back wall common with the house, where it will sleep through the cold side by side with the cannas. As with the cannas, the fever tree will reemerge with spring, adding its charm to the summer container garden.

Viburnum species, more familiar than *Pinckneya bracteata*, may be evergreen or deciduous, native or exotic. When selecting viburnums gardeners often focus on the flowers, yet there are a couple of deciduous species with pleasing foliage that I find useful as shrubs. These are not showstoppers; it is more that they are good at support, used en masse to provide a casual background. Arrowwood (*V. dentatum*) has prominently veined, coarsely toothed, dark green leaves, usually lustrous and shining. They form a pleasant, more or less neutral backdrop, which in some settings turns a clear bright red before falling. Hobblebush (*V. alnifolium*), also called alder-leaved viburnum, thrives in moist, shady woodlands and upland roadsides all the way from Maine to Georgia. The prominent veins feather out from the incised midrib, finishing at the points of the leaf's coarsely serrate edge. Leaves are an attractive medium green in summer, turning a clear claret red in autumn. Hobblebush grows 6 feet tall, sometimes more, so you must find the proper companions to set off its rich color. Consider the leaves of *Sassafras albidum*, each shaped somewhat like a mitten. Their autumn hues of luminous yellow, pumpkin-orange, and orange-red, with an occasional lingering flush of green at the base, do the job nicely. Spicebush (*Lindera benzoin*) thrives in the same type of moist woodland and has simple oval leaves that turn a radiant clear yellow. Add in the prostrate form of English yew (*Taxus baccata* 'Repandens') for a pleasing festival of autumn foliage. Like hobblebush, linden viburnum (*V. dilatatum*) has coarsely toothed leaves of a dull medium green, and in autumn they turn a russet red. This species, native to Japan and China, grows best in partial shade to full sun. It should be planted in groups for screening or as a backdrop for lower-growing plants. Mapleleaf viburnum (*V. acerifolium*) prefers partial to deep shade rather than full sun. The three-lobed, maplelike leaves are a quiet green in summer, turning purple in autumn. Many hostas have leaves that turn clear yellow, becoming translucent in the process, and these make a fine underplanting for mapleleaf viburnums. These same hostas, however, would seem boring if paired with spicebush, whose leaves are too similar in color.

GROUNDCOVERS

I have a woodland path lined with about twelve hundred poeticus daffodils (*Narcissus poeticus*). These are stupendous while in bloom but quickly do what spring bulbs seem best at: they go dormant. The path is in an area not especially close to my house, so watering is awkward. Consequently, when selecting a groundcover for the area I had to choose one that could thrive in dry conditions. Since the path is lengthy, I needed a large number of plants, more than I could set in the ground in one afternoon. I had to select a groundcover that could patiently wait while I planted first one contingent, then another. I decided upon periwinkle (*Vinca minor*). Early one April I bought a thousand bare-root plugs. They arrived in bundles of two hundred, wrapped in damp burlap. I opened the box, set it in the toolshed, and started planting one bundle at a time. The soil around my house is clay laced with rocks and roots, which means that before I could plant I had to do a little pickaxing and add compost. Some days I planted a hundred, some days more, and several days into this process I took a day off. The bundles of periwinkle didn't mind: their roots were kept cool and damp in the shade of the toolshed. Everything was planted within ten days. None rotted or wilted, all took hold, and now, three years later, I have a nice carpet of periwinkle that sets off the daffodils while they're in bloom, distracts attention from their withering foliage, and provides an attractive groundcover of oval, glossy, dark green leaves. I could have chosen a variegated form of *Vinca minor*—'Aureovariegata' with its gold-edged leaves, 'Argenteovariegata' or 'Sterling Silver' with their white-edged leaves—but I wanted something simple. I thought of cultivars such as 'Burgundy', which has wine-colored flowers, and 'Alba', which has white flowers. Their leaves look the same as those of the species, but I couldn't find them wholesale in the quantity I needed. In the end *Vinca minor* was the solution, as it had been in the shady area beneath the maples at my childhood home in Brooklyn.

I was pleased with how well the periwinkle covered the bare ground left by the dormant bulbs, especially at a site that is difficult to maintain, and I mentioned this to my friend M. M. "Dicky" Graaf, who has very strong opinions about plants and gardens. Too funereal, Dicky promptly replied. She would have chosen sweet woodruff (*Galium odoratum*) for its delicate texture and apple-green foliage laced with a froth of white flowers in spring. As a concept sweet woodruff would have be ideal, but in reality it would not have worked. It isn't available bare root because it cannot survive this way, so I would have had to buy potted plants at a much higher cost. Though tough once established, in its early stages sweet woodruff requires watering, a service difficult to provide in my situation. Ideas are invaluable, but it always helps to run a reality check before executing the concept.

I do use sweet woodruff in the woods near the drainage creek, where the soil remains damper than at the top of the slope. It is a good, territorially aggressive groundcover, and the original six pots have spread nicely into a weed-choking mat, shading the ground so well that even garlic mustard (*Alliaria petiolata*) and Japanese stilt grass (*Microstegium*) have difficulty germinating. Shrubs and sturdy perennials, however, such as medium to large hostas or the larger clump-forming ferns, emerge just fine from its embrace. Sweet woodruff is a winter-dormant groundcover, so its visual appeal is negligible in winter. Keep in mind too that its dainty appearance conceals its ability to spread efficiently. It is relatively easy to remove (just roll it up like a piece of carpet), but be careful where you dump it: a chunk tossed into that awkward neglected corner of the garden will root down and spread out from its new location.

Pachysandra terminalis gets bad press. It is overused and boring, it overruns paths, it vines its scandent way up into azaleas like some constricting anaconda—you've heard it all. Some of these problems, however, are caused by the gardener, not the plant. Maintenance is needed to keep any spreading plant confined to where it belongs. Planting huge swatches of anything will result in a poor design, whether it be a cornfield rolling over the Iowa countryside, an excessive, manicured acreage of turf, or pachysandra taking over some corporate office park. In Japan, where *P. terminalis* originates, it is used with more restraint, as an accent rather than a groundcover. There are a few selections with more refined habits or foliage interest. 'Green Carpet' has small, finely toothed, deep green leaves on compact, low-growing plants, while 'Green Sheen', more compact, has small, very glossy, dark green leaves. 'Silver Edge' features leaves of a lighter green, narrowly edged in white. Its habit is similar to the species, but it does not spread as rapidly.

My favorite species of *Pachysandra* is our native Allegheny spurge (*P. procumbens*). The larger, matte leaves appear in spring a soft green with silver spots, maturing to a grayed green with brown spots. Though this species is often described as semi-evergreen, the Allegheny spurge in my zone 6 garden seem to be wholly evergreen. My plants remained green even in the midst of a horrendous Connecticut winter in which temperatures dipped to −8° Fahrenheit (there was snow cover, but it was cold!). Allegheny spurge does not spread as rapidly as its Japanese cousin, *P. terminalis*, nor propagate quite so easily. I take summer cuttings, usually in late July. Before potting the cuttings individually I twist the end of each stem into a loose knot. This helps hold them upright in the pot (though whether it helps them root or not, I have no idea). Allegheny spurge partners very well with larger, spring-flowering bulbs and any other shade-tolerant, midsized perennial. Keep scale in mind: groundcovers of any kind will swamp primroses (*Primula vulgaris*). *Lamium* species are also useful groundcovers for shady places.

PERENNIALS

If this were a three-volume book, with supplements, there would be room to include many more, if not all, of the enormously diverse plants that gardeners grow. Plants flood into garden centers and nurseries, insinuate themselves into mailboxes after tempting catalogs arrive in profusion, and get passed along from one gardening friend to another. New introductions, old favorites: plant options can appear intimidatingly endless. I can't resist the lure of some new introduction any more than the next gardener; but at the same time, I hate to see worthwhile plants discarded merely because they are no longer brand-spanking new. Herbaceous plants are more subject to the cycles of fashion than are trees and shrubs.

As I've already mentioned, a garden consists of plants in combination. Now take a minute to reflect on that. In a first-rate garden plants are arranged so that they look better together than they do by themselves. In my work as a garden consultant I often see less-than-inspired gardens, wherein the design can be easily improved with the aid of a shovel and some rearrangement of existing plants. A good design will enhance a garden more than the addition of some trendy horticultural newcomer. Novelty does not guarantee superior qualities, in either looks or performance. Just think of the many introductions that sprout on the gardening scene only to vanish into that great compost heap of discarded plants. *Heuchera* 'Snowstorm', for example, with its white-spattered leaves displaying only a little green, was introduced with great fanfare. A new color break for heucheras, it was promoted with enthusiasm, but faded away as quickly as it arrived on the scene. It simply did not grow successfully in any region except the Pacific Northwest, where the summers are cool.

Besides, if you wait long enough you will see that what goes around comes around. Cannas were once passé but have regained popularity. Coleus (*Solenostemon scutellarioides*) suffered a name change, the genus *Coleus* becoming the genus *Solenostemon*, but recovered its reputation as a hot plant for the cool summer garden. I will mention a few newcomers, but I believe readers will be better served by suggestions for enhanced use of plants they either already have or can easily obtain.

Siberian bugloss, as *Brunnera macrophylla* is commonly called, is a dull enough name to put anyone off. I prefer to call it brunnera. But whatever you call it, this species is a workhorse for the shady garden. A cluster of heart-shaped, spadelike leaves emerges in spring, suitably scaled to the delicate bunches of blue flowers, similar in effect to those of forget-me-nots. After the flowers fade, the leaves continue to increase in size, reaching the dimensions of a coffee-cup saucer. Their soft surface appearance and sturdy constitution (they are deer resistant and remain weatherproof until a few hard frosts hit in late autumn or early winter) create a great foil to the lacey leaves of small to midsized ferns and astilbes, or to the coarser yet still compound foliage of epimediums. An alternate look can be created by pairing brunnera with the linear shapes of liriopes, shade-tolerant sedges (*Carex*), or Japanese roof irises (*Iris tectorum*). Brunnera is tolerant of abuse; it will endure poor soil, somewhat dry conditions, and heavy shade. Given suitable conditions of light to moderate shade and an open, moist yet well-drained soil with ample organic matter, the plants are more vigorous, more attractive, and multiply by self-sowing. Young plants move readily. Older plants, with a heavy system of sturdy, thonglike roots, dislike relocation.

In a first-rate garden plants are arranged so that they look better together than they do by themselves.

The crisp, clean white edge bordering each leaf of *Brunnera macrophylla* 'Variegata' is apparent as soon as leaves emerge in spring and remains until plants are cut down by frost. This creates a very bright, delicate effect in places where several plants are grouped together. Under stress—drought, for example—'Variegata' may revert to all-green. When this occurs, or if all-green seedlings are produced, any green-leaved portion must be removed, roots and all. The green-leaved plant will be more vigorous than its variegated counterpart, crowding it out and eventually displacing it altogether. 'Jack Frost' is a recently introduced brunnera cultivar whose whole leaf appears to be painted silver-gray, creating an elegant hoarfrost look (see Plate 48). If planting this in your garden you might keep the theory of leaf shape combinations in mind and, staying with the theme of gray, pair 'Jack Frost' with Japanese painted fern (*Athyrium nipponicum* 'Pictum').

Alternatively, you might contrast silver-gray with forest-green by also planting Christmas fern (*Polystichum acrostichoides*).

Even gardeners who avoid variegated plants seem to find the patterning on lungworts (*Pulmonaria*) charming and attractive (see Plate 27). Perhaps this is because the simple silver splotches seem to replicate sunlight dappling through an overhead canopy. Use lungworts to disguise the fading foliage of small bulbs. Pair its hairy leaves with the glossy, slick forest-green leaves of European ginger (*Asarum europaeum*). Japanese painted fern (*Athyrium nipponicum* 'Pictum') will make a willing partner where there is adequate moisture in the soil. Lungwort is also commonly called pulmonaria, naturally enough, and both names hint at the silver-spotted leaf of the most commonly grown species, Bethlehem sage (*P. saccharata*). The leaves of *P. saccharata* were traditionally thought to resemble tubercular lungs, and under the doctrine of signatures this meant that the plant had some curative value for lung problems. Whether this is true or not, it is safe to say this workhorse plant will be appreciated for its other features, including attractive foliage, springtime flowers, and an ability to tolerate dry shade. Keep in mind, though, that Bethlehem sage will grow most satisfactorily in average to moist soils, especially in hot weather. While it thrives with spring sunshine and appreciates morning light year-round, afternoon summer sun will quickly lead to wilting, droopy leaves. In hot-summer regions Bethlehem sage will often beat the heat by going into estivation. If lungworts begin to look shabby in hot summer weather, they can be easily rejuvenated. Cut back the leaves, right to ground level, water thoroughly, and fertilize lightly. This technique will be useful through July, resulting in a fresh new crop of leaves, but August is too late for such drastic treatment. Lungworts readily reseed in woodland gardens. The infant plants are easy to recognize: look for a pair of round, slightly cupped seed leaves and true leaves displaying spots just as soon as they emerge. Young plants are easy to move, but larger plants generally wilt. They are less apt to do so, however, if you cut the leaves back by half, removing half the length from tip back towards the stem. Also, rather surprisingly, lungworts seem most likely to move without wilting right at the height of summer. Perhaps it is merely that by summer the leaves are tougher, more mature than tender spring growth. Should a seedling crop up with extraordinary appeal, perhaps a greater or lesser degree of spotting, you may clone it through division in spring or late summer. Root cuttings taken in early summer also work well. Luckily, mammalian vermin such as deer, rabbits, and woodchucks leave lungworts alone (those hairy leaves probably tickle too much going down); nor have I found slugs to be a problem, even in damp weather.

Blue lungwort (*Pulmonaria angustifolia*) has unspotted, lanceolate, 7-inch-long leaves and bright blue flowers that appear in spring. The leaves of red lungwort (*P. rubra*), also unspotted, grow only 5 to 7 inches long and are nearly evergreen. They are also pointed and quite hairy, as are the stems. Red flowers appear very early in spring and last for an extended period. *Pulmonaria rubra* 'David Ward' is a cultivar with apple- to mint-green leaves nicely edged in white. *Pulmonaria longifolia* has dark green, silver-spotted, long, narrow leaves, 9 to 18 inches long, that mound into a dense clump. There are several interesting varieties: *P. longifolia* var. *cevennensis*, with extremely long, nicely spotted leaves; *P. longifolia* 'Bertram Anderson', with especially long, narrow leaves and distinct silver spotting; *P. longifolia* 'Dordogne', with lanceolate leaves larger than those of the species and heavily spotted with silver; and *P. longifolia* 'Little Blue', selected for its profuse blue flowers. Jerusalem cowslip (*P. officinalis*) has heart-shaped leaves covered with hairs and usually freckled or spotted white. Like Bethlehem sage, it was used to treat lung problems in the late medieval period.

Bethlehem sage (*Pulmonaria saccharata*) features white-spotted, medium green, widely oval leaves that are more or less evergreen. Given the propensity for lungworts to hybridize with each other, the ancestry of some *P. saccharata* cultivars is problematical. Older cultivars still worth growing include 'Mrs. Moon', with large leaves and blue flowers that open from pink buds (unfortunately, however, this cultivar gets mildew in hot, humid weather, and lookalike seedlings may be found under the same name); 'Janet Fisk', with large, apple-green, very nicely spotted leaves nearly marbled with silver and lavender-pink flowers; and 'Sissinghurst White', very showy, with wide, silver-spotted leaves and white flowers. More recent cultivars include several gray- or silver-leaved cultivars: 'British Sterling' is nearly entirely silver-white with a narrow green margin, 'Cotton Cool' has narrow, all-silver leaves, 'Excaliber' has very silver-white leaves narrowly edged in dark green, 'Majeste' has silver-gray leaves with just a hint of a narrow green border, and 'Spilled Milk' has wide, heavily silvered leaves on a compact dwarf plant that grows to about 9 inches tall. Other popular *P. saccharata* cultivars include several selected for their flowers but which also have good foliage: 'Blausemeer' features long leaves freckled with small silver spots, and dark blue flowers, 'Coral Springs' has long leaves attractively spotted gray-white, and deep purple-pink flower buds opening to coral-pink flowers; and 'Dora Bielefeld' has medium green leaves spotted with silver gray, topped off with pink flowers.

The species and cultivars of *Astilbe* are deservedly popular plants for the shade garden, their fernlike foliage providing interest well beyond their two weeks of early summer bloom. Astilbes prefer adequate moisture, a rich free-draining soil high in organic matter, and light or dappled shade. Use them on the banks of a pond or along a stream, making sure the roots are not in the water. Varieties of *A.* ×*arendsii* with deep pink to red flowers may start the season with copper to bronze foliage, though they all mature to a pleasing medium green. *Astilbe chinensis* 'Pumila' is a low-growing, spreading plant that functions as a groundcover, its dark green leaves overlapping in a tidy manner. *Astilbe simplicifolia* and its cultivars, such as 'Dunkellanchs', 'Heinie Graafland', and 'Sprite', offer the gardener low-growing plants with very glossy foliage. Similar in foliage but grander in scale than the garden hybrids is our native species, *A. biternata*, called false goatsbeard. It grows 3 feet tall, forming a moderately dense mound of medium green leaves, two or three times ternately divided. This means that each leaf is divided into three leaflets, and since it is biternate, each leaflet is again divided into three parts. The appearance is very similar to goatsbeard (*Aruncus dioicus*), which has two-pinnate leaves that are twice as large as those of false goatsbeard, and which at 6 feet high can reach the bulk of a small shrub.

Precisely because they are so similar in effect, astilbe and goatsbeard should not be planted together. Fern, cimicifuga, doll's eye (*Actaea pachypoda*), baneberry (*A. rubra*), and blue cohosh (*Caulophyllum thalictroides*) would also be poor choices to plant with astilbes because of their airy, divided foliage. Bolder, bulkier leaves play better. Brunnera, with its heart-shaped leaves, is one easy option. There are a diversity of hostas as well: small cultivars for the tiny astilbes, medium cultivars for the other astilbes and the actaeas, large cultivars for the bulky false goatsbeards (as well as for *Aruncus dioicus*). Astilbes also partner well with *Astilboides tabularis*, which features very large, shield-shaped, peltate leaves and stalks attached at the center of each leaf's underside. The astilboides will need a moist, rich soil in partial shade to be coaxed into its most sizeable display.

TENDER PERENNIALS

Caladiums are tropical tubers, and so lumpy that determining which side of a dormant individual is supposed to go up can be a real quandary. To keep happy, caladiums must be provided with heat—*lots* of heat—and high humidity, along with a moist yet freely draining soil high in organic matter. Although shade used to be a sine qua non, I often see these plants out in the broiling sun. Apparently, if they are started off in sunny conditions as they break dormancy, and if they are given sufficient moisture, caladiums can, like mad dogs and Englishmen, go out in the noonday sun. Of course, that's in the relatively temperate conditions of the Northeast. Caladiums do not thrive in the Pacific Northwest, where summer temperatures are too cool, nor in the arid Southwest, where their thin, tender, arrowhead-shaped leaves shrivel in the dry air. Gardeners are frequently restricted to the limited selection of caladiums offered by their local nurseries. This usually includes large white-leaved plants with green veins, translucent pink-leaved plants with opaque red veins, and perhaps one or two other varieties, such as a white-spattered form with hot fuchsia-pink veins. This really is a pity, as specialty growers in Florida offer dozens of cultivars. Slow to get going, caladiums like an early start to the season. If planting-out time is mid to late May, you'll want to get your caladium going indoors in February, making sure it has a bottom warmth and temperatures of about 70° Fahrenheit. In these energy-conscious times, this is probably warmer than many of us keep our homes—which brings us back to the circumscribed options at the local garden center. As ever, good design is the solution: make the best of whatever you have available.

Caladium has a thin-textured, strong, blocky, arrowhead-shaped leaf. The lance-leaf type is narrower, with more substance. Pairing caladiums with hostas is tempting, given their colorful appearances. Combine *Caladium bicolor* 'Candidum', a white-veined, white-margined, dark green, frequently sold cultivar, with *Hosta plantaginea*, whose deeply veined leaves, green as a Granny Smith apple, provide a nice contrast, accentuated when the hosta's fragrant white flowers appear in August. Sprinkle in a few white impatiens for an easy-maintenance planting that lightens a shady corner (see Plate 67). Keeping in mind what you know about using foliage shapes, you could also plant a dark green fern, perhaps Christmas fern (*Polystichum acrostichoides*), whose lacy fronds play against the caladium's bold shape and accent its margin and veining. Set *C. bicolor* 'June Bride', whose leaves are entirely white, among a groundcover of periwinkle (*Vinca minor*) to lighten the somber green. Remember, though, that caladiums need moisture. 'June Bride' would look stunning along my forest path, where periwinkle covers the ground over dormant daffodils, but conditions there would be too dry.

Caladium bicolor 'Freida Hemple' is more moderate in size than 'Candidum' or 'June Bride' and features clear cardinal-red, slightly ruffled leaves. 'Freida Hemple' blends well with *Heuchera micrantha* var. *diversifolia* 'Palace Purple', the red perking up the purple, and with black mondo grass (*Ophiopogon planiscapus* 'Nigrescens'), with its thin, ribbonlike, truly black leaves (see Plate 45). This striking bijou combination should be placed for suitably intimate observation, perhaps raised into prominence in a container set next to a bench. If instead of *H. micrantha* var. *diversifolia* 'Palace Purple', you were to select *H.* 'Can-Can', with its ruffled, intensely silvered leaves, then Japanese painted fern (A*thyrium nipponicum* 'Pictum') would be an obvious match, along with black mondo grass. Should your caladium have bright pink leaves—as with *C. bicolor* 'Fannie Munson', for example—then think about combining it with pink-flowered astilbes. The fernlike leaves will create a quiet summertime foliage partnership, elevated into prominence when the astilbe is in flower. Pink can be a tricky color. If it has even a hint of blue about it, it is a cool pink and will clash with any pink warmed up by a breath of yellow. Precisely matching foliage to flower is a guessing game, since flower color changes with age and is influenced by weather conditions. Consider *Astilbe* ×*arendsii* 'Bressingham Beauty', with its bright pink flowers, but also consider the more softly pink *A.* ×*arendsii* 'Grete Pungel', which might be more suitable.

DESIGNING FOR SHADY GARDENS

Plants are the materials; design is the method. Begin with a concept, some notion of what effect you are after. Develop your ideas at a leisurely pace, with patience. Gardening should not be about instant gratification. Pity the poor corporate executive who never spends more than a year or two in each house before moving on, and have sympathy for his or her transient, abandoned garden. Remember that gardening is the slowest of art forms, incorporating the fourth dimension of time. Wait to elaborate on the project until you see how the original plants settle in together. Allow them time to grow into their places, permitting the garden itself to suggest changes. Do you need more ferns? Should they sweep behind the hostas or remain adjacent to them? Do the hellebores fail to thrive?

Perhaps you wish to praise the woodlands surrounding your Virginia home. Oaks and tulip poplars form the canopy, and mountain laurels sweep over the hillside. Several ferns and wild gingers (*Asarum*) are already present, along with Jack-in-the-pulpit (*Arisaema triphyllum*) and bloodroot (*Sanguinaria canadensis*). Chary of buying native flowers such as trillium that might have been collected from the wild, you seek out perennials that will look at home whether they are native or not. Bear's foot hellebore (*Helleborus foetidus*) has dark green, narrow-fingered leaflets in a pedatisect arrangement. *Euphorbia amygdaloides* var. *robbiae*, a wood spurge, also has dark green leaves, rounded and ovulate, which contrast nicely to those of the hellebore. It would be best to place a lighter green between these two, to set them off with more clarity. Siberian bugloss (*Brunnera macrophylla*) has a strong, blocky, ace-of-spades shape in a medium green and is further distinguished by its roughly pubescent, slightly hairy texture, in contrast to the slick surfaces of the hellebore and the wood spurge. Hostas are also a possibility, their deeply incised veins creating a pleasing accentuation to the leaf—though in this example those with plain green leaves are preferable, such as the medium dark green *Hosta ventricosa*. Viridescent hostas are those with leaves that appear white- or yellow-variegated as they emerge in spring but that become entirely green as they mature, and these are another option. *Hosta fortunei* var. *albopicta* is an excellent example.

Moving up the path and out of the woods, towards the house, brings us to a terrace, a more obviously cultivated site. This area allows us to play with horticultural forms of plants already in use: *Brunnera macrophylla* 'Langtrees', perhaps, with its silver-spotted leaves, and *Hosta* 'Citation' with its light green leaves and wavy white margins. Impatiens might find a place here, but they should be planted in irregular small groups rather than en masse as carpet bedding or in soldierly rows. Arriving at the house, any and all plants are suitable for fair use, from a block planting of impatiens to vividly colored coleus (*Solenostemon scutellarioides*) and anything else that takes the homeowner's fancy. Containers announce the cultivated nature of their contents equally well.

Masonry buildings, concrete sidewalks, and pavement provide the ambience for a Brooklyn brownstone where the neighbors are never out of view. Golden shrubs add light and warmth to a shady space, with coleus (*Solenostemon scutellarioides*) and caladiums providing summer color. Spring bulbs add early color, their absence disguised by a carpet of pachysandra. In Manhattan a stylish formal garden with a handkerchief-sized lawn is bounded by precise conifer accents and a low hedge of box (*Buxus*) or yew (*Taxus*). A finishing ribbon of English ivy (*Hedera helix*) or periwinkle (*Vinca minor*) creates a quiet space in which to retreat from a frantic workaday world.

You can also create your own little woodland hideaway without even leaving home. Use a flowering dogwood (*Cornus florida*), an alder-leaved serviceberry (*Amelanchier alnifolia*), or a green-leaved form of Japanese maple (*Acer palmatum*) as the "forest." Assuming you have room for a couple of shrubs, choose one that is deciduous and one that is evergreen, for winter interest. Rather than selecting the typical evergreen azalea, try a native species such as flame azalea (*Rhododendron calendulaceum*). It flowers later in the season than its evergreen cousins and its fall color is often a rich orange. *Leucothoe axillaris* has a mounding habit that plays against the more upright form of flame azalea. Add sturdy, shade-tolerant, herbaceous perennials, remembering that since their spring flowers are fleeting you will need good foliage to sustain the garden into summer and beyond.

New Orleans has that tropical ambiance of walled gardens, lacy ironwork fences, and balcony railings. Heat and rain make the gardens grow and grow, but gardening isn't something you can do during the daytime in summer. Keeping plants in their place begins with selecting appropriate, slower-growing plants. Crape myrtle (*Lagerstroemia indica*) has elegant, exfoliating, snakeskin-mottled bark, glossy leaves, and white, pink, red, or lavender flowers. Train one to a single-trunk standard rather than allowing it a boisterous, unhousebroken exuberance as a multistemmed shrub. Japanese holly fern (*Cyrtomium falcatum*) has shiny, bright green, evergreen fronds made up of hollylike leaflets. Match this with cast iron plant (*Aspidistra elatior*), whose architectural, oval, dark green leaves are carried on long sturdy petioles for more height. Or try *A. elatior* 'Variegata', with streaky white variegation that seems to vary from leaf to leaf. White caladiums show up ghostly pale at night, whether lit by the moon or by a streetlamp. Back these up with *Pittosporum tobira* 'Variegatum', whose gray-green leaves, edged in white, have a cool look even on the hottest nights. Allow this shrub to softly billow as it pleases, or clip it into a precise background for the herbaceous plants. If you simply must have flowers, stick with white impatiens.

First you contemplate, then you garden, using foliage as a firm foundation to support your dreamy reveries and make them real.

CHAPTER 4

❧

Golden Treasures

There is a vogue for monotone flower gardens—gardens with perhaps only blue flowers, or moon gardens in which every plant has white flowers. The same conceit can be accomplished with foliage. Russell Page, for example, designed an all-yellow garden at the PepsiCo Sculpture Gardens (see Plate 29). He incorporated upright, pyramidal golden conifers and other moplike spreaders, as well as gold-leaved deciduous trees and shrubs. The only portion of the garden that isn't gold is a carpet of green grass. I first saw this garden in the bright sunshine of a late spring day, when the leaves were at their brightest, and it sparkled. On another visit, during an overcast early autumn day, the garden had an even more buoyant, if less vivid, effect, its golden foliage acting as a substitute for sunshine.

Conifers displayed at the PepsiCo garden include the slow-growing golden hinoki cypress (*Chamaecyparis obtusa* 'Crippsii'), which eventually reaches 20 feet tall or more and features handsomely textured, bright golden yellow, scalelike foliage and a pyramidal or broadly conical shape. The much smaller *C. obtusa* 'Tetragona Aurea' is also displayed. This bright golden pyramidal dwarf has gracefully curving, fernlike main branches and serves as a reminder that with conifers the word "dwarf" might be more properly translated as "slow growing." *Chamaecyparis pisifera* 'Filifera Aurea Nana' is a golden form of Sawara cypress with weeping, threadlike branches and scalelike needles pressed tightly to the stem. It is a low-growing cultivar and looks something like a pile of gold wires, remaining gold year-round unless grown in heavy shade. It eventually reaches 6 feet high. *Chamaecyparis pisifera* 'Juniperoides Aurea' is a low-growing, compact, tidy, globose dwarf with finely textured, plumose foliage. It has only been in cultivation since 1965 and is very much a collector's plant.

Moving on to other conifer genera on display, we have golden arborvitae, juniper, and spruce. Sudworth golden arborvitae (*Thuja occidentalis* 'Lutea') is a tidy, slender, conical tree that eventually reaches 45 feet tall. New growth is a soft creamy yellow that ripens to gold and eventually turns green. Oriental arborvitae (*Platycladus orientalis*) is an Asian relative. Its dwarf golden cultivar, *P. orientalis* 'Aurea Nana', is a rounded shrub that rarely grows more than 5 feet tall. The scalelike needles on its tightly packed branches are arranged in a vertical plane like the pages of a book standing on its spine. In spring the needles have a glowing yellow-green hue, often shifting towards brown in winter. The form and color of this shrub are striking, and its price is rather modest. As a result, 'Aurea Nana' frequently shows up at garden centers and discount stores. There is nothing wrong with that, of course, but the result is that gardeners often purchase 'Aurea Nana' on impulse and plug it into a situation in which it doesn't belong. It ends up a poorly placed yellow blob, either plopped in the lawn for an unwittingly shrieking effect, paired up by a front door or garden gate, or planted in a row that marches along the property line.

Golden Norway spruce (*Picea abies* 'Aurea'), which can also be found in the PepsiCo garden, is a striking tree with stiff golden yellow needles that turn greener as summer arrives. The upright form is accentuated by more pendulous branchlets. *Juniperus chinensis* 'Gold Coast', known as gold coast juniper, is very similar to *J. chinensis* 'Golden Armstrong'. Both full, blocky shrubs reach 4 feet tall, are more compact than the ubiquitous pfitzer juniper (*J. chinensis* 'Pfitzeriana Aurea'), and have feathery branches armed with needle-sharp golden foliage.

In contrast with its upright and rounded conifers, which provide finely textured foliage for year-round interest, Russell Page's garden includes the broad-leaved, evergreen *Euonymus fortunei* 'Emerald 'n' Gold', which features leathery leaves splashed with yellow. Rather than climbing or trailing, as do many of its relatives, this cultivar forms a bushy shrub. It is instructive to note, too, that Russell Page was as willing to use ordinary shrubs like *E. fortunei* 'Emerald 'n' Gold' and *Platycladus orientalis* 'Aurea Nana' as he was to choose rarities. His selections were based on the qualities each plant offered, rather than on some snobbish reliance on rarity. Golden vicaryi privet (*Ligustrum ×vicaryi*) is another widely used shrub that Page included in his design, and with excellent results. Slower growing and wider spreading than either parent, when planted in a sunny site this hybrid of *L. ovalifolium* 'Aureomarginatum' and *L. vulgare* displays golden yellow foliage throughout the growing season, looking especially bright in early summer. Though deciduous in northern regions, golden vicaryi privet remains semi-evergreen in milder climates. There are two strains of this shrub, true vicaryi and hillside vicaryi, and both are present in the PepsiCo garden. True vicaryi is brighter than hillside vicaryi, which was originally selected for use in Minnesota and is cold hardy down to zone 4.

Deciduous trees and shrubs for seasonal accents include several with finely textured lacy foliage. Though our native American elderberry (*Sambucus canadensis*) is most often seen as a scruffy, green-leaved inhabitant of damp roadside ditches, there is a gold-leaved form that responds nicely to care and cultivation. *Sambucus canadensis* 'Aurea' has pinnately compound leaves that remain bright golden yellow to yellow-green throughout the summer, creating a strong accent on this 10- to 12-foot-tall shrub.

Sunburst honey locust (*Gleditsia triacanthos* 'Sunburst') is a popular lawn tree because the light shade cast by its finely textured, pinnately compound leaves allows grass to grow right up to its base. A tall tree, it will rather quickly reach 30 to 40 feet tall, with an open crown spreading from a short trunk. It is brightest in spring when the new leaves, with as many as one hundred inch-long leaflets pinnately arranged on a single leaf, are a glowing golden yellow. Young foliage on the branch tips remains yellow all season long, creating a softly blended contrast against the green older leaves. In addition, 'Sunburst' is seedless, eliminating the cleanup problem resulting from the 18-inch-long, twisted, leathery seedpods produced by the species. Golden locust (*Robinia pseudoacacia* 'Frisia') is equally tall with similar finely textured, pinnately compound leaves, which remain yellow throughout the summer in cooler regions. Hardy from zones 3 to 8, this tree is affected by summer heat, which seems to fatigue the foliage, turning it from gold to green. The leaflets of both *G. triacanthos* 'Sunburst' and *R. pseudoacacia* 'Frisia' are so fine and light when they fall in autumn that they are best sucked up by a lawnmower rather than raked. Golden rain tree (*Koelreuteria paniculata*) is the odd one out in this garden of gold foliage: the seven to fifteen leaflets of its pinnate foliage are a rich dark green. It does, however, offer masses of yellow flowers in early summer and, on occasion, acceptable yellow fall color.

Golden mock orange (*Philadelphus coronarius* 'Aureus') and mellow yellow bridal wreath (*Spiraea thunbergii* 'Ogon') are alike in that both pair gold foliage with white flowers. Foliage color on the mock orange remains a more glowing yellow to chartreuse in cooler climates, turning greener where summer heat is the normal situation. Mellow yellow bridal wreath has the willow-like leaves typical of *S. thunbergii*, but they are yellow to chartreuse-yellow rather than light green. Leaves appear after the flowers and make this shrub, at 3 to 5 feet high and wide, a pleasing mound of sunny foliage.

Golden barberry (*Berberis thunbergii* 'Aurea') is a mainstay shrub for yellow foliage. It holds its clear yellow color right through the dog days of August, making a neat and tidy mound of finely textured oval leaves. It can be clipped into a mound, made into a small hedge, or placed into an herbaceous border as a color note.

What a marvelous concept Russell Page devised: tall deciduous trees acting as a sunny backdrop, elegant golden conifers marching in pyramidal geometry or mounding softly, shrubs adding a seasonal warmth of yellow leaves from spring to fall. Everything comes together: the play of shape and texture, the subtle shifts of color from the vivid yellows of spring to the more subtle, subdued golds and greens of summer.

> Plants with yellow leaves can be used to lighten a shady area, adding a sense of brightness where things are dim.

Plants with yellow leaves can be used to lighten a shady area, adding a sense of brightness where things are dim. They make a refreshing contrast to green foliage, from the dark forest-green of bear's foot hellebore (*Helleborus foetidus*) to the pale apple-green of *Hosta plantaginea*, and a vivid disparity for plants with purple, plum, copper, or bronze foliage. Since yellow-leaved plants are capable of photosynthesis, they remain healthy, grow well, and need no special care.

Yellow coloration is most vivid in spring on new growth. This is especially true with coniferous shrubs, though it also applies to some yellow-leaved perennials—Bowles golden grass (*Milium effusum* 'Aureum'), for one. Many yellow-leaved plants turn greener as the season progresses, especially as temperatures rise in summer. This is why a plant like *Philadelphus coronarius* 'Aureus' may be better suited to cooler regions such as the Pacific Northwest than to zone 8 gardens in Georgia or Louisiana. Some plants, however, such as the yellow-leaved hostas, remain as bright in summer as when they first emerged in spring.

It is a personal matter as to whether you like yellow-leaved plants or loathe them. Some plants with yellow foliage look sickly, as if diseased or chlorotic, and I find that yellow-leaved plants with pink flowers, such as golden bleeding heart (*Dicentra spectabilis* 'Gold Heart'), have a dissonance that sets my teeth on edge. Clearly, though, there is another point of view. Minnesota nurseryman Steve Kelley tells me he cannot keep 'Gold Heart' in stock—they "just fly out the door." Although I don't care much for that particular plant, I do enjoy golden barberry (*Berberis thunbergii* 'Aurea') and golden creeping Jenny (*Lysimachia nummularia* 'Aurea').

DECIDUOUS TREES

Golden moon (*Acer shirasawanum* 'Aureum'), also known as yellow moon maple, was known as *A. japonicum* 'Aureum' as recently as 1984. It is an elegant little tree eventually reaching 20 feet tall with a compact, densely branched habit. Orbicular leaves are 3 to 4 inches across, with nine to eleven shallow lobes. Leaf color is a warm golden yellow, darkening with maturity. Slow growing in its youth and difficult to propagate, it remains on the expensive side of things even though readily available. Since the delicate foliage is prone to sun scorch in exposed sunny sites, it is more safely sited in a shaded situation, such as at the edge of a woodland, in zones 5b to 8b.

Catalpa bignonioides 'Aurea' is a bright yellow-leaved cultivar of Indian bean tree, which is native to southeastern United States. The typical green-leaved species is hardy from zones 5a to 9a and has even naturalized much further north of its native range, Georgia to Mississippi and Florida. Widely adaptable to heat or cold, wet soil or dry soil, this large tree with bold, coarse texture and tropical, showy, early-summer flowers is not a popular landscape choice. This is probably due to the messy litter of stiff seedpods, which can be as much as 15 inches long, that drop at their leisure all fall and winter. In addition, the leaf-eating larvae of the catalpa sphinx moth (*Ceratomia catalpae*), commonly called catalpa worms, can be a problem (though, incidentally, catalpa worms are much prized by fishermen, who use them for bait).

Catalpa bignonioides 'Aurea' is often managed by stooling or pollarding, firstly to control its size but even more so to increase the size of its leaves. Since this deletes any possibility of flowers, it also takes care of the litter problem. The two techniques are similar in that both involve severely cutting back the branches of a tree on a regular, even yearly basis. The resulting smaller size of the tree also simplifies management of any leaf-eating caterpillars. In warmer climates 'Aurea' is most strikingly colored from spring until early summer, turning green later in the season. Its rich yellow color remains throughout the growing season in cooler climates such as the Pacific Northwest.

Honey locust (*Gleditsia triacanthos*) is tolerant of heat, wind, compacted soil, road salt, cold down to −15° Fahrenheit, and even some drought. All this would make this tough tree suitable for urban situations, but it also features clusters of stiff 4-inch-long thorns up and down its trunk. Fortunately, *G. triacanthos* f. *inermis* is thornless. And refining our selection even further brings us to our old friend *G. triacanthos* 'Sunburst'.

DECIDUOUS SHRUBS

Berberis thunbergii 'Aurea' is a finely textured shrub with a slower habit of growth than the species, and bright yellow leaves when grown in full sun. Its tidy habit and orderly appearance, coupled with its restrained size of 3 to 4 feet tall and wide, make it suitable for placement in the herbaceous border. The yellow foliage combines nicely with yellow to orange flowers and acts as a foil to blue ones. In addition, the shrub's dense and twiggy bare branches offer some interest in winter, adding structure when perennials are dormant. Full sun is necessary to maintain the brightest color—leaves will green up if the site is even somewhat shaded.

The most readily available European hazel (*Corylus avellana*) is Harry Lauder's walking stick (*C. avellana* 'Contorta'). Its distorted, twisted growth is most pleasing when the shrub is bare in winter, as even the leaves have a contorted habit, looking as if they were accidentally damaged by herbicide. A better choice would be *C. avellana* 'Aurea', which lacks the crooked habit but makes up for it with pleasing chartreuse-yellow leaves in spring and early summer. By midsummer, as temperatures heat up, leaves change to green, turning a nice clear yellow in fall. Slow growing and 12 to 20 feet high and wide, 'Aurea' is not as vigorous as the species, and is suitable for zones 4b to 8b.

Privets (*Ligustrum*), often classed as "trailer park plants," are in disrepute for the very adaptability that makes them popular with chain store garden centers. Their ease of cultivation makes them ubiquitous and commonplace. Keep in mind that good design makes skillful use of plants—the plants alone cannot turn a poor design into a better one. Semi-evergreen to deciduous, golden vicaryi privet (*L.* ×*vicaryi*) is a slower-growing, wider-spreading shrub than its parents, *L. ovalifolium* 'Aureomarginatum' and *L. vulgare*. The lustrous, leathery leaves are golden yellow throughout the growing season if the plant is grown in full sun, and especially bright in early summer as new foliage matures. *Ligustrum* ×*vicaryi* can brighten dull overcast days, so frequent in the Pacific Northwest, or be clipped into topiary or used as a hedge. It is hardy from zones 5b to 8b, and *L.* ×*vicaryi* 'Hillside' is hardy down to zone 4b, making it useful in Minnesota. A superb hedge I saw pictured once in a magazine article had golden vicaryi privets placed as buttresses, geometrically spaced with precision against a tall green hedge, all the shrubs clipped into a living version of a masonry wall.

The common name for *Philadelphus coronarius*, mock orange, hints at the sweet perfume of its white flowers. While flowering is most generous in full sun, mock orange will happily take partial shade (a fortunate fact, as the young foliage of *P. coronarius* 'Aureus' is likely to burn in full sun). In shade the color is softer, closer to chartreuse or a delicate lime-green than to the bright yellow hue developed in full sun. Whether mock orange is grown in sun or light shade, in summer its leaves are green. It is hardy from zones 4a to 7b, its best color most easily maintained in the cooler portion of the range. This shrub needs room to grow. Regular pruning out of some of the oldest stems, right to ground level, will keep it shapely. Though less vigorous than the species, which can grow 10 to 12 feet high and wide, 'Aureus' will still reach 7 feet tall.

Eastern ninebark (*Physocarpus opulifolius*) is a cold-tolerant shrub hardy from zones 3b to 7. It features coarse foliage, up to 3 inches long with three to five lobes, and peeling bark, for a modicum of winter interest. Resistant to both pests and diseases, eastern ninebark is a sturdy choice for those tough sites where other shrubs might not make it. There are two yellow-leaved forms, 'Dart's Gold' and 'Luteus'. The older cultivar, 'Luteus', has leaves that are yellow-green as they emerge in spring, later changing to green. It is a large shrub, reaching 8 to 10 feet tall and wide. 'Dart's Gold' is a better choice: the color is brighter and longer lasting (though it too turns green in hot summer weather), and it makes a more compact shrub.

American elderberry (*Sambucus canadensis*) is a roadside shrub found throughout eastern United States but only noticed when in bloom or in berry. Large platelike clusters of tiny white flowers appear in early summer, followed by massive clusters of small purplish black fruits in August and September. The flowers can add a wild flavor to currant jelly, and the fruits themselves can make a tasty jelly or wine, but these are usually collected from the wild rather than given space in the orchard. Happiest in full sun and moist soil, American elderberry would be suitable for a wildlife habitat garden just about anywhere it is hardy, from zones 3 to 9. Though resistant to pests and diseases, it does need maintenance pruning: the 9- to 10-foot-tall, pithy, hollow stems are weak enough that a heavy berry crop will pull them over. A quick cutting back in early spring of broken or winter-damaged branches will help this shrub maintain a more pleasing form, but *S. canadensis* 'Aurea' is more suitable for ornamental use.

Spiraea japonica 'Goldflame' and *S. japonica* 'Lime Mound' are small shrubs that tuck neatly into the herbaceous border as partners for perennials. The leaves on 'Goldflame' are a rich orangey bronze-red when young, softening to yellow in summer and turning back to orange and copper in autumn. It is unfortunate that the flowers are a bright rosy pink, but these can be pruned off before the buds open. Growing to approximately 3 feet tall and over 3 feet wide, this is the only plant I've found to face down crown imperial (*Fritillaria imperialis*), which is taller than any other April-flowering perennial, reaching 3 feet in height. Crown imperial features a circlet of large orange bells beneath a crowning tuft of leaves. *Spiraea japonica* 'Goldflame' is well suited to screen the bulb's stem, enhance its flowers, and disguise any fading foliage. It is a good match for tulips as well. I planted 'Goldflame' and purple-leaved *Berberis thunbergii* 'Atropurpurea Nana' behind soft orange *Tulipa* 'Prinses Irene', feathered with faded purple, for an elegant spring display. Other *S. japonica* cultivars include 'Gold Mound', which has green leaves in summer, and 'Lime Mound', a great little Japanese cultivar with lime-green leaves flushed with rusty red as they unfold in spring, warming again to orange in autumn.

Weigela 'Rubidor' features bright canary-yellow leaves and vivid magenta flowers, and if you can avoid the harsh contrast between the two by arranging your vacation for the May–June bloom period, so much the better. This is an old-fashioned shrub, popular for its hardiness (it is cold hardy down to zone 4) and tolerance of neglect. It has an arching habit resulting in a roundish mound from 5 to 10 feet tall and wide. *Weigela* 'Rubidor' grows most vigorously with moist yet well-drained soil and full sun, but will accept most anything except full shade. Any pruning needed to remove dead branches and control the size of this shrub is best done after flowering is over.

EVERGREEN SHRUBS

Heaths (*Erica*) and heathers (*Calluna*) are readily distinguished from each other: the first has needlelike leaves, and the second has scalelike foliage. *Calluna vulgaris* is a wildly variable species, available in an array of foliage and flower colors. The low-growing shrub is hardy to zone 4b in places where snow cover is reliable in winter, hardy to 5b in places without such protection from wind and drying out. *Calluna vulgaris*, like heaths, prefers conditions of peaty, acid, well-drained soil, but it dislikes drying out. Moderate temperatures suit it best, along with relatively high humidity and full sun—a tricky set of conditions to achieve outside of northern states, or at elevation in the Appalachian Mountains. There are several cultivars of *C. vulgaris*, including 'Aurea', 'Blazeaway', 'Cuprea', and 'Gold Haze', which feature yellow to orange-yellow scalelike foliage that is at its brightest in spring, changing to yellow in summer, and turning orange-red to bronze in winter. Unfortunately these cultivars also have purple-mauve flowers, creating a deplorable color combination. Still, their winter foliage coloration makes them most welcome where they can be grown and appreciated (snow cover may keep them alive but it also conceals them from view).

Sawara cypress (*Chamaecyparis pisifera*) is one of those Japanese plants with a seemingly endless chain of cultivars selected over the centuries. When you compare the species, which reaches 75 feet tall at maturity, to the widely popular *C. pisifera* 'Golden Mop', which remains under 3½ feet tall its first decade, the range of options begins to become apparent. 'Filifera Aurea Nana', like 'Golden Mop', remains under 3½ feet tall, spreading more widely all the time, for ten years or more. 'Filifera Aurea' is larger but will stay under 10 feet tall for a long period. 'Squarrosa Aurea Nana' is a dwarf form with yellow needles. 'Plumosa Aurea Compacta' is a pretty yellow pyramid when young, but it loses its shape with age (something many of us can relate to!). There are three subgroups of Sawara cypress, each distinguished by their foliage: thread Sawara cypress, plume Sawara cypress, and moss Sawara cypress. Thread Sawara cypress belong to the filifera group and have a very fine, stringy texture produced by threadlike, pendent branches. Plume Sawara cypress belong to the plumosa group and have scalelike leaves that spread out from the stem, creating an effect like the fluffed tail of an annoyed cat. Moss Sawara cypress belong to the squarrosa group and feature soft needlelike leaves that spread widely from the stem, like a bottlebrush, to produce a mossy appearance.

There are other elegant golden cypress to choose from, including *Chamaecyparis obtusa* 'Nana Aurea', an aristocratic dwarf with tightly packed shell-like sprays of yellow foliage, and *C. obtusa* 'Tetragona Aurea', with its narrow upright habit clad in spreading yellow fans of foliage. Rarely more than 2 feet wide, it will in time reach 15 feet tall, even more in favorable locations. It made quite a sensation in England when it was introduced there from Japan around 1870.

Native to Mexico, and commonly named Mexican orange for its fragrant flowers, *Choisya ternata* is a heat- and drought-tolerant evergreen shrub that is hardy in zones 8b to 9a or above (and, if protected, in zones 7b and 8a). It grows 6 to 10 feet tall and features dense-growing dark green oval leaflets, clustered in threes, that make it a great choice for a foliage screen. While good air circulation is desirable, exposed sites or windy conditions can result in winter damage. However, Mexican orange does respond quickly to being pruned back. Sun or light shade are acceptable, and this shrub will need a light, moist yet freely draining acid soil. *Choisya ternata* 'Sundance' is a vibrant selection with bright yellow leaves. Though only introduced in 1986, Mexican orange is so easy to propagate from cuttings that 'Sundance' is widely available at moderate prices.

Chinese juniper (*Juniperus chinensis*) has great variability. Varieties range from 50-foot-tall trees to wide-spreading shrubs only 18 inches high, all hardy from zones 4 to 9. 'Old Gold' and 'Pfitzeriana Aurea' are both shrubby types, similar in that the tips of their branches turn a bright golden yellow in spring and summer when new growth is exposed to sunlight. In winter 'Pfitzeriana Aurea' turns yellowish green, while 'Old Gold' turns more of a golden bronze. More compact, 'Old Gold' reaches 2 to 3 feet tall at maturity with a spread of 4 to 6 feet. 'Pfitzeriana Aurea' will eventually reach 7 to 10 feet tall and spread 14 to 20 feet wide. Though it cannot be sheared, careful pruning can maintain 'Pfitzeriana Aurea' at a smaller size. Pruned or not, however, it will need room to grow or it will eventually have to be ripped out. 'Gold Coast', as previously mentioned, is a compact shrub growing about 4 feet tall and 4 to 6 feet wide. Its new growth is a particularly warm, bright yellow.

Privet honeysuckle (*Lonicera pileata*), also called boxleaf honeysuckle, is a vigorous, finely textured evergreen shrub suited for sun or shade in zones 7b to 9a or above. *Lonicera nitida* 'Baggesen's Gold' is more cold tolerant, down to zone 6a. It has bright yellow foliage when grown in full sun, and as you might expect, the color is strongest in spring. 'Baggesen's Gold' can be used for a finely textured small hedge or parterre (it grows about 3 feet tall). In *Ornamental Shrubs, Climbers and Bamboos*, Graham Stuart Thomas suggests using *L. nitida* to fill in where deer have eaten out the foliage at the base of yew. As he points out, "At a distance—green or yellow—the two plants look much alike." When shopping for these plants, keep in mind that there is some taxonomic back-and-forth about *L. nitida*. The *Index of Garden Plants*, which I have selected as my authority, lists 'Baggesen's Gold' under this species name; others say *L. nitida* is a synonym for *L. pileata* f. *yunnanensis*, mentioning that the two similar species are often confused.

American arborvitae (*Thuja occidentalis*), also called eastern white cedar, is a cold-hardy evergreen tree resentful of heat and humidity but tolerant of the crummiest of soils. It is commonly used as a hedge or in foundation planting but is occasionally seen as a free-standing, isolated specimen. Suitable for zones 2 to 7, American arborvitae may suffer from winter burn in the colder portion of its range, and freezing may result in a disfiguring dieback of the branch tips. These problems may be avoided if the shrub is situated so as to avoid first morning sunlight; it prefers conditions alternating between sun and shade. Shrubby forms of American arborvitae that lack a leader are apt to be damaged by heavy snow and ice, which load the branches and force them apart, eventually splitting the wood. There are a couple of nicely yellow cultivars, including *T. occidentalis* 'Rheingold', which forms a handsome golden pyramid over time, reaching perhaps 10 feet tall in twenty years, nicely pointed at the tip with a broadly swelling base. Rather different in appearance, *T. occidentalis* 'Golden Globe' forms a dense rounded globe only 3 to 4 feet tall, with bright yellow foliage.

Hardy from zones 6 to 8, oriental arborvitae (*Platycladus orientalis*) is much more heat tolerant than American arborvitae, but accepts only minimal cold. One of the most popular, most readily available of the golden conifers, *P. orientalis* 'Aurea Nana' looks like a fat pyramidal book resting on its spine, its flat pages slightly ruffled. Its new growth is bright golden yellow in spring, softening to yellow-green in summer. Though frequently offered for sale as a cute little golden shrub in a 3-gallon pot, 'Aurea Nana' settles into the landscape and will easily reach 5 feet tall—in fact, it is capable of doubling that height. As previously mentioned, "dwarf" is a relative term when it comes to conifers, the idea being that something that reaches 10 feet tall at maturity is significantly smaller than a 60-foot-tall tree. Also, the shrubby dwarf type will take longer to reach its mature height than will the species.

VINES

Hedera helix 'Buttercup' is a sweet English ivy that shows its bright side only when grown in partial sun. If given too much shade, its 3-inch-long, five-lobed leaves sulk and lose their golden color, becoming a dull lime-green; if given too much sun, they scorch and develop ugly brown patches. Grow 'Buttercup' in a north-facing site open to the sky with good light (think of an artist's atelier). Under these conditions the most exposed leaves will be completely yellow, while those overlaid by other leaves will be chartreuse. Imagine 'Buttercup' spilling over the edge of a container, perhaps with a bronze *Phormium* cultivar and a coleus (*Solenostemon scutellarioides*) with red leaves edged in gold. Ivies usually propagate quite easily. However, 'Buttercup' roots best from shade-grown, more green-leaved portions. It will take a year or so to show its true colors, but should be worth the wait.

Golden hop vine (*Humulus lupulus* 'Aureus') is strictly herbaceous and retreats underground each winter (see Plate 35). Leaves are a radiant yellow-green in spring and lime-yellow to chartreuse in summer. I once rooted some cuttings of golden hop vine that were included in a bouquet given to me in Portland, Oregon. After bringing these home to Connecticut, where we lived at the time, my husband built a nice trellis for them at the corner of the house. A 2-by-4-inch pressure-treated board extended from ground to eaves, with the space between the support and the corner of the house filled in with white plastic-coated wire fencing. The first year the vine made a scraggly little attempt to climb and looked very silly. The second year it did somewhat better. The third year it reached the gutter, and in subsequent years it has snaked out along the power line towards the street. Mind you, this is all one season's growth, since this vine dies back to the ground each winter. Like they say, "The first year it sleeps, the second year it creeps, and the third year it leaps!" Leaves are raspy, like a cat's tongue, so golden hop vine should not be sited in close proximity to bare-armed gardeners. It makes a pleasing accent in the herbaceous border when provided with a support to raise it above lower-growing neighbors, such as a more formal tuteur or a rustic pole tripod (though golden hop vine will completely conceal the support in every season but winter). This rambunctious vine may run about underground once well established.

Virginia creeper (*Parthenocissus quinquefolia*) is a familiar sight on the East Coast, growing on tall highway sound barriers or draped across equally self-planted field cedars (*Juniperus virginiana*). It remains "that green viny stuff" until autumn, when the five-fingered leaves blaze with superbly rich red color. The effect is quite nice, but whether or not you'll want Virginia creeper in your garden will depend on how large a wall or chain link fence you intend to cover. Constant maintenance is required to keep windows clear of this vine's questing tendrils. There is an equally vigorous relative, *P. tricuspidata*, commonly called Boston ivy despite having originated in Japan and China. This species is adaptable to a range of growing conditions from the warmer portion of zone 4 to zone 8, doing well in sun or shade. Boston ivy is self-fastening, clinging to walls and trees by means of aerial sucker discs. Lacking a support, it will ramble like a groundcover. *Parthenocissus tricuspidata* 'Fenway Park' is a new selection introduced by the Arnold Arboretum of Harvard University. Golden yellow three-lobed leaves keep their sunny color all summer long, turning a bright orange-red in autumn. Permit 'Fenway Park' to scramble up any handy, good-sized deciduous tree, allowing it to brighten a shaded woodland site; but keep it away from smaller trees such as flowering dogwood (*Cornus florida*) and Japanese maple (*Acer palmatum*), neither of which have the stature to support such a vigorous vine.

PERENNIALS

Hostas exist in droves, with new cultivars arriving yearly. A mutable genus, *Hosta* encompasses large, small, and medium plants with green, yellow, bluish, and variegated leaves. Though sturdy and self-reliant, hostas have one major drawback in that they are extremely popular with deer, who regard the plant as a culinary treat rather than an object of horticultural veneration (see Plates 36 and 37). Unfortunately, where deer are a problem there are no quick and easy solutions. There are two schools of thought concerning plants popular with deer (what I like to call "salad bar plants"). Some gardeners prefer to group all such plants together, reasoning that this will make life easier as far as spraying and other treatments are concerned. Others prefer to scatter them around the garden in the hopes that at least a few will be overlooked. I cannot say that I have found one or the other method more successful. Deer are creatures of habit, and this includes both how they travel and what they eat. They do have a certain inquisitiveness, and this is what will inevitably lead them to that choice specimen of *Hosta tokudama* f. *aureonebulosa* that you just planted in the last twenty-four hours.

It is possible to create a garden of plants that deer generally do not eat. However, if deer populations are high enough, deer will eat anything, even otherwise normally unpalatable plants such as cannas, ferns, and ornamental grasses. The same holds true under stressful conditions such as drought. Fencing often works as a deterrent. Use either heavy-duty plastic mesh, which, at 8 to 10 feet high, deer cannot jump over, or lower, 2½- to 3-foot-tall paired fences constructed of high-tensile wire connected to a stock fence charger. Keep in mind, though, that not all sites are suitable for enclosure, and moving people and vehicles through the gates of such an enclosure can be a nuisance.

Repellants will work to a certain extent, but before you begin a spray program, there are a few things to consider. First, try to begin the program before damage occurs: once deer learn there is something tasty to eat, they will be back. Remember too that rain or irrigation will wash the repellant off the leaves and necessitate another application, and that you will need to spray again as plants grow and new leaves are left unprotected. Lastly, deer become inured to a repellant if it is used constantly, so it is important to mix and match. Use a scent repellant followed by one based on taste, alternating a putrefied egg spray with one based on chili pepper or higher fatty acids (that's soap, to the nonchemist). There are commercially available egg sprays, but you can also make your own. Though odoriferous to deer, their aroma is not apparent to our less sensitive olfactory capabilities. Processed sewerage sludge also works as a scent repellent, as does dried blood, which is sold as an organic nitrogen fertilizer. My absolute favorite was the old version of Magic Circle, based on bone tar oil; but alas, it is no longer available in the United States. A more diluted formula is available in the United Kingdom under the brand name Reynardine.

Hostas with golden leaves are a stable color form. Say you have a nice clump of *Hosta* 'Frances Williams', a large-leaved bluish green hosta with a golden edge. Because it is an attractive hosta, you want more of it, and so you regularly divide it. Eventually you have enough, and you stop propagating it. Surprisingly, one such established clump suddenly produces a shoot with entirely yellow leaves. You lift and divide the plant to separate the completely yellow portion, and it continues to maintain the all-yellow color. Some spontaneously arisen yellow group forms have been given cultivar names, including *H*. 'Golden Mammoth' and *H*. 'Golden Sunburst'.

Yellow-leaved hostas need some direct sunlight in order to produce their brightest color. Morning and afternoon light is preferred, as the more intense midday sun (especially in southerly parts of the country) may burn the leaves. Remember too that when hostas are exposed to extra sunlight, they need constant moisture at their roots to replenish what is lost by transpiration.

There are many, many cultivars available. *Hosta* 'Sum and Substance' is the classic choice for super-sized, gold-leaved hostas. Though most often forming a 5-foot-wide clump, there is one legendary specimen that measures an astonishing 9 feet wide. Huge leaves with good substance, up to 20 inches long by 15 inches wide, make this cultivar an excellent choice as a specimen plant. Some direct sunlight is necessary for best color development; otherwise leaves will be chartreuse, a green tint overlaying the yellow. *Hosta* 'Daybreak' has chartreuse leaves that also color best with some direct sunlight. Prominent veins on its leaves, 12 inches long and 8 inches wide, add to its appeal, and the plant makes a 3-foot-wide clump just under 2 feet high. *Hosta* 'Sun Power' is more moderate in size, with leaves 10 inches long by 7½ inches wide, forming a mounding, 3-foot-wide clump about 2 feet high. *Hosta* 'Zounds' has bright yellow heart-shaped leaves 11 inches long by 8½ inches wide, and forms a clump 30 inches wide by 16 inches high. The award-winning *H*. 'Piedmont Gold' has clear yellow leaves 11 inches long by 8 inches wide. It makes a nice 40-inch-wide clump 20 inches high. *Hosta* 'Midas Touch' has an almost metallic sheen to its golden yellow leaves, which are 9 inches long by 8 inches wide, mounding to form a 28-inch-wide clump that is 22 inches high. *Hosta* 'Gold Regal' (no relation to *H*. 'Krossa Regal') has chartreuse-gold leaves 7 inches long by 5 inches wide, and makes a 2-foot-wide clump just over 18 inches high. The yellow leaves of *H*. 'Wogon Gold' are a modest 4 inches long by 1½ inches wide, forming a dainty 12-inch-wide clump only 6 inches high.

Spotted dead nettle (*Lamium maculatum*) is a popular shade-tolerant groundcover and includes 'Beedham's White', an interesting cultivar featuring yellow leaves marked by a little white stripe down their center. White flowers complement the foliage of 'Beedham's White', lighting up a shady area. This selection does not spread with the same enthusiasm as other *L. maculatum* cultivars, but rampant spreading is not always desirable. I find 'Beedham's White' a pleasing choice for containers or for refined, more congested areas.

Golden creeping Jenny (*Lysimachia nummularia* 'Aurea'), in contrast, makes a vigorously spreading groundcover. I once used a few plants in the window boxes on my toolshed and was pleasantly surprised the next spring to find some growing where it had fallen to the ground beneath and easily wintered over. Golden creeping Jenny features paired, rounded, yellow to chartreuse leaves. Though it prefers moist soil, a wide range of conditions is acceptable, and it will grow well in sun to partial shade. Keep in mind that the typically green form of creeping Jenny has naturalized in eastern North America, and watch the gold-leaved cultivar for similar escapist tendencies.

Feverfew (*Tanacetum parthenium*) is a charming, small daisy once favored by Victorian gardeners. Its feathery leaves have a pungent odor. Golden feverfew (*Tanacetum parthenium* 'Aureum') is a form with yellow-chartreuse leaves. Plants can grow in full sun to light shade, in average to moist or somewhat dry sites. I let it spread around my casual hillside garden, weeding out any that plant themselves in an inconvenient place. Golden feverfew is fine for a casual country or cottage garden, but its self-sowing habits make it a problem in more formal designs. Seedlings all come true, and any you care to pot up are generally welcome at garden club plant sales.

TENDER PERENNIALS

Mostly grown for its colorful foliage, *Alternanthera ficoidea* needs full sun and average moisture for best results, along with periodic clipping back to keep it low and compact. The 1-foot-tall plants should be spaced as closely as 6 to 10 inches so that they may quickly fill in for the carpet bedding effect loved by Victorian gardeners. In colder climates, wait to plant *A. ficoidea* until tomato planting time, when the soil has warmed up. 'Aurea Nana' is a low-growing form with yellow splotches on its leaves. 'Yellow Wide Leaf' and 'Yellow Fine Leaf' are descriptive but invalid names for a couple of popular bedding forms.

There are some stunning container combinations in the catalog for Beds and Borders, a wholesale grower in Laurel, New York. In one splendid stone urn, gold-leaved sweet potato (*Ipomoea batatas* 'Margarita') mingles with silver-gray foliage plants. There are the large furry leaves of *Salvia argentea*, the refined texture of *Helichrysum splendidum*, the whitish green fluff of *Lotus berthelotii* with its needle-fine leaves creating a texture like that of Spanish moss, and *Pelargonium sidoides* with its densely packed small gray leaves. There are a couple of flowering plants as well (*Petunia* 'Surfinia Blue Vein' and *Verbena* 'Chatto's Lavender'), but in this lush container the large golden leaves of the ornamental sweet potato are what balances and anchors the design.

A neighbor who grew up near the New Jersey shore, where sweet potatoes are grown as a field crop, recounted to me how the summer sun would heat the sandy soil to the extent that he could not walk barefoot between the rows. Ornamental sweet potatoes also prefer heat and sandy soil, and need at least a monthly heading back in summer to keep their trailing stems under control. Provide them with sufficient water and they'll even do well with the heat and sun of southwestern states. *Ipomoea batatas* 'Margarita' has large spade-shaped chartreuse leaves up to 6 inches wide. A great foliage plant for hanging out of baskets, dripping over the edges of large containers, or sprawling out of flowerbeds to trip up unwary passersby, 'Margarita' looks great in combination with orange to dull red, dark purple, or silver foliage. Deer seem to prefer this attractive cultivar to its black-leaved siblings. In my garden, they do not prune it back but simply eat the leaves off the petioles.

Many if not most of the coleus (*Solenostemon scutellarioides*) so popular today are variations on a theme of purplish burgundy and merlot, or brighter hues of cardinal and fuchsia. Sometimes more subtle colors are needed and a simple cool yellow, pineapple, or chartreuse might be just the thing to cool off warmer, more vivid reds and oranges, to brighten and polish dark purple or maroon, or to accentuate glaucous blues and silver grays. Among the *S. scutellarioides* cultivars is 'Amazon', which has a relatively narrow, more upright habit and deeply scalloped bright yellow leaves. 'Golden Wizard' reaches only about 1 foot tall, growing equally well in sun or shade, and features lots of densely packed sunny yellow foliage. The ruffled leaves of 'Yellow Frills' are a medium yellow suffused with a tint of green when grown in full to partial shade, a richer yellow when grown in full sun.

Plain green elephant's-ears (*Xanthosoma*) have long been popular in southern gardens, and even as summer ornamentals in cooler places. These plants have huge leaves on long stalks, like some giant caladium on megadoses of vegetable steroids. They thrive in rich mucky soils and wet places with ample water, even in shallow standing water at the edges of ponds, and need warm weather and filtered shade to thrive. In tropical regions *X. sagittifolium* grows so big that a typical adult can stand under its huge, 4- to 5-foot-long, broadly sagittate, typically green leaves. My friend Jerry Barad keeps a form of *X. sagittifolium* in a container in his New Jersey garden, and it is more modest in size than the species. This may be ascribed to a couple of factors. Firstly, any plant grown in a pot will have more limited dimensions than the same thing growing in the ground. Secondly, New Jersey may be hot and muggy in the summer, but it is no match for the tropics. The chartreuse-yellow leaves of Jerry's elephant's-ear are about 18 inches long, and the plant itself reaches about 3 feet tall after sitting in his koi pond all summer. It makes a superb contrast to the black elephant's-ear (*Colocasia esculenta* 'Jet Black Wonder', see Plate 47) and papyrus

(*Cyperus papyrus*) growing beside it. The new, rare, and elegant (not always synonymous) *X. sagittifolium* 'Chartreuse Giant' has large, sagittate, yellow-green leaves.

With the tropical look becoming increasing popular, suddenly there are refinements and details of nomenclature to be learned. *Xanthosoma* looks much like *Alocasia*, and neither is too different from *Colocasia* or *Schismatoglottis*. All have cormlike tubers, though some have more side shoots and others have fewer, and their leaves are variations on a theme, either sagittate, hastate, or cordate. To top it off, *Alocasia*, *Colocasia*, and *Xanthosoma* are all commonly known as elephant's-ear. But why worry? If it appeals to you, buy it. We gardeners will grow the plants and let the taxonomists sort out the details.

DESIGNING WITH GOLDEN FOLIAGE

I can offer advice, options, suggestions, and possibilities, and it's fine if you disagree because, getting right down to it, you are the only person your garden needs to please. Russell Page's golden garden at PepsiCo is a splendid tour de force. As public space set in a broad landscape, it creates an impressive visual effect for visitors who are here today, gone tomorrow, and back again at another time of year. I enjoy the skillfully designed combination of trees and shrubs, evergreen and deciduous plants, each time I see it, and without the least urge to replicate it in whole or in part.

Gardens are places to explore your creativity. Sure, it helps to do research by visiting gardens and sifting through books, but ultimately you should decide for yourself. Move a plant from here to there, then step back and think about how that changes the look of things. If you really want to plant nine different hosta cultivars, all with golden leaves, go for it. Even a triune planting of large-, medium-, and small-leaved hostas doesn't quite hold my attention, but that is just my opinion. If I suggest that different plants, all with golden leaves but each different in shape, would have a more interesting look, again, that is just an opinion.

Keeping this in mind, let's imagine just such a little golden garden. First we'll set the conditions, which should be suitable for the hostas. Our garden should be in a sunny to partially shaded site, somewhere in zone 6, with good soil that is high in organic matter and moist yet well drained. Just to keep things interesting, let's say all the plants must be herbaceous, like the hostas. Since hostas are a favorite plant, begin with a couple of yellow varieties, both of different sizes, say *Hosta* 'Piedmont Gold' and *H.* 'Wogon Gold'. Place the luminous 'Piedmont Gold' at the back of the garden next to a golden bleeding heart

(*Dicentra spectabilis* 'Gold Heart'), whose fernlike foliage will offer a nice contrast. Several plants of *H.* 'Wogon Gold' will fit nicely in the foreground as edging plants, along with Bowles golden grass (*Milium effusum* 'Aureum') for its linear texture and soft chartreuse-yellow spring color (though I concede it does become greener as summer progresses). Golden creeping Jenny (*Lysimachia nummularia* 'Aurea') can ramble around nicely as a groundcover in front of the little hosta and the grass, spilling over the edge of the planting bed onto the path. Fill the space between front and back with golden feverfew (*Tanacetum parthenium* 'Aureum') and a coleus, perhaps *Solenostemon scutellarioides* 'The Line', for summer interest (the coleus does have a burgundy center, but the line is barely penciled in). *Enfin*, we are there. We have a garden that is, to me, better than a simple collection of hosta cultivars (though still not what I would consider the best garden possible for these conditions).

But what if the little hosta in front were *Hosta* 'Kabitan', with a thin green edge to its little golden leaf? And what if the golden grass beside it was Japanese forest grass (*Hakonechloa macra* 'Aureola'), whose arching golden blades are penciled in with thin green lines? Too close to the pattern of *Hosta* 'Kabitan'? No problem. Consider *Liriope muscari* with its straplike dark green leaves of good substance. Let's switch the hosta at the rear from *H.* 'Piedmont Gold' to *H. plantaginea*, with its shiny leaves as green as a Granny Smith apple. Do you like it? Do you not like it? Can you explain why? There are many options when it comes to hostas; it all comes down to what you prefer. You might try something like *H. sieboldiana*, with large glaucous blue leaves of great substance, or you might prefer a hosta with entirely green leaves, a variegated hosta whose leaves have a golden edge or a golden center, or a hosta whose yellow leaves have a white edge. You might want to invest in precious metals, so to speak, by combining gold-leaved plants and silver-leaved plants (see Plate 53). Japanese painted fern (*Athyrium nipponicum* 'Pictum') with its silver fronds, *Heuchera* 'Can-Can' with its silvery ruffled leaves—not to my taste, but I'd love to see what you come up with.

Yellow foliage works best for me as an accent. I may brighten up my herbaceous border with golden barberry (*Berberis thunbergii* 'Aurea') and *Canna* 'Bengal Tiger' with its green-striped yellow leaves. Gold lightens a shady area, but I prefer it as a dappled effect rather than a pool. I prefer to use gold as an

> You might want to invest in precious metals, so to speak, by combining gold-leaved plants and silver-leaved plants.

accent with greens, from dark forest-green to pale apple-green, perhaps adding some gold-variegated plants for a transition between the two. I might set a small golden hosta such as *Hosta* 'Wogon Gold' to glow against the dark British-racing-green ribbonlike leaves of *Liriope muscari* and finish with the lacy fronds of Christmas fern (*Polystichum acrostichoides*) or bear's foot helle-bore (*Helleborus foetidus*).

Thinking about these options gets me daydreaming, and I imagine that perhaps golden foliage could work in my tropical border with plants in con-tainers. I may exchange the deep plum-black coleus (*Solenostemon scutellari-oides*) that front the peach, orange, red, purple, dark green leaves of my *Canna* 'Tropicanna' for some cultivars in sunny yellow. They say if it isn't broken, don't fix it, but there's nothing wrong with having a little fun in the garden.

"Suit yourself," my mother used to say when I didn't take her advice. More gently, I'd rather suggest that, above all, to thine own self be true.

Plate 28. The sunny look of golden conifers is strongest as new growth develops in spring, as exemplified by this marvelous specimen of golden spruce (*Picea orientalis* 'Aurea') seen at the New York Botanical Garden in early May.

Plate 29. A view of Russell Page's golden garden at the PepsiCo Sculpture Gardens. More than a decade after they were first planted, these golden conifers have swelled in size and are softly merging.

Plate 30. Japanese forest grass (*Hakonechloa macra* 'Aureola') is valued for its attractive arching golden blades, which create a soft mound that looks as tidy as if it were combed by the wind. Its sunny color lights up shady areas, where this plant prefers to grow.

Plate 31. The narrow blades of Japanese forest grass (*Hakonechloa macra* 'Aureola') contrast with the massive gold-edged leaves of *Hosta* 'Frances Williams'.

Plate 32. This pairing of Japanese forest grass (*Hakonechloa macra* 'Aureola') and European ginger (*Asarum europaeum*) plays dark against bright and dull against shiny.

Plate 33. The golden ribbonlike leaves of Japanese forest grass (*Hakonechloa macra* 'Aureola') face down the bolder dark green leaves of a rhododendron, illustrating how woody plants and perennials can act as partners, contributing foliage interest to lighten shady gardens.

Plate 34. A splendid fusion of herbaceous perennial and small shrub: a dwarf purple-leaved barberry, *Berberis thunbergii* 'Atropurpurea Nana', serves as the backdrop to the pinnate golden foliage of queen of the meadows (*Filipendula ulmaria* 'Aurea').

Plate 35. Golden hop vine (*Humulus lupulus* 'Aureus') is a cheerful thug whose chartreuse color is best when given some shade.

Plate 36. When deer eat the leaves off your hostas, it may be difficult to think of foliage as something to enhance the garden.

Plate 37. Bambi's mother looks in through my kitchen window. Perhaps she'd like a cup of coffee to round out the meal she's just eaten in the garden.

Plate 38. The bright violet-purple leaves of *Tradescantia pallida* 'Purple Heart' pair nicely with the somber black foliage of *Solenostemon scutellarioides* 'Black Emperor'. They are saved from becoming a light-absorbing black hole by the gold-tipped leaves of *S. scutellarioides* 'Robyn' and orange-yellow flowers of a *Lantana* species.

Plate 39. Color combinations tip the balance. The dark plum leaves of *Alternanthera dentata* 'Rubiginosa' meander through *Solenostemon scutellarioides* 'Alabama Sunset', toning down the crushed-strawberry-pink and gold foliage of the coleus.

Plate 40. *Solenostemon scutellarioides* 'Alabama Sunset' has a much lighter feel when paired with *Berberis thunbergii* 'Aurea', which accentuates the golden notes in the coleus foliage.

Plate 41. The vividly red, willow-leaved *Amaranthus tricolor* 'Salicifolius Splendens' creates a stoplight effect when paired with petunias of a matching color.

Plate 42. The matching warm colors of *Canna* 'Tropicanna' and *Solenostemon scutellarioides* 'Camilla' give cool early-morning summer sunlight the glowing shades of sundown.

Plate 43. A much subtler effect is created when the dark merlot ribbons of *Pennisetum setaceum* 'Rubrum' tone down the bold sunset-hued foliage of *Canna* 'Tropicanna'.

Plate 44. The bold olive-drab leaves of *Heuchera micrantha* var. *diversifolia* 'Palace Purple' are nicely balanced with the straplike inky black foliage of *Ophiopogon planiscapus* 'Nigrescens'. A simple handful of scarlet impatiens enlivens the summer season.

Plate 45. The same color effect can be created with foliage, replacing the red impatiens with *Caladium bicolor* 'Freida Hemple'. While the intensity is the same, the balance of shape is not as strong.

Plate 46. Like a bonfire licking at a stake, the fiery red-tipped blades of *Imperata cylindrica* 'Rubra' ring this decorative steeple at Craig Bergmann's Country Garden in Wilmette, Illinois.

Plate 47. The bold, somber leaves of black elephant's-ear (*Colocasia esculenta* 'Jet Black Wonder') make a magnificent accent for the summer water garden, holding their own against the dancing ripples of sunlight on water.

Plate 48. Bold, enticing silver leaves and ease of cultivation make *Brunnera macrophylla* 'Jack Frost' a highly desirable plant for the shady garden.

Plate 49. Always think first of leaf shape. Soft, finely textured *Artemisia schmidtiana* 'Silver Mound', seen flowering on the right, is too close a match for lavender cotton (*Santolina chamaecyparissus*), growing on the left. Why bother to use two different plants when they look so much alike?

Plate 50. *Plectranthus argentatus* has a polished look when combined in a summer container with the thread-fine texture of *Centaurea cineraria*.

Plate 51. An elegant duo just made to shimmer in the shade: the glaucous blue leaves of *Hosta* 'Blue Cadet' and the silver-netted foliage of *Lamium galeobdolon* 'Hermann's Pride'.

Plate 52. *Hosta sieboldiana* var. *elegans* is equally effective at lighting up shady areas. The seersucker texture of its coarse glaucous blue leaves is enriched by the lacy silver fronds of Japanese painted fern (*Athyrium nipponicum* 'Pictum').

Plate 53. Try pairing silver-leaved plants with gold-leaved plants. Here, Japanese painted fern (*Athyrium nipponicum* 'Pictum') combines nicely with a golden hosta.

Plate 54. The silver foliage of weeping willowleaf pear (*Pyrus salicifolia* 'Pendula') gently dominates the Nancy Bryan Luce Herb Garden, designed by Penelope Hobhouse for the New York Botanical Garden. At once a focal point and an anchor, the ornamental pear plays off against the green boxwood parterres and spring flowers.

Plate 55. It's easy to learn the language of plants. The numerous hairs on the leaves of beach wormwood (*Artemisia stelleriana*) indicate that this plant prefers full sun and a sandy, well-drained site.

CHAPTER 5

❧

Dusky Delights

Plum, purple, copper, bronze, red, even black—these colors are all possibilities for both temperate and tropical foliage. Take heed, though, that they can function like a black hole, sucking up light and making a dim shady garden appear even darker. Indeed, these colors need the proper foliage and flower partners to really dance, even in sunlight, where these deeper hues develop more richly. Silver or gold foliage and clear scarlet-red foliage or flowers add sparkle and bring these somber shades to life. Chartreuse flowers such as those featured by *Nicotiana langsdorffii* or *Zinnia* 'Envy' provide some lift, as do flowers of soft orange, gentle pink, lavender, or violet. White against plum or purple is another option, though sometimes such a pairing appears slightly harsh. A careful blurring of the distinction between the two colors, most easily achieved using softer tones of brown foliage, will subdue the contrast.

Dusky foliage colors (plum, purple, copper, bronze, red, and black) give an exuberant tropical feel to summer gardens, regardless of location. I recently created a grouping of tender perennials in containers that I find so eminently satisfactory that I plan to repeat it, with variations, for years to come. Starting at the left, I have a three-year-old, overgrown, shrubby Persian shield (*Strobilanthes dyeriana*), its intense fuchsia leaves overlaid with a metallic tint. In front of this is a pot of black elephant's-ear (*Colocasia esculenta* 'Jet Black Wonder'). The great thing about having these two plants in pots is that I can start the summer off with them situated as I've described; then, as the elephant's-ear gets, well, elephantine, I can reverse their positioning. Next are two 22-inch-diameter pots of *Canna* 'Tropicanna', whose large sunset-hued leaves look hot, hot, hot, especially side by side with the purple leaves of *Tradescantia pallida* 'Purple Heart', an old-fashioned grandmother's plant (well, I qualify five times over to be a grandmother!) that is again popular and easy to obtain. When I got my start of *T. pallida* 'Purple Heart' over twenty years ago, it was by crawling under a bench in a greenhouse and taking a cutting from the "weed" growing in the gravel floor. In autumn I use a hand truck to wheel the cannas into my unheated attached garage where they and the tradescantias happily sleep the winter away at about 38° Fahrenheit. They make this move just before I anticipate a black frost, which usually arrives on a clear night with a full moon, when temperatures drop to 28° Fahrenheit or lower. The containers, though sturdy, are just cheap white matte-finished plastic pots purchased from a hardware store. Since they appear so glaringly bright in the morning sunlight, I've made a scrim of bronze fly screening to soften and dignify their appearance until they are concealed by trailing plants.

Next is a pot of *Artemisia vulgaris* 'Oriental Limelight', a mugwort with soft green and creamy yellow leaves on semi-trailing stems. Frankly, this plant scares me silly since the typically green species is such a god-awful pest. 'Oriental Limelight' seems to be just as vigorous, so I don't dare turn it loose by planting it in the ground and won't even dispose of it in the compost heap. Instead I've used an upended clay pot as a plinth, providing some elevation to what is basically a groundcover plant. Next to this I've placed a pink, cream, and green phormium with handsome straplike foliage. The questing branches of the mugwort look attractive weaving into this neighbor.

Then there's naranjilla (*Solanum quitoense*), one of those gothic-looking nightshades, featuring thorn-studded purple-veined large leaves, 18 inches long and just about as wide. Its baby leaves are covered with purple trichomes, the same sort that make lamb's ear (*Stachys byzantina*) silver. Next to this is a phormium with large copper-hued leaves, followed by red Abyssinian banana (*Ensete ventricosum* 'Maurelii'). Rather than leave the banana in its pot, this year I planted it in the ground, letting *Tradescantia pallida* 'Purple Heart' grow around its base like a skirt. I didn't actually have to plant the tradescantia, mind you: lengths of it had broken loose as I was wheeling pots around and dropped themselves into place, after which some mulch had been thrown over them. (If this gives you the idea that *T. pallida* 'Purple Heart' roots easily, you are absolutely correct.) Since I had several plants of *Ipomoea batatas* 'Ace of Spades', these found a home here as well. The spade-shaped black leaves of this

> Then there's naranjilla (*Solanum quitoense*), one of those gothic-looking nightshades, featuring thorn-studded purple-veined large leaves.

ornamental sweet potato make an appropriate repetitive accent for the black elephant's-ear (*Colocasia esculenta* 'Jet Black Wonder'), a grace note on a smaller scale. The last pot on the right holds a *Dracaena* specimen with narrow red leaves. This was purchased in a 10-inch flimsy black plastic pot for less than eight dollars at a discount store; and believe me, it looks much better since it was transplanted into a handsome rounded Malaysian bowl with a russet glaze. Lastly, there are various black coleus (*Solenostemon scutellarioides*) here and there in the ground, placed wherever there was a gap I could plug them into.

This part of the garden gets only morning sun. The *Canna* 'Tropicanna' and *Ensete ventricosum* 'Maurelii' are shaded by about 10:30 A.M. , which gives them four and a half hours of direct sun, and strong light for the rest of the day. The shade creeps over the other pots over the course of the next hour, with the left- and right-most pots shaded last. These are plants in very active growth and so I water and fertilize regularly. As you may have gathered, my grouping is a madcap mix of "common" and "choice" tender perennials. Each plant is selected and placed for the attractive shapes, textures, and strong colors of its foliage, all of which, in combination, make for a striking, colorful display in a summer garden.

This tropical border is highly visible from the deck along the back of my house. One thing that makes it work so well is that to the left of these pots, on a slope rising up from the lawn, I have incorporated purple-leaved shrubs among the flowering perennials. Thus the colors of the tropical plants' leaves carry through year-round, just not in as concentrated a manner. Included among the shrubs are purple-leaved smokebush (*Cotinus coggygria* 'Royal Purple'), *Weigela florida* 'Alexandra' (often sold as WINE AND ROSES™), *Physocarpus opulifolius* 'Diablo', and a couple of purple-leaved barberries, *Berberis thunbergii* f. *atropurpurea* and *B. thunbergii* 'Gentry' (often sold as ROYAL BURGANDY™).

The barberries are placed apart from each other and kept softly clipped into roundish mounds, adding structure and providing colorful accents in my herbaceous border. *Berberis thunbergii* f. *atropurpurea* is paired with the coppery orange new growth of *Spiraea japonica* 'Goldflame', both of which act as a spring backdrop for *Tulipa* 'Prinses Irene', a soft apricot-orange and light lavender cultivar. The tulips are replaced by red geraniums (*Pelargonium*) in summer, by which time the leaves of *S. japonica* 'Goldflame' have turned greenish. *Berberis thunbergii* 'Gentry', further up the slope, is fronted with *Euphorbia dulcis* 'Chameleon', whose foliage remains a rich brownish purple all summer long. Between the two shrubs is an unknown bearded iris with brown standards and brown-edged white falls. Nearby this is a shrub-sized bowman's root (*Gillenia trifoliata*), which in June adds a froth of finely textured, small-petalled white flowers that play off the bearded iris.

The same games can be played with herbaceous plants. I use a canna (possibly *Canna* 'Intrigue') with graceful, relatively narrow purple leaves and small apricot flowers as a backdrop for *Hemerocallis* 'Heart of Africa', which has deep plum flowers, and *Dahlia* 'Bishop of Llandaff', which has clear red flowers. Edith Eddleman, curator of the herbaceous borders at the J. C. Raulston Arboretum in Raleigh, North Carolina, gave me a start of this canna years ago (as you can imagine, her own garden is crammed full of many good plants).

Dark-leaved cannas work nicely almost anywhere. I saw a broad-leaved cultivar, possibly *Canna* 'Red King Humbert', combined with shaggy orange dahlias in the hot border at Sissinghurst, arguably the best known of the great English gardens. And at the New York Botanical Garden a planting combined a purple-leaved canna with copper-leaved, pink-flowered *Begonia* 'Vodka' and silvery dusty miller (*Senecio cineraria*) for a great take on Victorian carpet bedding.

One summer I came upon a fabulous foliage border at Longwood Gardens in Kennett Square, Pennsylvania (see Plate 17). It massed 4- to 5-foot-tall *Hibiscus acetosella* 'Red Shield' at the back of the bed, its glossy, maroon, lobed leaves providing a somber effect. A large group of *Tradescantia pallida* 'Purple Heart' was placed in front. Diffusely covered with soft hairs for a modest silvery overlay, the oblong, trough-shaped, deeply mauve-purple leaves of 'Purple Heart' were brighter in appearance than those of the hibiscus. An equal mass of the rounded, bright silver leaves of *Senecio cineraria* 'Cirrus' butted up against the tradescantia, an absolute necessity for lifting this otherwise dull planting into gay lightness. Some tall blue-flowered cultivar of *Salvia farinacea* planted off to the right was the only flowering accent.

There is a superb combination of purple-leaved trees at Wave Hill in the Bronx (perhaps the finest public garden on the East Coast). Marco Polo Stufano, the former director of horticulture there, developed the gardens with an ardent love of plants and a keen eye for color and combination. For this planting he chose *Prunus cerasifera* 'Pissardii', an older selection of the species but still among the best cultivars. He partnered it with purple-leaved smoke-bush (*Cotinus coggygria* 'Royal Purple') and the lacelike, finely textured, bronze-leaved honey locust *Gleditsia triacanthos* 'Ruby Lace'. Stooling was employed to control size and encourage larger leaves. The play of shape and shade produced by these woodies is entrancing, and they act as a backdrop to flowers with similar shades, most notably daylilies, bearded irises, and June-flowering Asiatic lilies. Red to wine leaf color may occur only at a certain time of year, as particular trees and shrubs with summer green foliage blaze with color in autumn.

TREES

There are a number of Japanese maples (*Acer palmatum*) with purple foliage. Leaves may start off deep purple in spring and turn green in summer, or they may remain deep purple right through the growing season. Whichever form you choose will depend on what effect you want. Japanese maples are elegant little understory trees, growing in the wild under the canopy shade of larger trees. In cultivation the tendency is to place them out in the lawn in full sunlight. The risk here, however, is that careless lawn mowing or use of a string trimmer may damage the tree's thin bark. Strike a balance by planting these little maples at the edge of a forest or, where the landscape does not permit such placement, where some midday shade will shelter the tree when summer sun is at its strongest. Typically, Japanese maples form a broadly rounded silhouette, with a gracefully layered branching pattern. Major branches form quite close to the ground, giving a multi-trunk appearance. Though slow growing, Japanese maples add distinction to the garden even at an early age. Because they are so slow, however, specimens with some size to them are expensive. In 2001 I visited a Connecticut nursery that had 6- to 7-foot-tall *A. palmatum* 'Bloodgood' priced at $450, and the next size up, 8-foot 'Bloodgood', priced at $650. If instant landscaping had been in my budget, I could have purchased a 12- to 14-foot specimen for a hefty $2200.

Japanese maples have been popular in Japan since the earliest days of gardening, and there is a seemingly endless list of cultivars from which to make a selection. There are seven groups, some of which can be further subdivided. They are grouped first by the number of lobes on their finely drawn leaves, then by color. Group 1b, for example, contains those Japanese maples with five-lobed, occasionally seven-lobed, red-purple leaves, including those that fade to dark green. *Acer palmatum* 'Atropurpureum' is an outstanding cultivar in this group, having purple leaves in spring that become darker in summer before turning scarlet-red in autumn. The leaves of *A. palmatum* 'Crimson Prince' are dark purple in spring, becoming lighter (but not green) in summer. *Acer palmatum* 'Fireglow' is a readily propagated Italian cultivar with a nice growth habit and leaves similar to those of *A. palmatum* 'Bloodgood'. Introduced around 1977, it is not yet widely available. The older (1874), slow-growing, upright *A. palmatum* 'Purpureum' originated in Great Britain. As its leaves unfold in spring they are dark purple, turning dull purple-green in summer and scarlet in autumn.

Group 2b Japanese maples feature seven-lobed, occasionally nine-lobed, red-purple leaves that are more deeply divided than those of group 1b, to half of the leaf blade or even slightly more. This category includes the outstanding

Acer palmatum 'Bloodgood', the most widely available cultivar and the most deeply colored of the purple-leaved Japanese maples. Color remains consistent throughout the growing season, and leaves experience no special color change before they fall in autumn.

Group 3b Japanese maples are more like shrubs in that they grow as wide as they are tall, or even wider, with deeply divided seven- or nine-lobed leaves. *Acer palmatum* 'Burgundy Lace' is a gorgeous example, with deeply divided seven-lobed burgundy leaves handsomely serrate along the margins.

Group 4, the Dissectum Group (and I'll stop here even though there are three more groups), includes toadstool-shaped trees with sinuous branches and finely cut dissected leaves. *Maples of the World* lists *Acer palmatum* 'Crimson Queen' as "a truly outstanding cultivar" and "one of the very best Japanese maples available today." Young leaves are very dark purple-red from the time they unfold in spring until late summer, when they lighten and turn reddish purple. The deep purple leaves of *A. palmatum* 'Garnet' are not as deeply cut as those of 'Crimson Queen', but the color is similar. Young trees have a gawky, open, leggy adolescence before maturing at 12 to 15 feet, making 'Garnet' one of the largest Dissectum Group cultivars. *Acer palmatum* 'Red Dragon' has a mounding habit accentuated by trailing, weeping branches. The deep purple leaves are even darker than those of 'Crimson Queen' and hold their color quite late into fall. Dark red-purple *A. palmatum* 'Red Filigree Lace' is an exceptionally lacy-leaved cultivar that holds its color throughout the growing season, turning a glowing crimson in autumn. It would be much more popular were it not for its extremely slow growth, which makes scion wood for propagation limited in availability.

Above all, try to use Japanese maples well. I remember once seeing a long driveway to an estate lined with a dozen or more mature specimens of purple cut-leaf Japanese maple (*Acer palmatum* f. *dissectum*). It was a prime example of Thorstein Veblen's "conspicuous consumption," which he promulgated in *The Theory of the Leisure Class*. As he states in chapter 6, "It comes about that a beautiful article which is not expensive is accounted not beautiful." In the end those cut-leaf Japanese maples had more to say about the owner's deep pockets than about his or her horticultural taste. Used in this manner, they were not even attractive. Trees used to create an allée should provide a frame, a sense of structure and enclosure to guide visitors towards a destination. These poor maples were treated more like speed bumps. If the owners had simply wanted purple foliage, purple-leaved plum (*Prunus cerasifera* 'Atropurpurea'), also called Pissard plum, would have been a more suitable (though plebeian) tree. My neighbors Peter and Ellen Kluber used fifteen of these midsized 20-foot-tall trees to line a portion of the 1500-foot-long driveway to their country farm house. Veblen would have approved.

Should space and time allow, go for *Fagus sylvatica* 'Dawyck Purple', a fastigiate European beech with an elegantly columnar form and purple leaves. It will mature as a superior vertical accent for our exercise in grandiose estatehood. Less costly than Japanese maples, 'Dawyck Purple' is also slow growing. An 8- to 9-foot-tall slender stripling costs about $300, but a 3½- to 4-inch-caliper specimen, priced at $650, will look a bit more like a tree.

Such exceptional small trees as cut-leaf Japanese maples (*Acer palmatum* f. *dissectum*) should be given pride of place and a proper display. Consider surrounding a single specimen with a carpet of *Ajuga reptans* 'Atropurpurea' or *A. reptans* 'Bronze Beauty', whose burgundy leaves will mimic the color of the maple (see Plate 26). Use scarlet flowers as a summer accent, with just a handful of impatiens or fibrous-rooted begonias. An excellent option is *Begonia* 'Vodka', a begonia from the Cocktail Series with very dark copper-red leaves and red flowers. Using this cultivar will maintain a harmony among foliage colors, whereas a green-leaved begonia would be disruptive.

At all costs avoid the purple-leaved forms of Norway maple (*Acer platanoides*) such as 'Crimson King', 'Royal Red', and 'Schwedleri'. In fact, extend that caution to any and all Norway maples, whatever their leaf color. Yes, they are readily available. Yes, they need little maintenance and are nearly pest- and disease-free, excepting a susceptibility to verticillium wilt in some areas. But these trees are thugs with territorially aggressive habits, and they reseed by the thousands. Norway maples form a dense canopy, casting stygian gloom on the ground beneath them. An extensive shallow root system sucks up all moisture and nutrients. Even such tough groundcovers as pachysandra, periwinkle (*Vinca minor*), and ivy (*Hedera*) struggle to survive. If you accidentally acquired a few Norway maples when you bought your property, allow me to suggest their removal.

Cercis canadensis 'Forest Pansy' is an attractive form of eastern redbud. Clusters of small, vivid magenta flowers appear first, shaped like the flowers on a pea plant. Avoid an unfortunate combination by keeping 'Forest Pansy' away from azaleas with warm pink flowers or yellow forms of *Forsythia*. As the flowers finish, heart-shaped leaves appear, opening a bright crimson-red and maturing to a deep reddish purple, becoming a duller greenish bronze-purple with summer heat. While the spring appearance of 'Forest Pansy' is remarkable, like all eastern redbuds, this cultivar is subject to verticillium wilt, which can spot or discolor the leaves in late summer. Furthermore, trees produce numerous 2- to 4-inch-long persistent seedpods that are not especially attractive. Eastern redbud is also difficult to transplant and best moved as a balled and burlapped specimen while still dormant in early spring. That said, 'Forest Pansy' is a striking understory tree, growing 20 to 30 feet tall, with a wider, rounded crown. Adaptable from woodland edge to open situations in zones 4 through 9, it accepts acid to alkaline soils and prefers moist situations, disliking both drought and wet conditions as well as exposed, windy sites.

SHRUBS

Related to sumac (*Rhus*), smokebush (*Cotinus coggygria*) has several purple-leaved cultivars, including 'Royal Purple' and 'Velvet Cloak', the two most available cultivars (though it is possible these are pseudonyms for the same plant), and 'Nordine' and 'Notcutt's Variety'. All four (or three, as the case may be) have maroon to reddish purple, rounded leaves. With smokebush, gardeners have two options. Left unpruned, *C. coggygria* will grow as a small tree or a large, mounding, rounded shrub, producing billows of finely textured pink flower panicles in early summer that look like smoke or fog streaming off the plant. The fruiting effect will be much the same, adding to the smokelike appearance. Leaves will be moderate in size and intensity of color. The second option employs stooling. Once the young shrub has been established, any main shoots less than an inch in diameter are cut back to a foot or less in early spring, resulting in production of vigorous upright shoots, easily reaching 6 feet tall. As this is juvenile growth, the leaves will be larger and, more importantly, more vividly colored than they would be if left unpruned. Flowering, however, will not be an option. Stooling is not suitable for older, well-established plants, as developing a suitable framework or branch structure is not possible.

Purple-leaved cultivars of smokebush (*Cotinus coggygria*) are slightly less hardy than green-leaved cultivars and are useful from zones 5 to 7. Choose a site in full sun with good drainage and only moderate fertility, as extra nitrogen will result in greener leaves. Silver foliage, chartreuse foliage, or green flowers make attractive partners for these cultivars, as do flowers in the related hues of violet, lavender, blue, or soft purple. I find the lavender spikes of *Liatris spicata* work well. Geraniums (*Pelargonium*) make a good choice since they thrive in the same sort of sunny, well-drained sites and since their scarlet flowers pop out against the plum-purple leaves of smokebush. Dahlias also pair well. *Dahlia* 'Bishop of Llandaff' features dark foliage, which corresponds well with the purple foliage of the smokebush, and warm red flowers.

Purple-leaved sand cherry (*Prunus* ×*cistena*) is a hybrid of *P. pumila* and *P. cerasifera*, growing 7 to 10 feet tall but not as wide. It is a tough survivor, enduring zone 3 winters in only semi-protected sites and tolerating severe pruning and tip dieback. Yet this sturdy shrub is sometimes belittled as a "builder's special," as though the fact that it is sold in DIY discount plant shops and used in the gardens of fast-food restaurants somehow makes it a low-class shrub. Remember that it is not what you plant, but how you use those plants, that will have anything to say about your high-style or low-class garden. But enough said. Young purple-leaved sand cherries suffer more from tip burn in harsh winters than do older, more established plants. Since this plant tends to have vertical shoots, tip burn in winter or tip pruning in spring encourages production of side shoots, resulting in a fuller, bushier shape. Full sun is needed to produce the best color, as leaves will green up in light shade.

Barberries (*Berberis thunbergii*) present a bit of an ethical dilemma. The green-leaved form is an invader, its bright red berries eaten by birds who disseminate the seeds far and wide. I prefer to keep exotic shrubs in the captivity of a garden rather than allowing them to escape to the wild. The purple-leaved forms in my garden do not seem to produce that many seeds, however, perhaps because I clip back the new growth several times each growing season. Though various purple-leaved cultivars of *B. thunbergii*, such as 'Cardinal', 'Humber Red', 'Redbird', and 'Sheridan Red', originated in Canada, they are now banned from that country, having been labeled a host for black stem wheat rust. It would be prudent to check with local cooperative extension agents in the grain-growing states of the Midwest as to whether you should avoid planting barberries, or, indeed, if doing so may be illegal.

The leaves of *Berberis thunbergii* f. *atropurpurea* turn an intense red-purple when the shrub is planted in full sun, dark green when it is grown in shade. This holds true for all purple-leaved barberries. *Berberis thunbergii* 'Atropurpurea Nana' is a dwarf selection that grows 3½ feet tall but spreads more widely. Use it as an accent in the flower garden or for low hedges. 'Gentry' is smaller, at 2 to 3 feet high, and has a deeper burgundy color. 'Bagatelle' is a compact, slow-growing selection that may eventually reach 30 inches tall over fifteen years, but can easily be kept at 18 inches tall or less. 'Rose Glow' undergoes a color shift as the season progresses: the first leaves in spring are a deep purple, with subsequent shoots bearing rose-pink leaves mottled and speckled with purple and cream. Encourage its sparkling habit by pruning it back by as much as a third each spring before growth begins. A larger shrub, 'Rose Glow' grows to 5 or 6 feet tall and wide.

Common elder (*Sambucus nigra*), also called black elder or European elder, grows 10 to 20 feet tall and has pinnate leaves with five (though sometimes three or seven) leaflets. Plants prefer moist to wet sites. Though common elder is considered a weed in Europe, there are some handsome, colorful, garden-worthy variants, including those of the Porphyrifolia Group (a catchall name for purple-leaved forms). The leaves of *S. nigra* 'Guincho Purple', for example, are green when they first appear but quickly develop into a rich wine-purple when grown in full sun. Keep in mind that while the species is hardy in zones 5 through 8, hot summers are a problem for Porphyrifolia Group cultivars. Cut away any broken or winter-damaged branches, and remove a few mature shoots every year or two to encourage new growth and maintain a more attractive form.

Heavenly bamboo (*Nandina domestica*) is a popular evergreen shrub in zones 7 through 9, though it will also grow in zone 6 if given a sheltered, protected site. The leathery leaflets, each drawn to a sharp point, are bronze to red when they unfurl in spring. A double or triple compound leaf habit results in an attractive, open, bamboolike patterning, which is accentuated by the sparse branching of the canes. When planted in a sunny place, heavenly bamboo turns a bright red to dull reddish purple in fall. While the species grows 6 to 8 feet tall, *N. domestica* 'Fire Power' is more compact, reaching 2 feet tall. This dense-growing cultivar features red-tinted leaves all summer and especially vivid winter color. The foliage of *N. domestica* 'Nana Purpurea' retains a red-purple flush throughout the growing season and is especially attractive because its leaf segments are larger, if fewer in number, than those of the species. Heavenly bamboo and low-growing, glossy-leaved sweet box (*Sarcococca hookeriana* var. *humilis*) make an attractive combination for shady sites. In a sunny situation, consider planting a variegated cultivar of maiden grass (*Miscanthus sinensis*) behind the heavenly bamboo.

Corylopsis sinensis var. *sinensis* 'Spring Purple' is another shrub with coppery purple leaves, but these make their colorful display only in spring, greening up in summer. It is hardy from zones 6 to 9 and dislikes dry sites or exposure to wind. Late spring frosts will damage the early flowers, which appear before the leaves. Unfortunately, I am unable to suggest a source for this hard-to-find rarity, since it is absent from the lists of my usual sources. But this leads to an important consideration. Gardening is about growing plants. Reading of hitherto unknown plants serves an important purpose, bringing new plants within the gardener's ken. If we do not learn about new plants, something unfamiliar but potentially delightful might be overlooked and left behind at the nursery. However, if the plant is unobtainable, intellectual descriptions may only incite horticultural lust that cannot be readily satisfied. On top of that, catalogs may have lurid descriptions of plants said to be new and rare when in fact they are more or less familiar and commonplace. In the end it is probably best to consider a plant purely for its value in your own garden, noting how it grows amongst its companions.

Filberts (*Corylus maxima*) are hardy from zones 5 through 8 and are said to bear delicious nuts. However, gardeners of my acquaintance who have grown these large shrubs—which, at 15 to 20 feet tall, function as small trees for modest gardens—report that squirrels are more efficient at harvesting the nuts than are people. Red-leaved filbert (*C. maxima* 'Rote Zeller') is marginally more available than *Corylopsis sinensis* var. *sinensis* 'Spring Purple'. Its large leaves are an attractive red-purple in spring, turning bronzy green in summer. *Corylus maxima* 'Purpurea' has dark purple-maroon leaves that are at their brightest in spring, turning darker and duller in summer. Although it is able to grow in partial shade, 'Purpurea' needs full sun to develop its richest color.

Weigela florida is an old-fashioned shrub, a workhorse plant that continually grows and flowers, remaining resistant to pests and diseases and needing little care. This is why we see them flourishing around shabby old houses—planted when the house was new, the 7-foot-high green mound patiently continues to bear pink flowers in late spring, year after year. In the past, gardeners used *W. florida* 'Foliis Purpureis', which features purplish leaves in early summer that later turn more green. Its best feature was said to be its dwarf stature, as it remains less than 5 feet tall. Now there is *W. florida* 'Alexandra'. Its glossy leaves are the rich dark shade of burgundy wine and keep their deep hue throughout the growing season, making a fine foil for the shrub's own pink flowers. At 4 to 5 feet tall, 'Alexandra' makes a good accent in the perennial border for the flowers and foliage of other plants.

Deer leave my *Weigela florida* alone, but the same cannot be said of the nearby purple-leaved eastern ninebark (*Physocarpus opulifolius* 'Diablo'), which gets chewed back in spring. However, this may only happen when the does are pregnant and nursing, for they seem to leave the plant alone when summer arrives. Pregnancy cravings perhaps? It may be a good thing then that eastern ninebark has a moderate to rapid rate of growth. In fact, one method of rejuvenation involves cutting an established shrub back to ground level and letting it start all over again. Though *P. opulifolius* is native to North America, 'Diablo' is a German selection. Its wide, arching branches are covered with dark purple three-lobed leaves up to 3 inches long. Here is a contender for difficult urban sites: this cultivar will tolerate sun or partial shade, a wide pH range (though it prefers acid conditions), and a dry environment (though it prefers moisture), growing just about anywhere.

VINES

Vines are relaxed plants that need some support to take themselves off the ground. Some lovingly twine around trees and shrubs—occasionally with fatal results to the host, as when bittersweet (*Celastrus*) strangles a sapling. Others, such as Boston ivy (*Parthenocissus tricuspidata*), develop little suckering feet that cling to rough bark, masonry walls, or wooden fences. Similarly, poison ivy (*Toxicodendron radicans*) and English ivy (*Hedera helix*) employ their hairy rootlets as holdfasts all along their main stems. *Clematis* species use their leaf petioles to wind around a supporting twig or trellis, while grapes have specialized tendrils that coil like watch springs to hold young vines to their support. Whatever the mechanism, vines need some supporting structure on which to brace themselves. Roses and clematis are a traditional pairing. A convenient wall, fence, arbor, trellis, or pergola will work well as a fabricated support. Be careful, though, to match the habit of the vine with the sturdiness of the support: a rampaging wisteria might flatten what may easily sustain clematis.

Because the three-lobed leaves of Boston ivy (*Parthenocissus tricuspidata*) grow so densely, this plant makes a good screen when used as a fedge (see chapter 9). Branched tendrils with adhesive discs help it cling to brick or masonry wall, and vigorous growth makes it suitable for covering large buildings. Boston ivy covers windows with the same ease, so maintenance will be necessary to keep the glass clear. Remember too that this deciduous plant drops its leaves in winter. *Parthenocissus tricuspidata* 'Purpurea' features persistently purple leaves tinted with red, the color especially noticeable when they first unfold in spring. The large leaves of the vigorously growing *P. tricuspidata* 'Atropurpurea' are red in spring, changing in summer to green tinted with blue or purple.

No doubt grapes were grown for their fruit before they were ever treated as ornamentals. *Vitis vinifera* has been in cultivation for so long that its actual origins are uncertain, and it includes a large variety of table and wine grapes. This is a variable species, and diverse selections have been made for toothed, lobed, or otherwise attractive leaves. *Vitis vinifera* 'Purpurea', sometimes known as teinturier grape or claret vine, has young leaves fuzzed with a whitish down as they unfold in spring, quickly becoming plum-purple to claret as they mature. The deeply lobed foliage is dark to begin with but turns an even deeper dark purple as summer ends, and vivid crimson in autumn. Young leaves make an especially attractive contrast against the older, larger, dusky, deep purple leaves. Though gangly and sprawling with high climbing habits, teinturier grape can be kept under control through late winter pruning.

PERENNIALS

I am always interested in how plants develop status, whether a high grade or a low rank. Rarity has something to do with it, as does novelty if the plant is a recent arrival on the gardening scene. If it is both difficult to obtain and hard to grow, the more we gardeners will surely lust for it. I myself am beginning to appreciate the workhorse plants—those that do their job of growing without my having to fuss or bother, providing a neat appearance while keeping weeds from dominating their space. Of course, just as Dr. Dolittle can speak the language of animals, I would love to speak the language of plants: "You—spread only until you reach your neighbor, then stop." It would make bugleweed (*Ajuga*) that much easier to contain within bounds.

Ajuga reptans is an evergreen, generally rhizomatous (that's where the spreading comes in), sun- and shade-tolerant member of the mint family (Lamiaceae or Labiatae), and it remains untouched by deer, rabbits, and woodchucks. What's not to love? Well, it is also common and weedy. I use it to edge paths in my woodland garden—not solid ribbons of it, mind you, but a group here, next to some low-growing ferns, and another there, with liriope for a partner. Sure, it spreads out into the path, but it is also easy to remove. Another thing I've learned over the years is that just because we call a particular plant "perennial" does not mean it will be unsuitable for composting. Where *A. reptans* strays too far over the mossy branches that delineate the path, it is simply snipped and evicted. *Ajuga reptans* 'Bronze Beauty' has brilliant bronze leaves that make a fine foil for the silver lace of Japanese painted fern (*Athyrium nipponicum* 'Pictum'). *Ajuga reptans* 'Chocolate Chip' has a cachet of newness about it. It was introduced to the United States in 2001 by Terra Nova Nurseries, a wholesale vendor in Canby, Oregon, that specializes in forms of *Heuchera*, *Pulmonaria*, and every other herbaceous perennial with fascinating leaf color or variegated foliage. Their catalog describes 'Chocolate Chip' as a natural, dwarf, spreading groundcover only 2 to 3 inches tall with chocolate foliage suitable for sunny to shady sites in zones 4 through 9. No doubt it will remain popular until it becomes more widely available. And after that? Who knows. Only the sometimes fickle gardening public.

Cow parsley (*Anthriscus sylvestris*) is a relative of chervil (*A. cerefolium*), a popular herb. Both have similar flowers and fernlike three-pinnate leaves comparable to those of Queen Anne's lace (*Daucus carota*). The leaves of *A. sylvestris* 'Ravenswing' are green as they emerge in spring, soon changing to deep purple-black. This cultivar may have been a passing fancy, however, as it seems to have faded from the garden scene. Fortunately there are other options for purple-black lacy-leaved perennials. Mitsuba (*Cryptotaenia japonica*), also known as honewort, is, like *Anthriscus* and *Daucus*, a member of the Umbelliferae. It features biserrate to two- or three-lobed, heart-shaped leaves, which are used extensively as a vegetable in Japanese cooking. Purple mitsuba (*C. japonica* 'Atropurpurea') has—what else?—purple-black leaves, which seem most deeply colored when given extra sunlight, paling to a softer bronze in partial shade. This elegant cultivar partners nicely with glaucous blue or gold-leaved hostas. It isn't as widely offered as it should be, which probably explains why it is rarely seen in gardens. Purple mitsuba is hardy to zone 5.

At 5 to 6 feet tall, black-leaved snakeroots (*Cimicifuga ramosa*) are stately plants. *Cimicifuga ramosa* 'Brunette' is one example, with intense purplish black leaves, deeper in color than those of *C. ramosa* 'Atropurpurea'. The one- to three-ternate, lobed, serrate leaflets of 'Brunette' create a feathery look, making a soft mound of foliage. Plant it near a large yellow hosta for a shocking color contrast. Its leaves will look like deep shadows if placed close by the classic *Hosta* 'Sum and Substance', for instance. Some sun will be needed for the hosta to develop its strongest yellow, and in such a site the cimicifuga will require adequate moisture, especially in summer. For a softer, subtler combination, use a glaucous blue hosta such as *H.* 'Blue Umbrellas', with its immense, glossy blue-green leaves whose deeply indented veins create a seersucker texture. *Cimicifuga ramosa* 'Hillside Black Beauty' is a patented selection discovered by Mary Ann McGourty of Hillside Gardens, Connecticut. Its coppery purple-black leaves may be the darkest of all the purple-leaved cimicifugas (of course, as soon as that is said, there is sure to be a new contender).

Cimicifuga simplex 'Black Negligee' is smaller than *C. ramosa*, at 2 feet tall, and hardy from zones 5 to 9. Featuring lacy black foliage on dark stems, 'Black Negligee' was named by Ernie and Marietta O'Byrne of Northwest Garden Nursery in Eugene, Oregon, which specializes in perennials. The display border at the nursery makes excellent use of foliage and flowers. Marietta has a flair for visual excitement and has come up with superb combinations of purple and gold foliage, matching, for example, a pollarded purple-leaved smokebush (*Cotinus coggygria* 'Royal Purple') with a feathery gold-leaved elderberry (*Sambucus racemosa* 'Plumosa Aurea'). She likes to use the rusty black foliage of *Cryptotaenia* as, in her own words, "a referee between colors I wouldn't normally place next to each other, like pink and yellow."

Not all clematis are woody vines—a few are herbaceous, like other perennials. While *Clematis recta* does need some support, especially for the taller 6-foot-high forms, it is no more than what many back-of-the-border perennials require. Allow the deciduous vine to scramble up a tripod made from three bamboo canes about 6 feet long, use slender cedar saplings as poles, or create a more formal tuteur. *Clematis recta* var. *purpurea* has deep bronze-purple leaves that slowly turn green by summer's end. If kept clipped back during the growing season, this vine will continue to produce more deeply colored young shoots and leaves, though at the expense of the strongly scented white flowers that normally appear in June and July. Though the species will always produce some purple-leaved forms when raised from seed (approximately 10 percent), most will exhibit wishy-washy coloring. The best option is to purchase *C. recta* var. *purpurea*.

Riders of the Purple Sage was a popular Western by Zane Grey. The purple sage referred to is actually sagebrush, which belongs to *Artemisia*—all the more confusing because there is a true sage with purple leaves: *Salvia officinalis* 'Purpurascens'. The soft-textured reddish purple leaves of this cultivar make a great foil for gray, red, or glaucous blue leaves. When planted in the garden, it requires full sun and reasonably good drainage, as it dislikes wet roots. One year I used purple sage as part of an autumn planting for the pair of window boxes on my toolshed, in addition to a few other plants. *Imperata cylindrica* 'Rubra', a Japanese blood grass with a warm red color on the upper portion of its blades, provided a linear, upright accent. *Euphorbia amygdaloides* 'Rubra', a wood spurge with a compact habit and dark green leaves flushed with red-purple (especially in cold weather), made a nice sprawling mound. Finally, a few 4-inch pots of ornamental cabbage (*Brassica oleracea*) with pale fuchsia-pink hearts added their ruffled texture and bright color.

The leaves of cogongrass (*Imperata cylindrica*) are plain green, unlike its red-leaved cultivars. The species has gotten some bad press, as it has become widespread in subtropical and tropical regions, and has even made it onto the USDA's Federal Noxious Weed List. Ornamental cultivars, however, have not yet spread outside gardens. *Imperata cylindrica* 'Rubra' (see Plate 46) and *I. cylindrica* 'Red Baron' (both forms of Japanese blood grass) are cold tolerant, and there is some concern that they might hybridize with *I. cylindrica*. It would be prudent to avoid planting the ornamental forms in subtropical and tropical regions; as long as they are planted only in cold-winter regions where cogongrass does not grow, problems are unlikely to occur. Should a reversion to the green-leaved form occur in your garden, it would make sense to dig it out and destroy it. Kurt Blumel of Blumel Nurseries in Baldwin, Maryland, has two great sweeps of Japanese blood grass in his garden. Sizeable groups of the red-hued grass, offset from each other so that those on the left can never reach those on the right, alternate with the cool little lemon-yellow daisies of *Coreopsis verticillata* 'Moonbeam'. At one time Kurt partnered the grass with the sexy black ribbons of *Ophiopogon planiscapus* 'Nigrescens'.

The genus *Heuchera*, whose members are commonly known as coral bells, includes North American perennials that form dense mounds of lobed, rounded, or reniform evergreen foliage. Wiry stems carry many small white, pink, or red flowers. *Heuchera* ×*brizoides* cultivars were introduced first by Lemoine in France, then by Bressingham Gardens in England. These hybrids of *H. sanguinea*, *H. micrantha*, and possibly *H. americana* were first brought into gardens for their flowers. Then *H. micrantha* var. *diversifolia* 'Palace Purple' appeared on the scene, introduced by the Royal Botanic Gardens at Kew, London. With glossy deep bronze-purple leaves, red as a beet underneath, 'Palace Purple' was a resounding success. Technically, as a named cultivar it should have been propagated asexually, cloned through high-tech tissue culture or through a good old-fashioned method such as division. Soon, however, we were getting 'Palace Purple' with olive-drab leaves—the sort of phenomenon that gives cultivars a poor name. One suspects genetic mixing (as in seeds) had a role to play in this. It hardly matters, though, for *H. micrantha* var. *diversifolia* 'Palace Purple', whether true to name or not, is old hat, dull in comparison to *H. micrantha* var. *diversifolia* 'Bressingham Bronze' or *H. micrantha* var. *diversifolia* 'Chocolate Veil', with their intense color and shiny leaves. Dan Heims of Terra Nova Nurseries is at the forefront of heuchera introduction, offering what is arguably the most extensive selection worldwide. He has hybridized and selected some truly stunning cultivars.

Heucheras prefer a moist yet well-drained soil and partial shade, though in cool-summer regions such as the northern states and the Pacific Northwest, they can thrive in full sun. Ultimately you will need to find the appropriate balance for your garden, as a couple of hours of direct sun are needed to keep leaf color at its strongest. Hot, humid summers can be a problem. Deer enjoy heucheras but are easily repelled with a scattering of Milorganite, a granular sewerage sludge fertilizer produced in Milwaukee. Since the dark red and purple foliage of these plants is somber under low light conditions, I like to use silver foliage for bijou combinations and gold foliage for more vibrant effects.

Garnet-leaved *Heuchera* 'Montrose Ruby' was the hottest heuchera to come along after *H. micrantha* var. *diversifolia* 'Palace Purple', followed by the silver-flushed *H.* 'Dale's Selection'. Deep chocolatey purples with a burgundy overlay can be found in *H.* 'Checkers', *H.* 'Chocolate Ruffles', *H.* 'Crimson Curls', *H.* 'Plum Pudding', *H.* 'Purple Petticoats', *H.* 'Purple Sails', and *H.* 'Velvet Night', as well as in *H. micrantha* var. *diversifolia* 'Bressingham Bronze' and *H. micrantha* var. *diversifolia* 'Chocolate Veil'. Some are more ruffled and perhaps more deeply lobed, and there is variation in size from 4 to 7 inches.

Some heucheras feature a silver overlay, creating a frosty effect that can be accentuated with silver foliage such as Japanese painted fern (*Athyrium nipponicum* 'Pictum'). To my mind, golden leaves such as those of golden bleeding heart (*Dicentra spectabilis* 'Gold Heart') are not a good match, making too much of a mishmash with the silver-accented purple. *Heuchera* 'Amethyst Myst' features amethyst-purple leaves covered with a fog of silver. The leaves of *H.* 'Autumn Haze' have more of a purple flush in summer and are silver with purple veining in winter. *Heuchera* 'Regina' has burgundy leaves with a silver mist.

Another option is offered by cultivars such as *Heuchera* 'Mardi Gras', with variable coral to orange variegation. Some olive-green leaves display just a segment of the warmer color, while others are entirely salmon with small spatters of olive-green. The yellow color and linear form of Japanese forest grass (*Hakonechloa macra* 'Aureola') makes a pleasant pairing.

TENDER PERENNIALS

Where you live controls which plants you consider perennials and which you consider annuals. None of the plants in my tropical border would make it through the winter. Some years dusty miller (*Senecio cineraria*) and snapdragon (*Antirrhinum majus*) are perennial for me, though most years they function as annuals. My zone 6 garden is on the cusp of what such plants can endure in winter. Yet plants that I must treat as annuals can be treated as perennials elsewhere: the coleus (*Solenostemon scutellarioides*) and impatiens that are mainstays of summer gardens cooler than zone 10 are perennial where conditions suit their needs. And although gardeners often think of winter cold as being the limiting factor, those who garden in hot climates know that plants can be killed just as easily by summer heat.

Numerous tender perennials are available as options for the summer garden, and many are grown for their foliage attributes. Others are grown as houseplants and are brought outdoors in summer. There is nothing new in this. Writing about bloodleaf (*Iresine herbstii*) in 1965, Jean Hersey suggested gardeners "set the plant outdoors in summer, if possible." A Victorian favorite, bloodleaf, also known as chicken gizzard, used to be popular for carpet bedding, a formal style of patterned planting wherein plants are massed for a colorful tapestry like effect. Bloodleaf's red leaves with darker maroon markings require full sun and thrive in hot, humid conditions. Regular pinching keeps plants compact and bushy. Richard Iversen, author of *The Exotic Garden*, suggests it be used with *Alternanthera ficoidea*.

There are several different species and cultivars of *Alternanthera*, all popular for massing, or as edging plants trailing over the rim of a container. *Alternanthera ficoidea* 'Red Fine Leaf' is a low, bushy, spreading groundcover with bright burgundy, oval to linear leaves 1 to 2 inches long. *Alternanthera dentata* 'Rubiginosa' is a sprawling, weak-stemmed spreader with glossy, deep plum-purple leaves. At 3 feet tall it is much bigger than *A. ficoidea,* and some pruning will be needed if it is not given sufficient space to roam. Let it weave in and around golden barberry (*Berberis thunbergii* 'Aurea') for a vivid contrast, or mingle with crushed-raspberry-pink coleus (*Solenostemon scutellarioides*). Combine it with a copper or tricolored phormium, or let it shine against the metallic fuchsia-pink leaves of Persian shield (*Strobilanthes dyeriana*). Cut back and kept juvenile, a silver-blue eucalyptus would also make an attractive partner, adding the powdery appearance of its rounded leaves.

Think of using cannas with purple leaves to heat up an already hot border featuring red and orange flowers.

Some nurseries sell cannas by name, while garden centers and discount stores often sell them by flower or leaf color. Nevertheless, the plant knows who it is even if you don't. Remember that cannas want full sun and moist to wet soil. Some are tall, some are short. *Canna* 'Black Knight' and *C.* 'Pink Futurity' are dwarf forms with burgundy leaves, reaching 30 to 36 inches tall. *Canna* 'Purple Faiase' can reach 4 feet tall. *Canna* 'Red King Humbert' and *C.* 'Louis Cotton' grow 5 to 6 feet tall. *Canna* 'Intrigue' is a flaccida type with narrow lanceolate leaves of deep purple on plants capable of reaching 6 to 10 feet tall. Think of using cannas with purple leaves to heat up an already hot border featuring red and orange flowers. Try adding red fountain grass (*Pennisetum setaceum* 'Rubrum') to echo the color but add a change of shape. Cool things down with pink and green flowers or silver foliage.

The big oval leaves of our old friend *Canna* 'Tropicanna' are vividly colored, a stunning effect on 5- to 7-foot-tall plants. *Canna* 'Durban' is a midsized canna, at 4 to 5 feet tall. It also features large leaves, which unroll to display deep red and orange stripes radiating from a dark green main vein. As they mature the leaves become splashed with rose, gold, red, olive, and violet. The display is so colorful that 'Durban' makes a first-class accent plant for container or garden.

Most gardeners are familiar with caladiums: heat- and humidity-loving tubers with broad arrowhead-shaped leaves in shades and combinations of pink, red, white, and green. *Caladium* belongs to the aroid family (Araceae), as does *Colocasia*. Black elephant's-ear (*C. esculenta* 'Jet Black Wonder') has exotic, velvety, matte black leaves with purple undertones, as much as 3 feet long by 2 feet wide at their broadest point, on plants up to 5 feet tall. This cultivar needs warmth and is unsuitable for the Pacific Northwest and other regions with cool summer weather. Ample water and regular feeding are also important if plants are to do their best. Give the tubers a few weeks head start indoors, placing them in a warm spot or providing bottom warmth with a heat mat. They should be kept indoors until tomato-planting time or until nighttime temperatures are regularly above 65° Fahrenheit. In all except tropical regions, container culture is often easier than planting in the ground. Set the pot in sun or light shade, watering moderately until growth really begins to take off. Plants should be watered freely, even kept in shallow water in a pond, and never allowed to dry out while in growth. Reduce watering as autumn approaches. After a frost has withered the leaves, store the tubers dry, still in their pots, at a minimum temperature of 55° Fahrenheit. Castor bean (*Ricinus communis*) makes a stately partner, though one that must be given average soil rather than the mucky swamplike conditions preferred by *C. esculenta* 'Jet Black Wonder'. *Tradescantia pallida* 'Purple Heart' can sprawl around nearby, its lighter violet foliage providing an attractive grace note to the colocasia's deeper eggplant-black color.

The ornamental sweet potatoes *Ipomoea batatas* 'Blackie' and *I. batatas* 'Ace of Spades' are relatively recent introductions that have made the transition from vegetable garden to ornamental garden. 'Ace of Spades' has spade-shaped leaves, while 'Blackie' has lobed foliage. Long runners clothed in black foliage add a somber effect. Like their agricultural cousins, these ornamental sweet potatoes love sun and heat, and thrive in a sandy soil. Fortunately, deer seem to prefer the gold and variegated forms of sweet potato to these black-leaved cultivars. Both can act as a summer groundcover, soften the edge of large containers, or trail gracefully from a hanging basket. 'Ace of Spades' is more compact in habit than 'Blackie', which can become rambunctious, requiring regular cutting back to be kept within bounds. All ornamental sweet potatoes form tubers, which can be stored with some success. They also root easily from cuttings, which provide a source of smaller plants to grow indoors through the winter.

Red fountain grass (*Pennisetum setaceum* 'Rubrum') is a beautiful cultivar, though it may be helpful to point out, as Rick Darke does in *The Color Encyclopedia of Ornamental Grasses*, that there are some doubts as to whether it actually belongs to this species. Unfortunately, it does not tolerate prolonged periods at temperatures lower than 40° Fahrenheit, so it is not hardy below zone 9. Gardeners in lower zones may treat it as an annual, or, if suitable quarters are available, keep it contained for wheeling in and out as the season dictates. (It will not appreciate being dug up from the garden each winter.) A stately size makes this 4- to 5-foot-tall grass a candidate for back-of-the-border placement. Its linear texture contrasts well with bold or lacy foliage. Consider contrasting it with the jagged silver leaves of cardoon (*Cynara cardunculus*), for example, or with the prominent leaves of bananas or cannas. Its rich color pairs nicely with just about any end-of-summer daisies, which provide an opportunity for a final fling before cold weather sets in. I once saw *P. setaceum* 'Rubrum' used at a nursery to edge a massive group of *Lilium* 'Stargazer'. The effect was superb when I was there, in August, while the lilies were in flower; but I found myself wondering what would come next, after the flowers faded, and what it must have looked like before they had even bloomed.

Perhaps you would like something with a similar look but even taller. Sugarcane (*Saccharum officinarum*) easily reaches 8 feet tall as a summer annual in temperate regions when given warmth, sunshine, and ample moisture, and it grows over 16 feet tall in the tropics. *Saccharum officinarum* 'Pele's Smoke', named after the Hawaiian goddess of volcanoes, features glossy purple stems narrowly banded white at the nodes where the smoky purple leaf blades have fallen away. Give it a large container, the size of half a whiskey barrel, to provide adequate room for the roots. You may also think about warming the irrigation water. Either fill a watering can and let the water sit until it warms to ambient summer temperature, or add some warm water to chilly water from the tap. This will be less of a shock to the roots and help this tender tropical grass perform better.

New Zealand flax (*Phormium tenax*) is another linear, grasslike plant for summertime gardens. On a trip to Ireland, I became envious of the magnificent specimens that seemed to grow in every garden we went to, whether they were grand estates, public gardens, or smaller personal properties. Great swordlike leaves reached 5, 6, even 7 feet tall, and huge flowering stems erupted yet another 3 feet into the air. I coaxed the tour bus driver into stopping at a garden center or two and came home with a few small phormiums. They'll never reach the magnificent proportions of those I saw in Ireland (or of those I've seen in California and Washington), for my phormiums must live in pots and spend their winters indoors. *Phormium tenax* 'Purpureum' has a dull coppery color, something like an even overlay on gray-green. My potted specimen spends the summer outdoors in the tropical border. Its leaves are over 2 feet long and about 2 inches wide and flat at the tip, folding to an acute V at the base. Though hardy in zones 9 and 10, in zones 7 and 8 phormiums die to the ground and need a deep mulch of dry straw or leaves over the crown for winter protection. They do well in sun, shade, or something in between, and tolerate well-drained to wet soil. Phormiums evolved with cooler temperatures and lower rainfall. Hot, humid conditions are a problem, especially if such weather keeps on for extended periods. I keep them on the dry side in winter, having learned the hard way that too much water results in rot. My potted phormiums are kept on the cool side in winter, at 50° Fahrenheit or lower. They can remain outdoors until it is time to bring Christmas cactus and non-hardy azaleas inside, after night temperatures start dropping below 40° Fahrenheit. Other purple to copper phormiums include the rich purple-red *P.* 'Atropurpureum', which has 3- to 5-foot-long leaves, and *P.* 'Bronze Baby' and *P.* 'Tom Thumb', both of which feature dwarf (18-inch), narrow bronze leaves.

A coleus by any other name would be a solenostemon, a taxonomic revision that is all at once longer, more difficult to pronounce, and more easily misspelled. Nevertheless, we are all supposed to tug our forelocks and acquiesce. I wonder if coleus would have found its popular niche as a houseplant if we had been forced to call it solenostemon back in 1747 when Rumphius first described it in *Herbarium Amboinense*. In the mid to late nineteenth century, coleus were popular as decorative greenhouse plants and bedding plants. As the twentieth century rolled around, more plants were raised from seed than cloned from cultivars, and their quality declined. When I started gardening (not quite that long ago, but more years than I care to admit), coleus were raised from seed and sold in mixed colors. If you found one you especially liked, it was easy enough to take a stem cutting, root it in a jar of water, and keep it going. Coleus are seeing a resurgence in popularity, and there are numerous varieties available. Landcraft Environments, a wholesale nursery in Mattituck, New York, listed fifty different coleus in a recent catalog. Some have large oval leaves with a simple color scheme; others are compact with deeply lobed foliage. There are a range of colors, from *Solenostemon scutellarioides* 'Florida Gold' with its large, wide golden yellow leaves splashed and veined with red, to *S. scutellarioides* 'Inky Fingers', listed as "a cute compact grower having deep burgundy leaves and a green scalloped edge." *Solenostemon scutellarioides* 'Rex' is described as having a "black midrib fading to plum, magenta, lime, gold, and cream."

The catalog includes an interesting description of *Solenostemon scutellarioides* 'Black Blister' as well: "It has very long, narrow, deeply cut black leaves. On the leaf surface there are random blotches and puckers. The overall effect is that of a roasted tarantula. Choice." Having never roasted a tarantula, I'll have to take their word for it. Other black *S. scutellarioides* cultivars include 'Black Magic', with narrow black leaves scalloped in moss green along the edges; 'Dark Star', with wide, midsized, dark black leaves and violet-black stems; 'Purple Emperor', which looks like a purple basil, with velvety, deep purple, ruffled leaves; and 'Red

Velvet', an upright cultivar with narrow, curled, velvety, plum leaves scalloped in red at the edges. I enjoy using these black beauties with yellow or orange to red foliage in sunny places, and with silver foliage in the shady places.

If you prefer a coleus without the usually bushy habit, train one as a standard. Simply take a vigorous, well-rooted cutting of an upright form and encourage straight growth. Pinch off any side shoots, letting the upper leaves remain to nourish the plant. Place a thin bamboo cane next to the stem and tie it in two or three places for support. Use soft twine or raffia, and cross it between stem and stake in a figure eight. Check the ties periodically to see if they need to be loosened or tightened: if they are too tight they may damage the stem, and if they are too loose they won't provide adequate support. When the standard-to-be reaches 2 feet tall, pinch back the tip. Allow four side shoots to form at the top, to produce the head. Pinch back secondary side shoots after the second pair of leaves appear. This is also when the leaves up and down the stem can be removed. If you begin the process in spring, you should have a nice standard by midsummer.

While coleus need a moist soil and prefer partial shade, some newer cultivars will grow in full sun. Remember to provide adequate moisture, though. Coleus make a good indicator plant due to their readiness to wilt when sufficient water is lacking, a signal that other, more resistant plants are probably also thirsty. Consider pairing up purple coleus and heuchera, using silver foliage as a lighter accent. One season I paired a green and gold plectranthus with *Solenostemon scutellarioides* 'Inky Fingers' to accentuate the wine-colored stems of the plectranthus. Dark coleus look great in combination with purple and lavender flowers, as accent plants, with alternantheras in a carpet bedding scheme, in containers with small cannas, or planted in the shade with the golden blades of Japanese forest grass (*Hakonechloa macra* 'Aureola').

You would think that coleus thrive in hot steamy places like Florida, but unfortunately such is not the case. In these environments they quickly become tall and leggy, needing to be repeatedly cut back. Heat and humidity also make coleus vulnerable to all sorts of bacterial diseases, stem rots, nematodes, and soilborne diseases such as phytophthora and pythium. What to do? P. J. Klinger, a wholesale bedding plant grower in Longwood, Florida, decided to tackle the problem. The coleus he wanted to produce for use in Florida had to be disease resistant, short, self-branching, and colorful. Starting in 1999, he selected twenty-four of the most commonly grown cultivars and let pollinating insects do their stuff. Since coleus are widely variable, P. J. knew the resulting seed set from open pollination would produce highly diverse plants with a wide genetic range. The following year a hundred thousand seedlings were produced and grown in plug trays. One criterion for selection was good color—any seedling with entirely green leaves was promptly discarded. Plants were also considered for their formation of axillary buds and branching, as those with this feature would become compact and self-branching at maturity. By March 2000 the original number of seedlings was ruthlessly winnowed down to eight hundred plants, less than 1 percent of the original number. By August these were again rigorously culled, down to thirty-six plants, which were then vegetatively propagated. In September these thirty-six selections were taken to a meeting of the Florida Nurserymen and Growers Association, at which attendees were asked to choose the six plants they liked best. The final *Solenostemon scutellarioides* selections were named for Florida cities: 'Altoona', 'Bonifay', 'Immokalee', 'Micanopy', 'Yalaha', and 'Yulee'. 'Micanopy' has large, rather flat leaves the bright color of red wine vinegar, with an elegant lacing of green at the edge. Color is consistent in older foliage and new growth. 'Yulee' is a dense selection featuring ruffled, deeply lobed plum-black leaves. Lobes are tipped with yellow, producing a lighter touch over the compact, dark bulk of the plant. After the six selections were made, P. J. felt it was important to monitor their ability to survive in Florida as low-maintenance landscape plants. Some plants were so vigorous from the first culling that a shovel was needed to dig them out of the trial bed. They, and the thirty-six from the second selection, were planted out for a second round of seed production and selection. Thanks to P. J., Florida gardeners have some fine coleus for their landscapes.

By midsummer, the coleus you purchased last spring in a 4-inch pot will have reached the size of a small shrub. Even if you had the space to winter it over, this large plant would respond poorly to such disruptions as digging and potting. Fortunately, coleus roots from cuttings with the greatest of ease. A three- or four-node tip cutting taken in early August will root in five days while still wrapped in a damp paper towel thrust into a plastic bag. I usually remove the largest leaves, or at least shorten them by half, and pull off the lowest pair of shoots. It is a simple procedure, so if someone offers you a start, feel free to gratefully accept. Just remember to root some of your own coleus, and be similarly generous with garden visitors.

There are other tender perennials with purple foliage, including *Euphorbia cotinifolia*, a shrub with glowing purplish red, rounded leaves. It wants full sun and good drainage, and looks absolutely stunning in front of a mass of *Foeniculum vulgare* 'Purpurascens', the feathery bronze-green foliage of the fennel making a soft backdrop for the euphorbia's coin-shaped, sunburn-red leaves. Velvet plant (*Gynura aurantiaca*) is a fuzzy trailing houseplant with obnoxiously scented orange flowers. It is great in a container, where it can fall gracefully over the edge, and can function as a summer groundcover in sunny sites. The coriaceous, oval leaves of *Pseuderanthemum atropurpureum* are green and cream flushed with rose-pink. I found a few of these plants at a home and garden store once and brought them home. Humus-rich, moist soil and a partially shady location kept them growing nicely all summer long. Around Labor Day I made cuttings and was pleased with how easily they rooted in sand and peat moss mixed with some rooting hormone. I placed a thin clear plastic bag over the pot as a little intensive-care tent, and this seemed to help. This species, however, is very frost tender, and my plants died when the pot they were in stayed outdoors too late one year. Chocolate plant (*Pseuderanthemum alatum*) has larger, more papery, chocolate-brown leaves with a central silver blotch. I brought one home from Natchez, Mississippi, and have kept it for three years now, potted with *Oxalis regnellii*, a clover-leaved bulbous plant whose purple leaves are made even more vivid by a fuchsia blotch at the base of each triangular leaflet. The chocolate plant has gotten kind of leggy, so I prune it back. During winter it stays in my cool greenhouse, and I keep it on the dry side, watering when I decide it's time for it to wake up. At the garden center where I purchased the chocolate plant, they told me it would have tiny violet flowers and would sometimes self-sow. Perhaps in Natchez but not, I think, in New Jersey. Another summer planting I put together combined chocolate plant, a merlot-red coleus (*Solenostemon scutellarioides*) with a thin yellow-green margin to its crenate, lanceolate leaves, and a chili pepper (*Capsicum*) with elegant black leaves.

Persian shield (*Strobilanthes dyeriana*) is a fantastic foliage plant with a shimmering metallic overlay on intense fuchsia-pink leaves. It looks a bit unreal, almost computer-generated. I wedge it in a large container with *Ipomoea batatas* 'Ace of Spades', an ornamental sweet potato, which trails its black spade-shaped leaves over the edge for a good contrast. A couple of yellow-throated lavender petunias and some glowing fuchsia impatiens complete the grouping. Though the petunias and impatiens outnumber the Persian shield and sweet potato, the foliage plants are more substantial and provide the bulk of the display. Persian shield performs well in full sun or light shade.

ANNUALS

Remember that true annuals germinate from seed, reach flowering maturity, set seed themselves, then die—all in the space of one growing season. Among these plants, which must focus on their flowers so as to ensure the next generation, there are a few with purple leaves. Interestingly enough, the few I have in mind are edible or herbal plants: orach (*Atriplex hortensis*), including 'Cupreatorosea', 'Rosea', and var. *rubra*; the purple basils (*Ocimum basilicum* 'Dark Opal' and *O.*

basilicum 'Purple Ruffles'); shiso (*Perilla frutescens* 'Atropurpurea'); and tampala (*Amaranthus tricolor*), including 'Flaming Fountain', 'Molten Fire', and 'Splendens'.

DESIGNING WITH DUSKY FOLIAGE

When gardening with dusky-colored plants, keep in mind that dark leaves look even darker in low light situations. Use them in moderation, and accent with pale green and silver-gray leaves. Glaucous blue hostas such as *Hosta sieboldiana* with its wrinkled blue leaves, or the daintier *H.* 'Halcyon' or *H.* 'Blue Cadet', make fine partners for black, lacy-leaved herbaceous perennials such as the dark-leaved cultivars of *Cimicifuga*. Hostas with leaves that are pruinose (thickly dusted with white)—*H.* 'Frosted Jade', for example, with its white-edged gray-green leaves— also alleviate somber foliage. Choose a golden hosta such as *H.* 'Sum and Substance' if you want to pop the combination into manic gaiety. Use *Ophiopogon planiscapus* 'Nigrescens', with its black straps of leaves, and combine it with the silver lace of *Athyrium nipponicum* 'Pictum' or the frosty blue spade-shaped leaves of *H.* 'Hadspen Heron'—or perhaps combine it with both. Keep in mind that dark green foliage also has the effect of turning down the lights, making crimson, scarlet, purple, and raven-dark leaves in shady situations appear even darker. This is not only important to consider in woodland gardens and shaded city backyards: gardeners who spend long hours at the office should also decide if their weekends provide sufficient hours of daylight for appreciating gardens that disappear into dusk on weekdays.

Sunny situations are very different, though intense colors should still be employed with restraint. Use shrubs and small trees with copper or purple-red foliage as emphasis and not as the main feature. Sunlit sites do energize and, in effect, lighten up plum, sanguine, sooty, and inky leaves. Here is the place for saffron-yellow, gold, and pinkish copper to glow with shadow-hued foliage. Cannas, bananas, and wine-red coleus are three simple, temporary options for just about any sunny summer garden, if you like the tropical look. Owing to the fact that intensity of light mitigates the effect of dark foliage, gardens along the coast or in subtropical Florida can use a carnival intensity of color as the norm, though it would appear extreme in Maine or Minnesota. A potted garden permits a more whimsical, anything-goes approach to plant selection. Mix and match plants in containers to try out colors and textures before expanding their use into the wider landscape of the garden.

~❧~

CHAPTER 6

Shimmering Selections

Silver, gray, pewter, platinum—I love these foliage colors; and frosty glaucous blue leaves have a similar cooling look. Gardens planted in tones of lavender, violet, and purple with generous amounts of gray foliage are very lovely and restful in effect. Flowers colored these shades of purple gain a lambent glow at dusk and, when brought together with gray foliage, create a luminous, sterling display for an evening garden with panache. There is a physical foundation for this effect, as the eye's mechanisms for viewing color alter in lower light levels. There are two kinds of light receptors in the human eye: rods and cones. Cones are used in daylight vision and are best able to distinguish bright colors. As light grows dim, rods become more functional. A color of low intensity may actually appear to increase in brightness as light fades.

Gray and silver leaves, however, complement any flower color, not just lavender, violet, and purple. Pure blue flowers like gentians and delphiniums are not at their best when planted side by side but gain in appeal when matched with gray foliage. Pink, blush, carmine, or rose flowers are set off by many gray-leaved plants. White flowers and silver foliage create a tranquil impression, especially effective at night in a moon-viewing garden, but also capable of producing a cool look on a hot, sunny day. Envision a plant with silver, gray, pewter, or platinum leaves, perhaps a wormwood (*Artemisia*), paired with white shasta daisies (*Leucanthemum* ×*superbum*). The temperature of an August afternoon seems lower when you're surrounded by such plants, as compared with a brighter combination such as hot orange dahlias and purple foliage. Silver is the great mediator. Just picture the riot of color that occurs when combining plants of contrasting colors, such as purple heliotropes and yellow dahlias. Running a ribbon of silver dusty miller (*Senecio cineraria*) between the two warring hues will cool the conflict.

Remember that foliage color is a pragmatic matter for plants. The color gray, which gardeners appreciate for its attractiveness, is the result of a plant's attempts to protect itself against sunburn, water loss, cold night temperatures, and even chewing insects and animal predators. However, this applies to sun-tolerant plants; gray-leaved, shade-tolerant plants are gray through a different mechanism. Unfortunately, very few gray- and silver-leaved plants prefer shade over sun, so the options for the shady areas beneath trees are limited. While yellow foliage ranges from variegated leaves to completely yellow leaves, white foliage does not work the same way. A white-variegated plant such as English ivy (*Hedera helix*) will occasionally produce a shoot with totally white leaves, nourished by chlorophyll-containing leaves located elsewhere on the vine, but such white-leaved shoots cannot be rooted to grow on their own. Plants that attempt to grow with entirely white leaves are simply unable to make it on their own and soon die. They have no chlorophyll, you see. Certain caladiums—*Caladium bicolor* 'Candidum', for example—are nearly all white, but these have green edges and veins that keep them alive.

TREES

Approximately 150 kinds of the more than 500 different eucalyptus native to Australia and Tasmania are grown in the United States, primarily in the more arid states of Arizona and California. One popular use in regions where eucalyptus are tender is as summer bedding plants. Eucalyptus are large (over 100 feet tall at maturity) or small (10 or 12 feet tall at maturity), generally messy trees, dribbling bits of bark, slow-rotting leaves, and seedpods. That's in places where conditions are right for them to grow—not merely mild, sunny, dry climates like southern California, but climates where dry autumn weather will send the trees appropriate signals to go dormant. Too much moisture late in the year, as is often the case in the Pacific Northwest, will encourage eucalyptus to keep on growing, which lays the groundwork for frost injury. Reduce— or even better, withhold—fertilizers after early July, and discontinue irrigation. In sites with full sun and relatively limited precipitation, eucalyptus will thrive. They may be the most widely planted non-native trees in Arizona and California. Drought tolerance helps them adapt to arid regions. They are pest free, quick growing, and have attractive foliage, form, and texture. High in fragrant oils, eucalyptus can be dangerous when planted close to buildings in wildfire-prone regions.

Zoos that exhibit koalas need a steady supply of tender young eucalyptus shoots, as these hard-to-digest, toxic leaves are all the cuddly Australian critters eat. Some nurseries grow eucalyptus especially for these zoos, such as Rancho Jojoba Nursery in Lakeside, California, which provides eucalyptus for the San Diego Zoo, and a grower in Devon, England, who produces the plant for European zoos. Approximately forty *Eucalyptus* species are grown in the Devon nursery as hip-high pollards with whiplike shoots. The hardier species are grown out of doors, while the more tender species are grown in heated polytunnel greenhouses. The grower must match the seed source of various eucalyptus with the climate of his sloping, west-facing, twenty-acre property. The plants have a native range, and genetic variation makes those from the northern portion of their range a bit more cold tolerant than those from the southern portion. Nurseries selling eucalyptus often sell to florists as well. These nurseries must guard against mildew, which may be a problem in wet weather, and sucking, chewing insects that may attack young growth. While zoos require eucalyptus be free of pesticides, which might harm the koalas, florists demand pristine foliage.

Silver dollar eucalyptus (*Eucalyptus cinerea*) has silvery, circular juvenile leaves that fuse around the stem for a perfoliate appearance. In places where it is hardy it quickly grows 20 to 50 feet tall and just as wide, making an interesting midsized tree with an irregular form. Mature foliage is longer, more lanceolate, and not as striking in appearance and color. Pruning will encourage the growth of new branches with juvenile leaves and correct the sometimes scrawny, spindly habit. The foliage is popular for bouquets and dried use. Stringy reddish brown bark clothes the trunk, which is often too weak to support a sizeable canopy. Silver dollar eucalyptus is hardy to about 15° Fahrenheit. Frosts are likely to cause more damage in November than in January or February, by which time the tree will have become accustomed to colder weather. Older trees are more frost resistant than young ones.

Blue gum eucalyptus (*Eucalyptus globulus*) is a fast-growing tree with a straight trunk and is capable of reaching 150 to 200 feet tall. As is often the case with quick-growing trees, the branches are brittle and easily damaged by wind. Falling branches can be a problem in gardens or if the tree is placed near a street. Juvenile leaves are oval and have an attractive silvery appearance. Adult leaves are dark green, with a longer, sicklelike shape, and grow 6 to 10 inches in length. Fallen leaves are very rot resistant and can remain on the ground for ten years or longer, building up in a thick layer. This habit, coupled with a tendency to drop bits of bark and seed capsules, makes this a messy tree to have around. Given its great size at maturity, its need for deep soil, and its litter problems, blue gum eucalyptus seems best suited for a rural landscape. This is not a eucalyptus for desert conditions, as trees grow most satisfactorily on coastal slopes. Dwarf blue gum eucalyptus (*Eucalyptus globulus* 'Compacta') is relatively smaller, potentially reaching 65 feet high. With a rounder, more shrublike form produced by its multi-trunked habit, it can be kept sheared to 10 feet tall. As such, it makes a good windbreak in coastal regions with infrequent, brief periods of frost and low temperatures of 20° Fahrenheit.

Cider gum eucalyptus (*Eucalyptus gunnii*) is variable in height, growing from 40 to 75 feet tall (even taller in its native Tasmania) with a dense, upright habit. It is hardy down to 10° Fahrenheit, but wet conditions and autumn rains preclude its use in southeastern states and in the Pacific Northwest. Blue-green, circular, evergreen leaves up to 2½ inches across form a loose, open canopy that provides dappled shade. Mature leaves are lanceolate. Smooth, exfoliating, green and white bark has a mottled appearance like snakeskin. Flowers are a creamy yellow, like old ivory, and are borne in great numbers.

Kruse's Mallee (*Eucalyptus kruseana*) is a slow-growing dwarf eucalyptus that reaches only 5 to 8 feet tall. (Used as a garden term in reference to multi-stemmed, shrubby eucalyptus, *mallee* is the Australian Aboriginal word for a eucalyptus thicket.) Attractive, round, dainty, perfoliate leaves are only 1 inch across and appear dusted with silver-blue. The thin, angular stems should be frequently cut back to maintain the best foliage growth. Kruse's Mallee is elegant enough for the most refined setting, but its use is limited by its only slight resistance to light frost, from 25 to 28° Fahrenheit.

Snow gum eucalyptus (*Eucalyptus niphophila*) is native to high elevations in southeastern Australia and is hardy down to 10 to 0° Fahrenheit. However, before you rush out to plant one in Maine, remember that this tree accepts such low temperatures only as a passing aberration, a transient fling with wintry conditions. There is a big difference between bitter weather that keeps things solidly frozen for weeks on end and weather that plunges down to the same low temperature for only a few brief hours before climbing back up above freezing. Snow gum eucalyptus is a small, slow-growing, spreading tree that reaches about 20 feet tall with a picturesque crooked trunk and open crown. Leaves are silvery blue, lanceolate, and anywhere from 1½ to 4 inches long. Smooth white bark peels away, adding to an interesting appearance. Snow gum eucalyptus is tolerant of wind and dry conditions, and is recognized as a fine choice both for its good looks and its cold tolerance.

There are three specimens of weeping willowleaf pear (*Pyrus salicifolia* 'Pendula') in the herb garden at the New York Botanical Garden (see Plate 54). Gracefully trailing branches are clothed with narrow, willowlike, silvery gray leaves 1½ to 3½ inches long. The finely textured branches of this small, 15-foot-tall tree are pruned to an even level above the ground, giving it the appearance of a large, deep-crowned umbrella. Weeping willowleaf pears are long lived (there is a tree in the Arboretum Trompenburg, Rotterdam, that was planted in 1870) and slow growing. Though they look fragile, they are hardier than you might expect. Laura Louise Foster kept one at Millstream, the garden she and H. Lincoln Foster shared in Falls Village, Connecticut, where harsh winters put plants to the test. Weeping willowleaf pears are said to be hardy from zones 4 to 7 but will do best in the lowest zone if given a sheltered microclimate. A beautiful silver tree, this would make a lovely gift for a twenty-fifth wedding anniversary.

SHRUBS

A number of plants—lavender (*Lavandula*), sage (*Salvia*), Russian sage (*Perovskia*), and such—have woody lower branches that place them in the category of shrub. More often than not these herbs are tossed in with perennials, no doubt due to their refined structure and scale.

Dusty zenobia (*Zenobia pulverulenta*) was one of the more unusual shrubs planted in my Connecticut garden. Perfectly happy on its west-facing slope, an exceedingly well-drained site (sand and gravel 2 feet down, the most I had ever excavated in the spirit of scientific inquiry), it made a loose mound of 2-inch-long, leathery, blue-gray leaves much whitened underneath by a waxy bloom. Foliage was deciduous in a typical zone 6 winter (though it would be semi-evergreen in a milder climate). When we moved, my dusty zenobia was about 3 feet tall and over 3 feet wide. It is a slow-growing shrub, though, and would have eventually gained another foot in height and spread to about 4 feet by means of underground suckers. Native to the coastal plains of southeastern United States, this rarely seen plant needs full sun, good drainage, and an acid soil in order to thrive. In hot-summer regions it should be sited for midday shade. Dusty zenobia is related to heaths (*Erica*) and heathers (*Calluna*), and like them it requires acid soil, low pH, and adequate moisture coupled with good drainage. Lovely, anise-scented, white, bell-shaped flowers, similar to those of leucothoe and pieris, appear in late June or early July.

Calluna vulgaris 'Silver Queen' is a dwarf shrub with frosty, silvery, scalelike foliage. It reaches 1 foot tall, more under ideal conditions, and grows best in a sunny site with an open, free-draining, humus-rich soil. Humid summer weather may lead to fungal problems, which may be easily controlled with an old-fashioned dusting of sulfur at the first sign of browning foliage. A light clipping back of established plants early in spring will help keep them compact and tidy. Follow this with a topdressing consisting of half sand, half peat moss or compost, working it into the crown with your fingers much like you would scratch a cat or dog behind its ears. If winter snow cover is not reliable, cover 'Silver Queen' with pine boughs late in December to prevent sun scorch. There are other silver-gray *C. vulgaris* cultivars available, including 'Anthony Davis' and 'H. E. Beale', each reaching approximately 18 inches tall, and the dove-gray 'Sister Anne', which grows a scanty 9 inches tall. Heathers, as well as heaths, are best off planted in groups and masses. Accent their foliage with the smaller lepidote rhododendrons such as *Rhododendron* 'Purple Gem' or *R*. 'Ramapo', both featuring dainty leathery leaves that take on a bronze-purple hue in winter.

PERENNIALS FOR SHADE

Japanese painted fern (*Athyrium nipponicum* 'Pictum') has already been mentioned so many times that it seems redundant to mention it yet once more. I cannot resist, however, because I find this little fern to be a workhorse, one that I use again and again in the garden. I am not alone in my opinion, either: Japanese painted fern is arguably one of the most popular ferns in American gardens. This clump-forming, deciduous, modestly sized plant finds a place in gardens from zones 4 to 9. When it is given a moist, shaded site with loose open soil high in organic matter, new fronds may be produced right through summer and into early autumn. Fronds vary in length (ranging from 8 to 18 inches long) and intensity of color (some are more gray or metallic in tone than others). As Judith Jones, proprietor of Fancy Fronds Nursery in Gold Bar, Washington, once said with a smile and a shrug, "Raise ten thousand of them from spores and you'll see variation!" After selecting the Japanese painted fern that most pleases you, plant it in the type of location that suits it best. According to John Mickel, emeritus curator of ferns at the New York Botanical Garden and author of *Ferns for American Gardens*, the rhizome of *A. nipponicu*m 'Pictum' is "short-creeping and branches freely, providing many growing in each plant, generally doubling or tripling in a single year. Full plants can be dug up and divided into eight to fifteen plants, each with three or four growing points." Elsewhere in his book, Mickel mentions making four to eight divisions after three to four years, a more modest multiplication but one that is definitely worthwhile, especially as it ensures the yield of identical plants, since they are produced by cloning. Pair Japanese painted fern with moderately sized glaucous blue hostas such as *Hosta* 'Halcyon' or *H*. 'Blue Cadet' to intensify the cool effect, or combine it with silver-frosted heucheras. Contrast it with the straplike leaves of black mondo grass (*Ophiopogon planiscapus* 'Nigrescens'), then add to the funky display by including *H*. 'Gold Edger', a small yellow-leaved hosta. Plant Japanese painted fern in a window box or handsome blue-glazed pot with white caladiums and impatiens for a cooling effect in summer, moving the fern out into the garden when autumn arrives.

A few gray-leaved cultivars of *Ajuga reptans* make good groundcovers for shady sites (unlike the green-leaved cultivars, which prefer sun). 'Silver Carpet' has a metallic sheen to its silvery leaves, and 'Silver Beauty' features gray-green leaves edged with silver-white. 'Grey Lady' is an English cultivar not often seen in North America. These ajugas need good conditions of shade, moisture, and loose organic soil to make a really thick groundcover—which isn't to say they won't spread, of course. Far from it. Just try planting one. In spring it will send forth several horizontal stems, each with a few plantlets across its length and one at the end. These plantlets will happily root down and commence producing short rhizomes underground. By the next spring, they'll all get into the act. My favorite partner for gray-leaved ajugas is autumn-flowering cyclamen (*Cyclamen hederifolium*). In August the tubers of the cyclamen send up small pink or white shuttlecock flowers, each one dainty enough for a fairies' game of badminton. Its leaves will not appear for another month, so the ajuga can provide an attractive background that will also keep the flowers from becoming splashed with mud. Autumn-flowering cyclamen has dark green ivylike leaves, each tuber featuring a different pattern of highly variable silver markings, which are also enhanced by the gray leaves of the ajuga.

Though originally used as flowering plants, heucheras are now popular for their foliage, and several silver-leaved cultivars provide good value for the shady garden. *Heuchera* 'Mint Frost' has silver leaves accented with green veins radiating out from stem to edge. In cold weather the color shifts to purple, frosted and veined with silver. The leaves of *H.* 'Silver Scrolls' are more distinctly lobed than most and shaded with purple when they first emerge in spring; by maturity, they are strongly marbled and frosted with silver-gray and veined in purple-green. The intensely silver leaves of *H.* 'Can-Can' feature edges as ruffled as a dancer's petticoat at the Moulin Rouge. The leaves of *H.* 'Stormy Seas' are a subtle blend of silver, pewter, charcoal gray, and lavender, and, like 'Can-Can', have ruffled edges.

Heucheras are superb plants for woodland gardens, adaptable from light dappled shade to a fair amount of tree cover, especially in more southern regions. They do need good drainage, though they will not respond well to drought-stricken conditions. Semi-evergreen, they make pleasing partners for *Epimedium* species, small to medium ferns, *Actaea* species, and other lacy-leaved plants. And with their smooth surface, these silver cultivars contrast well with the fuzzier leaves of lungworts (*Pulmonaria*). Keep in mind that breeders such as Dan Heims of Terra Nova Nurseries in Oregon and Charles Oliver of

The Primrose Path in Pennsylvania are constantly refining heucheras and making new introductions. Whether you think the world needs more varieties will depend on how refined your sensibilities are to the sometimes subtle differences amongst of the ever-widening list of offerings. After a leaf-by-leaf comparison you may agree with Robert Popham of Fairweather Gardens in Greenwich, New Jersey, who feels that "most of them require a magnifying glass to find the differences between one and the next."

×*Heucherella*, a cross between *Heuchera* and the closely related *Tiarella*, has produced, among others, ×*Heucherella* 'Pink Frost', with deeply lobed, silver-frosted purple foliage and pink and white flowers lightly touched with lavender. ×*Heucherella* 'Silver Streak' is quite similar, with silver-frosted purple leaves and lavender-tinted white flowers.

Although the pewter-silver leaves of spotted dead nettles (*Lamium maculatum*) feature a little green edge, the overall effect is silver. Pink-flowered *L. maculatum* 'Beacon Silver' is the touchstone for the group, with its especially attractive, radiantly silver leaves edged in light green. Admittedly, when good drainage is not provided, and when heat and humidity rise, this cultivar tends to suffer from leaf spot as well as other blights. If supplemental watering is necessary, do so in the morning so that leaves dry as quickly as possible. Slugs like the leaves, so learn to distinguish between the mollusks' silvery slime trail and foliage markings. Leaves with holes are also diagnostic. White-flowered *L. maculatum* 'White Nancy' has similar leaves, while the leaves of *L. maculatum* 'Shell Pink' are greener and irregularly blotched with white in the center. To keep spotted dead nettles looking their best, cut them back in summer, after they flower. This will encourage fresh new growth and better-looking foliage for the rest of the season. They do well in light to moderate shade.

Glaucous hostas such as we tend to label "blue" are not true sky blue but more of a grayish green, green with a powdery surface coating like a cabbage. *Hosta* 'Big Daddy' is a large blue variety with glaucous blue, seersucker-textured, cupped leaves that reach 11 inches long by 9 inches wide. The leaves of *H.* 'Big Mama' are larger, at 13 inches long by 9 inches wide, and even bluer. *Hosta* 'Blue Angel' is larger yet, its faintly bluish gray-green leaves a respectable 16 inches long by 13 inches wide. When growing hostas, remember to plant different cultivars apart from each other. It is not merely that the repetition of shape is boring but that a very glaucous blue cultivar will make one that is less blue seem dull and faded. Consider leaf shape, try to stack shiny texture against a duller matte surface, and emphasize hostas with blue leaves by playing their color against a gamut of green, gold, or silver foliage.

Hosta 'Krossa Regal' is a grayish blue hosta with a vaselike form created by 12-inch-long, ovate to lanceolate, pruinose leaves on upright 10-inch-long petioles. The true beauty of this cultivar only appears on mature plants, since the vaselike form does not develop fully the first couple of years. I enjoy pairing 'Krossa Regal' with sweet cicely (*Myrrhis odorata*), whose finely two- to three-pinnate leaves, often blotched with white, have the same delicacy as Queen Anne's lace (*Daucus carota*). The distinct leaf shapes make an attractive, elegant combination, accentuated by sweet cicely's lacy white flowers in early summer.

Hostas in the Tardiana Group are very popular, moderate in size, easy to grow, and feature beautiful glaucous blue leaves. They are all derived from a one-time chance crossing of *Hosta sieboldiana* var. *elegans* and *H. tardiflora*, made by Eric Smith in 1961 when he was working at Hilliers Nursery in Winchester, England. The two parents could hardly have been more disparate. The first is a stately species with bluish gray-green, seersucker-textured leaves 10 to 16 inches long by 8 to 12 inches wide; the second is a late-blooming species with narrow, glossy, dark green leaves 3 to 6 inches long by only 2 to 2½ inches wide. A grex (from the Latin for herd, or hybrid swarm) is a group name for all plants derived from the crossing of the same two or more species. The term is most correctly applied to orchids and lilies, but Wolfram George Schmid, author of the monumental book *The Genus Hosta*, considers Tardiana Group hostas to be correctly named as a grex. *Hosta* 'Halcyon' is perhaps the best known and most popular of this group. With blue-green leaves 8 inches long by 5 inches wide, the rather moderately sized 'Halcyon' needs time to mature and develop its true form, which can be as much as 3 feet wide by 20 inches high.

Later breeding between the resulting offspring of *Hosta sieboldiana* var. *elegans* and *H. tardiflora* increased the number of cultivars without widening the gene pool. Over a decade after making the initial crossing, Eric Smith, then head gardener at Hadspen House, named several other blue Tardiana Group hostas. These remain as popular today as when they were first introduced: *Hosta* 'Hadspen Blue', a small to medium plant with heart-shaped, deep blue, glaucous leaves, *H.* 'Hadspen Heron', a small, low-growing, medium blue-green plant with lanceolate leaves rippled along the edges, and *H.* 'Hadspen Hawk', a dainty blue-green plant. Be cautioned: not all Hadspen hostas are blue. *Hosta* 'Hadspen Honey', for example, has yellow leaves.

Hosta 'Blue Dimples' is another second-generation Tardiana Group selection and is often considered one of the bluest hostas. Its moderately sized leaves are 7 inches long by 5 inches wide. *Hosta* 'Blue Moon' is slow growing and quite petite, with dainty glaucous blue leaves a scant 3 inches long by 2 inches wide.

Hosta 'Blue Cadet' is a midsized blue-green hosta of different lineage than those of the Tardiana Group. Leaves are 5 inches long by 4 inches wide and eventually bulk up to a clump over 2 feet wide and 16 inches tall. One beautiful combination pairs 'Blue Cadet' with the silver-netted leaves of *Lamium galeobdolon* 'Hermann's Pride' (see Plate 51).

Brunnera macrophylla has been mentioned several times for its shade- and drought-tolerant habits and sturdy, pest-resistant, heart-shaped leaves. *Brunnera macrophylla* 'Jack Frost' is an important new cultivar that is not merely splashed with silver but coated with it. Each astonishing silver leaf displays a fine tracery of green veining that lifts it from flatness. This plant would make a superb color contrast with a blue hosta such as *Hosta* 'Blue Cadet' or *H.* 'Halcyon'. Since their leaf shapes are so comparable, you'll want to separate the two with fernlike and linear leaves. Place *B. macrophylla* 'Jack Frost' next to the shiny, evergreen, medium green leaves of *Epimedium* ×*perralchicum* 'Frohnleiten', which is hardier than several reference books give it credit for. Add the stiff dark green blades of *Liriope muscari* and complete the grouping with the blue hosta. Remember that it is important to play with your plants. Set them out in their pots. Consider their placement and shift them around if you are not completely satisfied. It is better for all concerned if you do this while the plants are still in their pots, rather than in the ground.

PERENNIALS FOR SUN

Sun-loving silver-leaved plants require good drainage. Wormwoods (*Artemisia*), for example, though more tolerant of cold winters than they are of hot humid summers, will not accept wet feet in winter (see Plate 55). Yet when they are given the right conditions, their silver-gray to gray-green leaves make a fine accent for other perennials with green foliage, and flowers of any color.

Lamb's ear (*Stachys byzantina*) comes to mind as a prime example of silver foliage, with its mats of oval leaves felted with white hairs. Leaves suffer in humid summer weather, turning brown and mushy. Overhead watering will only aggravate the situation. The only solution is to cut them back hard and wait for new growth. Some gardeners object to the flower stalks, which feature tufts of wool and small magenta flowers, while others enjoy using them as a filler in flower arrangements. If you fall into the first category, it would be worthwhile to seek out *S. byzantina* 'Silver Carpet', a nonblooming cultivar. *Stachys byzantina* 'Silver Ball' is a good choice for flower arrangers since it includes the woolly clusters but has no flowers. *Stachys byzantina* 'Helene Von Stein' has especially large leaves, and in my experience it stands up to humid summer weather without suffering meltdown, probably because its silver foliage is not as furry as other varieties. *Stachys byzantina* 'Primrose Heron' is golden in spring but reverts to gray-green in summer. Since lamb's ear revives in autumn, I like to use it as a groundcover for *Colchicum* species, which flower in the fall with large lavender flowers, looking something like crocus on steroids. Colchicum foliage does not appear until spring. Rather coarse, like a squat corn plant, it collapses in late June, smothering its neighbors. Since the lamb's ear also disintegrates at this time, I just chop everything back and wait for a fresh silver carpet to appear. Lamb's ear is evergreen (or should I say ever*gray*) and makes an attractive edging to the flower border, barring its problems in summer.

Novice gardeners often confuse *Lychnis coronaria* (which, like *Senecio cineraria*, is commonly known as dusty miller) with lamb's ear. True, both have flannel-soft gray leaves in a basal clump. They even grow in similar conditions, both thriving in sunny sites with nutrient-poor, well-drained soil. However, if you look closely you will notice that the leaves of *L. coronaria* are smoother, and that they end in more of a point than do the blunt leaves of lamb's ear. And unlike lamb's ear, lychnis has pairs of leaves growing up each flower stem. The flowers themselves are a dead giveaway, larger and showier than those of lamb's ear, and an intense magenta-cerise, white, or white with a pink eye.

When well grown, *Artemisia schmidtiana* 'Silver Mound' forms a shapely dome of thread-fine leaves. However, it often falls apart in summer, becoming blackened and rotten through the center. Overwatering and overfertilizing will encourage excessive soft growth, which will rot in the heat and humidity of summer. Dig in some coarse gravel if the site is not already free draining, and mulch with gravel rather than wood chips or shredded leaves. It is a good idea to avoid fertilizing any plant that does not need it, but especially this one. Should 'Silver Mound' decay in your garden, cut it back hard to encourage new growth while you decide how to correct the underlying problem. Pair it with plants tolerant of similar growing conditions. Lamb's ear (*Stachys byzantina*), with its furry silver oval leaves, would be a better choice than lavender cotton (*Santolina chamaecyparissus*), which is too similar in appearance (see Plate 49).

Southernwood (*Artemisia abrotanum*) is aromatic, smelling like a cross between creosote and turpentine. No doubt this pungent odor is what makes its sage-green leaves so effective as a moth repellent. This is a wide-spreading species; even plants of *A. abrotanum* 'Nana', its dwarf form, should be spaced about 3 feet apart in sunny sites with poor, impoverished soil. Though south-ernwood is naturally a dense, shrubby sort of plant, cutting it back every spring just as the buds are swelling will keep it more compact and shapely.

I find the various cultivars of *Artemisia ludoviciana*—'Silver King', 'Silver Queen', and 'Valerie Finnis'—more attractive, and more invasive, than south-ernwood. Elegant silvery gray-white leaves, 1½ to 4 inches long, appear on upright stems. These would be superb foliage perennials were it not for their running roots, which quickly make a crowded thicket of stems. 'Silver King' is tallest, at 4 feet high, while 'Silver Queen' is smaller with broader, more divided leaves. 'Valerie Finnis' grows only 18 to 24 inches tall and has almost rectangu-lar leaves. When it comes to buying these plants, forget the labels and use your eyes instead: their names are often very much confused in the trade. Pair them with copper-leaved shrubs, with pink or white flowers, from roses to phlox, or with whatever else takes your fancy. For a pretty effect in May, combine 'Valerie Finnis' with ornamental onions such as the lower-growing *Allium karataviense*, which features gray-green pleated leaves and soft mauve flower heads as round as soap bubbles, *Geranium* 'Johnson's Blue', and small, intensely purple-black violas (*Viola cornuta*).

Those fortunate enough to have the right sort of garden conditions can grow *Artemisia* 'Powis Castle', a very attractive shrubby hybrid of *A. arborescens* and *A. absinthium* with filigree leaves. Alas, due to the cold wet winters and heavy clay soil of my own garden, when I plant 'Powis Castle' it sulks, goes into a decline, and dies. Some years I can get away with planting *A. stelleriana* 'Silver Brocade', a form of beach wormwood, with a trailing habit and deeply lobed leaves that are felted a silvery gray-white. I dig in lots of grit, trail the stems art-fully over a stone, and mulch with gravel where they must contact soil. It sur-vives for a couple of years, spreading widely, but then it dies. Beach wormwood (*A. stelleriana*) does much better for me in a hanging basket, though it needs frost-free yet chilly winter conditions that are difficult to provide when it is planted this way. Maritime gardeners can give it the sun and sand it needs for best results, and nonpurist rock gardeners might also enjoy it.

Snow-in-summer (*Cerastium tomentosum*) is a type of mouse-eared chick-weed (*Cerastium*). A mat of gray-white hairs coats the small evergreen leaves, which themselves are thick enough on the trailing stems to create a solid carpet. *Cerastium tomentosum* 'Silberteppich' is a German introduction that grows only 8 inches high; *C. tomentosum* 'Yo-Yo' grows even lower, reaching 6 inches. During his tenure at Wave Hill, Marco Polo Stufano used snow-in-summer to carpet the ground around autumn crocus (*Crocus speciosus*), protecting their naked flowers from mud spatters. This was a lovely partnership, but because it could only be appreciated for a brief moment each year, he added pig squeak (*Bergenia cordifolia*), whose large, slick, evergreen, very deep green leaves make a year-round display in tandem with the snow-in-summer.

The leaves of rue (*Ruta graveolens*), also called herb of grace, are said to have been the model for the suit of clubs seen on playing cards. A beautiful glaucous blue, the bipinnatisect (twice-cut) leaves are evergreen and provide year-round interest. Rue is popular in both herb gardens and herbaceous borders, and makes a fine foliage accent in either situation. Be careful when handling the foliage in hot sunny weather, especially if pruning is involved. The sap found in rue, and even the pungent oil glands on its leaves, may cause contact dermatitis in susceptible individuals. *Ruta graveolens* 'Jackman's Blue' is an especially blue cultivar. I find the summer trio of rue, *Canna* 'Pretoria' (see Plate 62), and *Allium flavum* especially pleasing. The little ornamental onion has glaucous blue stems and leaves, which play off against the foliage of the rue, and soft yellow flowers, which accent the bold, green-striped, yellow leaves of the canna.

Though generally classified as a perennial, *Salvia argentea* seems to be biennial or perhaps monocarpic. Its first year, the adolescent plant displays a great basal clump of large, somewhat toothed and lobed, fetchingly silver leaves that lay close to the ground. Within the next year or two the plant will flower, producing a sizeable set of branching stems supporting white flowers guarded by gray-white calyces. Once seed has been formed, this silver sage dies. Even if you keep the plant alive by deadheading as soon as the flowers begin to fade, it is really not worth it, as young plants have the best foliage. *Salvia argentea* makes an elegant addition to large containers, perhaps combined with more finely textured silver-leaved plants or plants with purple flowers. Full sun and good drainage are sine qua nons.

Verbascum bombyciferum is a biennial with great rosettes of lovely, oval, gray-white, felted leaves. It performs best with good drainage and full sun. I was astounded when a plant of *V. bombyciferum* survived through the winter in my rather heavy clay soil before flowering and dying its second season. An even greater surprise were the few self-sown seedlings I later discovered. 'Arctic Summer' and 'Silver Lining' are a couple of cultivars with paler, cool yellow flowers.

TENDER PERENNIALS

According to Alice Waters, founder and proprietor of Chez Panisse restaurant in Berkeley, California, and author of *Chez Panisse Vegetables*, cardoons (*Cynara cardunculus*) "are widely appreciated in Italy and France as a cultivated vegetable."

She goes on to say, "Just looking at a cardoon plant will probably not induce hunger. The young plants form rosettes of long, spiny leaves that may be several feet across." That's the difference between the cook and the gardener. In *Perennial Garden Plants, or The Modern Florilegium*, Graham Stuart Thomas calls cardoon "one of the most magnificent of all herbaceous plants. The leaves alone would warrant its inclusion in any large garden." He describes the 3- to 4-foot-long leaves as "silvery grey, pointed and deeply divided, recurving and extremely elegant, lasting well in water." It hardly sounds as if the two are discussing the same plant. She would serve a cardoon, cannellini bean, and artichoke ragout, while he would "just enjoy the great clump of incredibly impressive foliage, the grandest of all silverlings." Though said to be hardy from zones 6 to 10, cardoon seems more often to be grown as an annual. This may be because the leaves on younger plants are more attractive, or because mature plants, whose stout 6- to 8-foot-tall stalks are topped by huge thistlelike flowers, are difficult to site. Cardoons thrive in sunny, well-drained gravelly sites and grasslands. *Cynara cardunculus* 'Florist Cardy' is an English cultivar. Its leaves are an even brighter silver-gray than those of the species, and are more deeply cut and serrated.

Honey flower (*Melianthus major*) is a tender shrub that grows 3 to 4 feet tall. Robust and elegant, it features arching leaves with nine to eleven coarsely serrate oval leaflets arranged in an alternate, odd-pinnate manner. Coloring is sea-green and strongly glaucous. Honey flower has a fetid smell when bruised, so site it away from paths and benches. Hardy to zone 8 (and with protection, to zone 7), plants growing near their limit of hardiness may be killed back to the ground by frost, but these resprout in spring. Even if not damaged by frost, they should be cut back in all except zone 10 gardens, where they are evergreen.

I once heard a gardener in California complaining about licorice plant (*Helichrysum petiolare*). Her own shrub spread so vigorously that she had to keep it constantly pruned. One advantage of gardening beyond a plant's limit of hardiness is that winter will quickly put an end to such tendencies. Only hardy in zone 10, licorice plant is a popular addition to summer gardens. Three-foot-long arching branches are clothed in nicely silver-felted, oval, 1½-inch-long leaves arranged in pairs, and look great cascading out of containers. Where licorice plant is hardy, it can be placed to spill over a wall. Plants prefer an even moisture level and full sun, though they will tolerate a modicum of shade. My own licorice plants experience problems with leaf miners early in the season, but it is easy enough to handpick affected leaves and discard them in the trash. New growth quickly fills in. *Helichrysum petiolare* 'Limelight' has pale chartreuse-yellow leaves and does better with light shade rather than full sun. The variegated leaves of *H. petiolare* 'Variegata' are gray and pale green.

I am very fond of plectranthus, my favorite being perhaps *Plectranthus argentatus*. Cuttings made around Labor Day root easily and, with benign neglect, remain modest in size under grow lights in my basement. I plant them in the garden in mid May and by Labor Day they are 4 feet tall, self-branching, and self-supporting with sturdy, square, wine-flushed stems. Gray-green leaves have an elegant silver nap. I like to pair *P. argentatus* with the purple-leaved *Canna* aff. 'Intrigue'. Some years I add the peacock lily *Gladiolus callianthus* 'Murielae', whose white flowers bear a magenta blotch that matches the canna. The plectranthus is also great in a container, perhaps with other glaucous and gray-leaved plants. I once combined it with blue lyme grass (*Leymus arenarius*), which features arching blue blades, *Euphorbia myrsinites*, which trails its stems of spirally arranged, sharply pointed blue-gray leaves over the edge, and a dusty miller, *Senecio cineraria* 'Cirrus'. The bright, freshly polished silver hue of the dusty miller, with its felted, barely lobed leaves, made a pleasing accent to the sea-ice color of plectranthus.

Felt bush (*Kalanchoe beharensis*) is a popular succulent for indoor use. Scalloped, spear-shaped to triangular, 10- to 16-inch-long leaves are a fuzzy silver beneath and cinnamon brown above. While felt bush can grow 10 feet tall in its native Madagascar, such size is unlikely in most North American gardens; plants can be readily maintained at a more manageable height of 3 to 4 feet. Should the plant get unwieldy, it is easy to start over. Simply cut off a length of stem and set it aside in a shady place. When the end is completely dry, pot it up in a well-drained sandy loam with some grit added to it. Panda plant (*K. tomentosa*) grows to 1 foot tall. Its fat, juicy, oval, light gray leaves are covered in soft woolly fur and decorated at the tip with stitchlike brown dots that run along the edge. *Kalanchoe pumila* is another small succulent, reaching only 1 foot tall, with silver farina powdering its 1-inch-long leaves. The gentlest touch will disturb the coating, so handle only the pot when shifting it around. All three *Kalanchoe* species are able to store water in their leaves and stems, and will tolerate neglect. Although they all love sun, those that have been kept indoors will need a period of adjustment before being taken outside for the summer. For the first few days, place them in a shady site or shield them with an old window screen until they toughen up.

CHAPTER 7

❧

Varied Variegation

In *My Garden in Spring*, first published in 1914, E. A. Bowles describes a unique bed in his garden for plants with leaves other than green, what he called Tom Tiddler's ground. This particular part of his garden was arranged according to shade. Purple plants were kept at one end and gold plants at the other, with a wedge-shaped central group of variegated plants to divide the two, and with gray-leaved plants along the front. He writes, "I have never felt the disgust for variegated foliage evinced by so many good gardeners, and in many cases I warmly admire it," and goes on to enthuse over the gray-green swordlike leaves of *Iris pallida* 'Aureovariegata', with their cream and soft yellow variegation. Lungworts (specifically *Pulmonaria saccharata* and *P. officinalis*), spotted dead nettle (*Lamium maculatum*), and milk thistle (*Silybum marianum*) are mentioned as plants with "a regular design of white or grey marks on their leaves." And, he notes, there are far too many variegated shrubs to include them all.

In terms of design, this was not so much a garden as a conceit or contrivance. The overriding principle was to create groups of particular colors—purple here, yellow there. We accept a garden of entirely green-leaved plants because it is what we expect. A garden in which all the leaves are purple, yellow, or variegated, however, is exceptional.

Always keep in mind that the design of a foliage-based garden is begun by choosing plants with divergent leaf shapes. Color is the secondary level of enhancement; while it must also be chosen with care, it cannot rectify poor selection of foliage shapes. A design consisting of a variegated, shrubby dogwood, a variegated hosta, and a groundcover of variegated periwinkle (*Vinca minor*) would lack a focal point, everything blurring together. Use variegation as an accent—to emphasize and highlight, to serve as a contrast to green leaves.

As discussed in chapter 2, yellow-variegated plants can be almost as vigorous and quick growing as their green counterparts. White-variegated plants, on the other hand, lack pigment in the white portion of their leaves and therefore grow more slowly. Plants that are entirely white are unable to survive unless they are saprophytic, meaning that they feed on dead or decaying plant matter. Indian pipe (*Monotropa uniflora*), also called corpse plant, is a good example of this.

It is useful to remember a few minor points when gardening with variegated plants. Too much nitrogen can trigger chlorophyll production in the yellow-variegated portion of some plants' leaves. And the white-variegated portion of the leaves on other plants, such as *Canna* 'Stuttgart', is frequently much more delicate than the green portion and subject to scorch and sunburn. The most frequent maintenance required by variegated plants concerns their tendency to revert to all-green leaves. If the vigorous all-green shoots that arise on *Hemerocallis fulva* 'Kwanzo Variegata' are not removed, the crisply white-striped leaves will be crowded out. Watch for such entirely green, more vigorous, sometimes larger leaves on variegated plants, and remove such shoots back to the variegated portion of the plant.

Use variegation as an accent—to emphasize and highlight, to serve as a contrast to green leaves.

Variegation can be found in many guises. A leaf may have a tidy margin, as with the white-edged *Kerria japonica* 'Picta' or yellow-edged *Hosta* 'Frances Williams'. It may have a central white blotch like the leaves of *H. undulata* var. *univittata*, or a yellow blotch like those *Aucuba japonica* 'Picturata'. White spots are spattered over the leaves of *Hypoestes phyllostachya* 'White Splash', while the maplelike leaves of *Abutilon pictum* 'Thompsonii' are so freckled with yellow that they appear mottled.

Variegated plants should generally be propagated by asexual means, though not all methods are successful. Division is perhaps the simplest and most reliable means of multiplying perennials like hostas and irises. A large clump is dug up and separated into several plants, each with both shoots and roots. Propagated in this way, variegated forms such as *Iris pallida* 'Argenteovariegata' remain crisply white-variegated. Taking stem cuttings of herbaceous perennials is another easy method, as anyone who has kept jars of coleus cuttings along the kitchen windowsill knows. Roots that form with water as a substrate need to readjust when they are shifted to soil. It is best for the young plantlets if a more substantial medium is used for rooting. A vigorous, preferably nonflowering young shoot with several sets of leaves is severed from the parent plant. The lower two or three sets of leaves are removed, allowing two or three to remain. The leaf-free portion is inserted into a nice gritty potting mix, perhaps half peat moss and half coarse sand or perlite, which is kept moist. Almost magically, the leafless stem produces roots and a new plant, identical to the parent, is created. Coleus (*Solenostemon scutellarioides*) and flowering maple (*Abutilon*) are typically multiplied through cuttings. Remember too that root cuttings will only produce green-leaved plants

Seeds are a different story. For one thing, while it is obvious which plant is producing the seeds, there is the question of who the "father," or pollen parent, may be. If the plant has been self-pollinated, all of the ancestry will be variegated. If the plant has been open-pollinated, by some passing bee or butterfly, it will be anyone's guess. Certain plants are very promiscuous, such as columbines (*Aquilegia*), which will happily cross with any other columbines within flight range. Violets have both normal, showy, insect-pollinated flowers and cleistogamous flowers. Bob Brown of Cotswold Garden Flowers in Worcestershire, England, has been propagating herbaceous perennials from seed for many years. His records indicate that certain herbaceous plants come true from open-pollinated seed 100 percent of the time. The seedlings of *Euphorbia marginata* are always variegated. Those of *Helleborus argutifolius* 'Pacific Frost' always have white-flecked foliage. Variegated Japanese hop (*Humulus japonicus* 'Variegatus') always has white-splashed leaves as long as the seed parent is variegated. *Nicotiana langsdorffii* 'Cream Splash' always starts off green, developing a spattered variegation that settles down to a marginal marking.

Joe Sharman of Monksilver Nursery in Cambridgeshire, England, has been collecting plant data and keeping records for years, starting when he was a journeyman apprentice at various nurseries both in the United Kingdom and abroad. As he points out, variation in a wild population is normal and natural. However, the current system of botanical nomenclature depends on the idea of a type specimen, which is dried and preserved on an herbarium sheet. The collected type specimen is not always truly representative of the species as a whole. For example, the first pressed specimen of quamash (*Camassia leichtlinii*), a bulb native to the Pacific Northwest, had creamy white flowers. This became the type, setting the standard for all other *C. leichtlinii*. While white flowers occur through the population as a whole, blue to violet flowers are more common. This does not matter, though, since the off-white specimen was recognized first. When variations show up in the wild, taxonomists name them as a form or variety. When a variant shows up in a garden, it is considered a cultivar.

According to Joe Sharman, some type specimens of Japanese species were variegated or had double flowers. "In subsequent years," he says, "the true wild species have been found." Previously, type specimens have always referenced wild plants, and there has been no herbarium material supporting horticultural names. The Royal Horticultural Society, with headquarters in London, has started a system of standard specimens for cultivars, the ultimate goal being to build up a useful reference set of all plants in cultivation. This is, as Joe notes, a mammoth task, and one that will take decades. The standard specimens for cultivars are held in the herbarium at the Royal Horticultural Society's garden at Wisley, Surrey.

Joe Sharman also points out that "certain variegated plants will come true from seed. Chlorophyll replication in the plant cell takes place independently from the replication of chromosomes. Usually the chlorophyll in the seed is already present in the ovule and comes solely from the mother plant. No chlorophyll is present in the pollen. If there are errors in the genetic material that controls the production of chlorophyll, e.g. leading to golden leaves or white-speckled variegations, then these abnormalities will also occur in the seedling. Chimeral variegations will usually produce seedlings which are all-green or all-white (no chlorophyll, which is fatal)." Somehow we have no qualms about raising variant, perhaps variegated, annuals from seed. The white-flowered, variegated *Lunaria annua* 'Alba Variegata' comes 100 percent true from seed. *Tropaeolum majus* 'Variegatum' has 100 percent variegated offspring, as does *T. majus* 'Alaska', which is also available with five different flower colors.

When it comes to perennials, however, gardeners are often hesitant about raising cultivars from seed. According to Joe Sharman's records, *Aquilegia vulgaris* (Vervaeneana Group) produces 50 to 80 percent variegated seedlings, even when self-pollinated. The variegated form of *Arum italicum* ssp. *italicum* 'Marmoratum' only comes 20 percent true from seed, but most plants have pale veins; while *Asarum hartwegii*, a native evergreen ginger with white veins, comes 100 percent true. Most seedlings of *Brunnera macrophylla* 'Aluminum Spot' have silver spotting. Silver-leaved forms of *Cyclamen coum* have 60 percent or more silver-leaved offspring.

SHRUBS

Cornus alba 'Elegantissima' is a great shrub. Native to Siberia, Manchuria, northern China, and North Korea, this variegated form of Tartarian dogwood is cold hardy down to zone 3 and adaptable enough to thrive in the relatively torrid zone 8. While I would not push it into drought conditions and stygian gloom, 'Elegantissima' is adaptable where soil type, pH level, moisture, and even light conditions are concerned. Handsomely white-edged leaves are narrower than are those of the all-green type species. Think of this species as good support for seasonal shifts of partners, perhaps leading off with the ivory-white, green-feathered petals and green anthers of *Tulipa viridiflora* 'Spring Green' and the unfolding crosiers of Christmas fern (*Polystichum acrostichoides*). In summer create a simple combination of white Asiatic hybrid lily and upward-facing, cup-shaped flowers such as ivory-white *Lilium* 'Mont Blanc' or *L.* 'Sterling Star', both charmingly freckled at the base of the petals, or *L.* 'Apollo', with faintly green-blushed clean white petals. Add some white-flowered fibrous-rooted begonias with green, rather than copper-hued, leaves should you not want white impatiens to face down the ferns, which disguise the lilies' rather sparse foliage. Shift again in autumn, this time to white chrysanthemums and white-leaved ornamental kale, as an intimation of the snow that's on the way. *Cornus alba* 'Elegantissima' has reddish twigs from late summer until midautumn, at which point they become a brighter red, remaining this color until early spring, when, as new growth awakens, they change to green again. To enliven the winter scene of evergreen fern and dogwood twigs, add *Arum italicum* ssp. *italicum* 'Marmoratum'. Arrowhead-shaped leaves conspicuously marked with pale green to cream veins appear from early autumn into early winter. Should the cold be severe enough to kill them back, a second crop of leaves will appear in spring. Coblike clusters of orange-red berries provide another nice touch, appearing in early autumn before the leaves come into view. These make a pleasant accent to the dogwood's dull to rich red autumn foliage. The arum leaves are often plain green the first year after planting, developing their patterned markings in the second year.

Kerria japonica is another old-fashioned shrub often found inhabiting gardens in which plants have been passed along rather than selectively purchased. The most common variety is the plain green-leaved, double-flowered form, which happily tends to itself in sun or shade along a fence line or boundary. Interestingly enough, it is the double-flowered form that was first collected in Japan by Carl Peter Thunberg in the late eighteenth century, making it the type specimen, still held at the herbarium in Upsala, Sweden. Single flowers and crisply white-edged leaves make *K. japonica* 'Picta' more appealing to me, its variegation giving it an air of lightness not found in the species. It is moderate in size, mildly spreading, and best grown in shade, since the white portion of the leaves can brown and burn with too much sun. This is a useful shrub for the woodland edge. It has a tendency to revert, producing occasional all-green shoots when it leafs out in spring. These shoots will have larger leaves and more vigorous growth, and should be rubbed out as soon as they are noticed to prevent the prettily variegated shrub from becoming plain green.

The word "willow" calls to mind either the enormous weeping willow (*Salix babylonica*) used by farmers to drain soggy fields or that harbinger of spring, pussy willow (*S. caprea*). The 5-foot-tall dappled willow (*S. integra* 'Hakuro Nishiki') is completely different. Its light green leaves are brilliantly variegated with large white patches and touched with pink when they first appear. As with purple-leaved smokebush (*Cotinus coggygria* 'Royal Purple'), juvenile foliage provides the best show, and stooling results in an improved display. Once dappled willow is established, cut back hard each spring to within 6 inches of the ground. As is true of most willows, 'Hakuro Nishiki' does best with a moist to average soil. Midday shade will prevent its foliage frying to a crispy brown. One elegant style for more formal gardens finds this cultivar grown as a grafted standard, a ball-like pouf of prettily variegated foliage on a 5-foot-tall trunk. I saw it grown in this manner when I visited VanDusen Botanical Garden in Vancouver, B.C., one June, where it was labeled under the synonym *S. integra* 'Albomaculata'. The pendulous pink and white new growth made an exceedingly handsome accent near a rustic bothy.

Native to Japan and hardy to zone 6, dappled willow has a tropical counterpart in Hawaiian snowbush (*Breynia nivosa* 'Roseapicta'). The latter is reliably hardy only in zones 10 and 11, and marginally hardy in the warmer portion of zone 9 if given a protected microclimate. Oval leaves unfold almost entirely white when new. As they age they become spattered with pink, deepening to red and finally green. Placement in shade will result in loose, open growth and poor color, the leaves turning white and green rather than the pink and red that harmonize so nicely with the red stems. Choose a sunny site with well-drained, evenly moist soil. Trailing, pendent branches present the appearance of pinnate foliage, so neatly is the foliage arranged. Hawaiian snowbush makes an attractive plant for summer interest in colder regions and may be wintered over indoors.

There are several variegated cultivars of wintercreeper (*Euonymus fortunei*), ranging from the extraordinary to the commonplace. This evergreen species is variable in habit and includes prostrate plants useful as groundcovers, plants able to climb masonry walls and tree trunks (without harming the tree, I might add), and upright, shrubby plants. Useful in sunny sites or in partial shade, these cultivars prefer an evenly moist, loamy soil. *Euonymus fortunei* 'Silver Queen' grows to 5 feet tall, even taller if espaliered, with large dark green leaves displaying a clean ivory-white edge. This quick-growing shrub is cold hardy down to zone 6, and perhaps to the warmer portion of zone 5 in the right microclimate. More reliably hardy in zone 5, *E. fortunei* 'Emerald Gaiety' is another upright, spreading form with white-variegated leaves. *Euonymus fortunei* 'Emerald 'n' Gold' is a lower form, though still upright and shrubby, with yellow-variegated foliage. The lower-growing *E. fortunei* 'Blondy' reaches 18 to 24 inches tall and displays mostly yellow leaves. Its stems are also yellow, increasing the sunny effect. Said to be hardy to zone 5, this European introduction is increasingly popular in North America. *Euonymus fortunei* 'Harlequin' is a Brookside Gardens introduction that spreads 5 feet across but only reaches 1 to 2 feet high. Leaves are dark green dotted with crisp white splotches that become pink and red in cold winter weather. This cultivar will spread as a groundcover but will also cling to vertical surfaces. Light shade is best for its delicate foliage. *Euonymus fortunei* 'Sunspot' is a vining form that may also be used as a groundcover. Leaves feature a central yellow blotch. The widely available *E. fortunei* 'Gracilis' is an appealing groundcover. Leaves are variegated a creamy white and tinged with pink in cold weather.

Euonymus scale is a serious insect pest that must be controlled with appropriate sprays. Where it is a significant problem, regular attention will be important. Horticultural oil sprays applied in winter are not very effective against armored scale insects such as these. Instead use an insecticide containing neem oil (a botanical insecticide) or carbyl (a synthetic insecticide registered for euonymus). Plan to spray when immature insects are still crawling around in early summer, before they have settled down and grown their armor. In regions of the South with an extended season, spray again in August when the second hatching is active. Avoid planting wintercreeper against walls and buildings where air circulation is limited, as this often aggravates the situation. Also avoid planting it in places where deer like to nibble on woody plants, as this is a particular favorite.

VINES

Variegated porcelain berry vine (*Ampelopsis brevipedunculata* 'Elegans') is an undeniably elegant, hardy plant with green to turquoise berries that ripen to a brilliant blue. As attractive as it is, however, this vine is not an ecologically sound choice for gardens. Birds have discovered that the berries are good to eat, and bird-planted seedlings are becoming a problem, naturalizing around New York, New Jersey, and Connecticut. Unfortunately, these kinds of problems often take a decade or two to be recognized. Russian olive (*Elaeagnus angustifolia*), multiflora rose (*Rosa multiflora*), and the nefarious kudzu (*Pueraria triloba*) are three other invasive exotics that have become naturalized, crowding native plants out of their natural, ancestral landscapes.

When I first saw English ivy (*Hedera helix*) growing wild in Cheddar Gorge, England, I was overcome with a fit of giggles. The idea of this quintessential landscape plant growing as a native wild plant had simply never occurred to me. Like variegated porcelain berry vine (*Ampelopsis brevipedunculata* 'Elegans'), English ivy has proven to be an invasive presence in the woods, to the detriment of both native plants and wildlife. While it is the juvenile, nonfruiting forms that are most commonly cultivated, somehow these manage to break out of gardens, forming dense evergreen blankets that carpet the ground, smother shrubs, and climb trees. If you decide to grow English ivy, keep a vigilant watch over its perimeter. I have not yet heard of variegated forms escaping from the garden, but better safe than sorry. The possibility of escape will certainly be limited if ivies are used as trailing plants in containers or hanging baskets, or if they are kept indoors. If you choose to grow English ivy as a houseplant, pay attention to watering and find some way of increasing humidity if your house is dry in winter; this will go far in reducing infestations of red spider mite. One effective method involves simply setting the pot in a pebble-filled tray filled with water to just below the level of the pebbles.

Variegated forms of English ivy (*Hedera helix*) may have a white or yellow edge, white or yellow center, or be speckled with white or yellow. While an occasional ivy does display genetically induced variegation, as evidenced by an ability to come true from seed, most are chimeric, somatic variegations wherein cells do not produce chlorophyll. Periclinal chimeras have a white or yellow outer layer and a green inner core, which produces a white or yellow edge. If the outer layer is green and the inner core is yellow or white, the leaf edge appears green with a central blotch of yellow or white. The popular *H. helix* 'Glacier' has gray-green leaves with a creamy white edge, while *H. helix* 'Goldheart' has yellow leaves with a green edge. Many variegated English ivies are hardy to zone 6 or 7, while cultivars with entirely green leaves such as *H. helix* 'Baltica' are hardy to zone 5. Variegated cultivars are too numerous to list. Consult a catalog or monograph, or simply select from the houseplants at your local garden center.

Larger-leaved ivies tend to be less cold hardy. Algerian ivy (*Hedera algeriensis*), for example, whose evergreen leaves may reach a sizeable 6 inches wide by 6 inches long, is hardy from zone 8 or 9 to zone 10. *Hedera algeriensis* 'Souvenir de Marengo' has light green leaves with irregular, elegant, creamy white margins. I like to grow this cultivar in a pot raised on a concrete birdbath column sponge-painted a rusty red to match the local stone. Late in autumn, both potted plant and column come indoors for an attractive winter display. *Hedera algeriensis* 'Goldleaf' has glossy, deep forest-green leaves with a central yellow blotch, while *H. algeriensis* 'Marginomaculata', a sport of 'Souvenir de Marengo', has leaves suffused with a mottling of light green and cream. Persian ivy (*H. colchica*) is hardier, reputedly to zone 6, and smells a little like celery when crushed. The leaves of *H. colchica* 'Dentata', commonly named bullock's heart ivy, are entirely green and almost 10 inches wide. *Hedera colchica* 'Dentata Variegata' is a spectacular plant with large, drooping, light green leaves enhanced with gray-green mottling and creamy yellow margins the color of old ivory. *Hedera colchica* 'Sulphur Heart' has an irregular yellow-green center fanning out towards a wide green margin.

All these ivies are fine accent plants. The more vigorous plants may be used to cover walls and buildings or disguise a chain-link fence. Alternatively they may be used as a fedge (see chapter 9). Smaller ivies that are more restrained in growth can be used to conceal a stump or embellish a tree trunk. Keep in mind, though, that some variegated ivies lose their color when grown as groundcovers.

Boston ivy (*Parthenocissus tricuspidata*) has a lively new cultivar in 'Ginza Lights'. Glossy green three-lobed leaves are splashed with pink and white variegation, a showy effect that gardeners will either love or hate. Hardy to the colder portion of zone 5, 'Ginza Lights' is more restrained in its growth than the green-leaved type, and midday shade is useful in preventing leaf scorch. Fall color remains an intense red.

GROUNDCOVERS

Groundcovers are wonderfully unifying carpets for the garden, filling the ground beneath trees and shrubs. They make such a sturdy, undemanding alternative to turf that three of our choices—pachysandra, periwinkle, and ivy—are well nigh omnipresent, a hallmark of corporate parks, shopping malls, and suburbia, where they are generally seen in their standard green forms. Perceptive gardeners may wish to employ a higher standard by using variegated forms to accent their gardens. (Keep in mind, though, that substituting a variegated groundcover for the plain green version will not necessarily be an improvement—poor designs remain mediocre regardless of the plants used.)

E. A. Bowles says, in *My Garden in Spring*, "It has been said that no plain green form is known of *Pachysandra terminalis*, that strange Euphorbiaceous plant from Japan." He goes on to speculate that many introductions from Japan were garden forms, and the variegated pachysandra was most likely one of these. He had seen the green form at the Cambridge Botanic Garden and hoped that some day he would have it in his garden too. His statement is especially interesting in that the green form is now ubiquitous, and it is *P. terminalis* 'Variegata' that is the rarity. I find variegated pachysandra useful as a year-round accent plant in conjunction with an evergreen fern and dark green liriope, perhaps underplanted with white daffodils for emphasis in spring.

Periwinkle (*Vinca minor*) is one of the most popular groundcovers. It does not climb as ivy does and is therefore unable to wedge itself up into azaleas and other plants. Instead it remains a nice, low-growing carpet, spreading agreeably in shady sites such as beneath shallow-rooted trees, under shrubs, and along walkways. The small, oval, dark green, evergreen leaves make an attractive, glossy filler even in dry woods from zone 4 to zone 7 or 8. In spring each clump sets forth new runners. Some flower while others are vegetative and root down at their nodes. These can be used for propagation. Begin with a shallow tray filled with a loose soil mix high in organic matter and some added grit. Lay the runners over the surface and then scatter a thin dribble of the same soil mix over the stems without covering the leaves. Add water and keep the tray in a shady place outdoors, someplace where it will be easy to water in dry weather. Plant the periwinkle out in a new location when it is well rooted later in spring. Preparing the planting site, rather than just digging individual holes, will encourage new runners to root down as they go. Add topdressing with a loose, gritty, organic mix.

Variegated periwinkle cultivars are generally sold as individually potted plants, unlike the plain green-leaved species, which is often sold in trays of twenty-five plants or as bare-root plugs. *Vinca minor* 'Argenteovariegata' has irregularly creamy white and pale green leaves, and large light blue flowers. The leaves of *V. minor* 'Aureovariegata' are irregularly patterned in yellow along the margins. *Vinca minor* 'Golden' also has leaves patterned in yellow along the margins but features white flowers as well. *Vinca minor* 'Gold Heart' has leaves blotched with yellow in the center. *Vinca minor* 'Sterling Silver' has dark green leaves narrowly margined in white, and pale violet flowers. The foliage of *V. minor* 'Ralph Shugert' is similar to that of 'Sterling Silver', but the flowers are larger and more intensely blue-violet.

Greater periwinkle (*Vinca major*) has larger leaves and, at 8 to 18 inches high, is taller than common periwinkle (*V. minor*). Oval, matte, evergreen leaves reach up to 3 inches long and 1 inch wide. Plants are hardy from zones 6 to 9 and can survive in zone 5 if situated in a sheltered microclimate. *Vinca major* 'Variegata' is the white-edged form popularly used as a trailing plant in window boxes and in whiskey barrels filled with geraniums (*Pelargonium*). Yellow-veined *V. major* 'Reticulata' has a conspicuous netted look on its young leaves, which fade to green in summer. *Vinca major* 'Surrey Marble' has roundish leaves with a mustard-yellow central blotch.

PERENNIALS

Let's think about linear foliage such as grasses, sedges, irises, and daylilies, starting with variations of scale. *Iris pallida* 'Argenteovariegata' is shorter than *Miscanthus sinensis* 'Cabaret', but the iris leaves are much broader in proportion to their length than are those of the grass. The two plants are not interchangeable, even though their patterns of variegation are similar. *Hemerocallis fulva* 'Kwanzo Variegata' also has variegated white and green leaves, but they have less substance than those of the iris and more of an arching habit (see Plate 56). It is, as always, a matter of deciding on an effect and then selecting plants to provide the desired result. Variegated sweet flag (*Acorus calamus* 'Variegata') has 3-foot-long upright leaves smoothly striped in creamy white. It is hardy to zone 3 and an excellent choice for a shaded site that is damp to wet (it can even grow in shallow water). *Acorus gramineus* includes a number of variegated cultivars, each smaller than sweet flag and each with glossy leaves arranged in a fan and tapering to a fine point. *Acorus gramineus* 'Dwarf Himemasumune' is a dainty 4 inches high with glossy grasslike leaves neatly striped in white on the inner edge. *Acorus gramineus* 'Oborozuki' grows 8 to 10 inches tall with arching grasslike leaves striped in yellow-gold. Sun will bleach its color, so plant this cultivar in partial shade, preferably in a damp to quite wet site. The leaves of *A. gramineus* 'Ogon' are cream and chartreuse. The dark green *A. gramineus* 'Variegatus' is nicely striped in white, grows 12 to 18 inches tall, and thrives in shady sites with damp to moist soil. Ample moisture is necessary for it to grow in sunny sites without leaf damage.

Yellow flag (*Iris pseudacorus*) is a Eurasian species that has naturalized in damp ditches and wet sites in the Northeast. Though woven into the tapestry of our natural landscapes, it is not as invasive as such wetland thugs as *Lythrum salicaria*. Attractively marked with creamy yellow variegation, *I. pseudacorus* 'Variegata' looks beautiful when grown in shallow water, where it can cast reflections of its spring foliage. Leaves fade to all-green about the time yellow flowers appear in early summer. Japanese irises (*I. laevigata* 'Variegata' and *I. ensata* 'Variegata') have narrow, swordlike leaves permanently striped in white, a handsome contrast to their purple or pale blue flowers. *Iris pallida* includes two variegated cultivars: 'Argenteovariegata' with crisp green and white foliage, and 'Aureovariegata' with rich, soft buttery yellow and green foliage.

Members of the genus *Liriope* are often called lily turf or monkey grass, though I prefer to call them liriopes. Shade-tolerant, evergreen, and grasslike, these plants may be used as an accent or massed as a groundcover. *Liriope spicata* 'Silver Dragon' has narrow white-striped leaves, though they are often entirely white when they first appear in spring, and makes an elegant container plant in a blue-glazed bonsai pot. It is said to be hardy to zone 4. The dark green leaves of *L. muscari* 'Variegata' are boldly striped with yellow at the edge, while those of *L. muscari* 'Gold Band' are green at the edge with a yellow stripe down the center.

The genus *Hosta* includes a bemusing assortment of variegated plants. There are cultivars with glaucous blue-gray or green leaves featuring white edges, white centers, yellow edges, or yellow centers. There are even yellow-leaved hostas with white margins. The dainty *H.* 'Anne Arett' has small, ribbon-like leaves 5 inches long and 1 inch wide. *Hosta* 'Lunar Eclipse', a sport of *H.* 'August Moon', has white-edged chartreuse to yellow leaves that grow 6 inches long by 5 inches wide. The leaves of *H.* 'Golden Sunburst' have white margins and grow 9 inches long by 6 inches wide. Both *H.* 'Moon Glow' and *H.* 'Moonlight' have white-edged yellow leaves that reach 7 inches long by 5 inches wide. The dainty yellow leaves of *H.* 'Platinum Tiara' (a mutation of *H.* 'Golden Tiara') are 4 inches long by 3 inches wide and narrowly edged in white. The American Hosta Society named 'Platinum Tiara' the Alex J. Summers Distinguished Merit Hosta in 1989.

> White-edged yellow leaves require an obvious garden setting, something formal in style. Variegation of a plainer type is frequently more useful.

The extravagant patterning found on many variegated hostas calls for careful placement. White-edged yellow leaves require an obvious garden setting, something formal in style. Variegation of a plainer type is frequently more useful. A green hosta with non-green edges (or a non-green hosta with green edges) may not belong in a wild or naturalistic design, but it will fit nicely into a casual or country-style garden.

Hosta 'Frances Williams' features large leaves with a creamy golden yellow edge. With its green-edged yellow leaves, the smaller *H.* 'Kabitan' makes a handsome edge for a woodland path, perhaps in combination with liriopes (either entirely green or gold-variegated) and yellow-flowered primroses (*Primula vulgaris*). The undulating, twisted leaves of *H. undulata* var. *univittata* are dark green with a creamy white central stripe. A light green patterning provides transition between the two stronger colors. This variety can be used to accent a corner or line a path, or it can be partnered with white flowers to lighten a shady area. *Hosta decorata* is a Japanese species that was introduced to the West sometime before 1900. In Japan it was named *otafuku-giboshi*, the moon-faced hosta, for its distinctly rounded leaves narrowly edged with white. Simple, sturdy, and popular, it is moderately stoloniferous and makes as excellent a groundcover as it does a specimen plant.

TENDER PERENNIALS

Members of *Abutilon* are commonly known as flowering maples because of their maple-shaped foliage and nodding, bell-like flowers. In addition to numerous green-leaved cultivars and hybrids, the genus includes a few attractively variegated selections. A neat white margin adorns the green leaves of *A*. 'Souvenir de Bonn', a vigorous grower capable of reaching 6 feet tall. It has an upright habit and can be trained as a standard. The leaves of *A*. 'Savitzii' feature broad bands of white, which in places reduce the green portion of the leaf to a central blotch. This cultivar was given an Award of Garden Merit by the Royal Horticultural Society in September 1999. Its bushy growth makes it equally useful in the garden and in a container. *Abutilon pictum* includes several cultivars with yellow or cream mottling, an effect caused by a stable virus. Most readily available is *A. pictum* 'Thompsonii', a compact, upright shrub with deeply lobed leaves flecked and mottled with yellow.

Native to South and Central America, flowering maples (*Abutilon*) grow in the wild in lightly shaded woodland edges. In gardens they perform well in dappled shade but are equally happy in full sun. Though tender, they will not swoon with the first frost. Indeed, flowering maples can tolerate temperatures as low as 25° Fahrenheit before showing signs of damage. In late summer I take cuttings of half-ripe wood, which root quite easily. These are carried over under grow lights and planted out the following spring. By summer's end a cutting of *A. pictum* 'Thompsonii' will have grown into a respectable shrub, easily 3 feet tall and nearly as wide. It looks particularly fine in combination with *Canna* 'Pretoria', a short, 3-foot-tall canna with broad green leaves handsomely penciled in yellow. The divergent foliage shapes and contrast between the mottled yellow pattern of 'Thompsonii' and striping of 'Pretoria' play out quite nicely.

The foliage of *Canna* 'Stuttgart' is also especially handsome, its long, relatively narrow gray-green leaves elegantly blotched with white. However, care must be taken to protect this tender beauty from the sun. Bright light, perhaps some morning sun, is all that is needed; otherwise unsightly brown blotches will form on the white portions of its leaves. Early growth may be distorted as the rhizomes break dormancy in spring, producing a constriction where white and gray-green portions of the leaf meet at the edge. Plants soon settle down, however, and growth will be fine later in the season. 'Stuttgart' is a tall plant, easily reaching 6 feet or more. Be stingy with fertilizer, especially nitrogen, to prevent stems falling over. I like to use this canna as a container plant, choosing one at least 18 or 20 inches in diameter. After a hard frost turns the aboveground growth to limp blackened mush, I trim it away and drag the pot full of rhizomes

into an attached, unheated garage. The temperature can dip as low as 38°
Fahrenheit but the canna rhizomes do just fine. One year I planted variegated
Japanese hop (*Humulus japonicus* 'Variegatus') in the same pot with 'Stuttgart',
allowing the rough-stemmed vine to twine upwards on the canna. Its green and
white maplelike leaves made a pleasant addition. Of course, the next spring I
had variegated Japanese hop seedlings volunteering hither and thither, but it
was easy enough to transplant the few I wanted and weed out the rest.

Covered with measlelike spots, *Hypoestes phyllostachya* is the popular polka
dot plant. *Hypoestes phyllostachya* 'White Splash' is an interesting white-spotted
selection, less common than forms with pink or red spots, which contrast more
with the dark green leaves. Though usually sold as a dainty 6- to 8-inch-tall
plant in a 3-inch pot, polka dot plant is actually a soft-stemmed shrub and
capable of reaching 3 feet tall—something to keep in mind when planting it out
in the summer garden. Pinch back new shoots as it grows to prevent it becoming thin and leggy. Plants are tolerant of sun or light shade and great in combination with ferns or other contrasting foliage plants. You might think coleus
(*Solenostemon scutellarioides*) would make a good partner, considering its different color patterning, but the shape of polka dot plant's ovate, softly downy
leaves is too close for comfort.

CHAPTER 8

꩜

Herbs and Edible Ornamentals

I do not think of my garden as being specifically an herb garden, but it does include lavender and lavender cotton, sage and thyme, beebalm and rue, catmint and agastache, a large potted rosemary and a potted bay laurel. Sure, I clip them to use in the kitchen, but they were originally included among the other herbaceous perennials for their good looks rather than their good flavors. Parsley, sage, rosemary, and thyme are popular tuneful herbs, along with lavender blue, dilly, dilly, and sweet violets. They are also garden favorites. The number of unsung herbs found at nurseries and garden centers is always increasing; and at nurseries specializing in herbs, the selection can be mind-boggling. Well-Sweep Herb Farm in Port Murray, New Jersey, lists eleven varieties of rue (*Ruta graveolens*), ten varieties of culinary sage (*Salvia officinalis*), sixty-nine varieties of creeping thyme (*Thymus*), and sixty-two upright or prostrate varieties of rosemary (*Rosmarinus*) with white, pink, or blue flowers.

It is often said, "What goes around, comes around." What was popular, innovative, and fresh at one time is sure to be popular, innovative, and fresh again. Before grocery stores and pharmacies existed, people were more or less on their own for food and medications. Herbs were necessarily popular plants, used for treating sickness and injury as well as for flavoring food. They had a place in the gardens of monasteries and manor houses. Their orderly arrangement was part of the contemporary garden style. Today herbs are grown for their good looks and pest-resistant habits as much as for their culinary and medicinal uses. Picture the lime-yellow leaves of *Chrysanthemum parthenium* 'Aureum' (which, like *Tanacetum parthenium* 'Aureum', is commonly known as golden feverfew), with their feathery patterns like hoarfrost on a window. Pair this cultivar with the swordlike green leaves of a dwarf iris, the dark green carpet of a creeping thyme, or the pebbly oval leaves of a sage, perhaps even *Salvia officinalis* 'Icterina' with its gold and green leaves. Sweet fern (*Comptonia peregrina*) is a useful fragrant shrub for a sunny dry spot. Scented geraniums, particularly the large, velvety-leaved peppermint geranium (*Pelargonium tomentosum*), are popular for their tactile, aromatic summer foliage, as is lavender.

How would you go about designing an herb garden, or even deciding on what herbs to grow? Selection will most likely be predicated on the herbs you want to use. This was Paul Gervais's thinking when he and his partner bought a sixteenth-century Tuscan villa in 1981. His charming book, *A Garden in Lucca*, describes his adventures. Finding he was more interested in culinary herbs than medicinal ones, he selected "the obvious: rosemary, mint, parsley, chives, coriander, chamomile, sage, marjoram, salad burnet, alpine strawberries, and three or four different species of thyme. I added among these the less delicious tansy, angelica, sweet woodruff, and bergamot." Unfortunately the results were not what he wanted. The herbs grew well, but in midsummer the garden looked like a meadow. He also found that the herbs quickly declined and weeds began to grow. Ten years later he planted grass in the eight boxwood-edged beds.

> Instead of creating a hodgepodge of this and that, try planting herbs in a way that shows off their ornamental value.

Different herbs have different habits. To begin with, some, such as coriander, parsley, and dill, are annual. It will simplify things if herbs needing a yearly replacement are grouped together rather than scattered among perennial herbs such as thyme, sage, and rosemary. Beebalm, mint, and sweet woodruff are territorially aggressive. These galloping spreaders will quickly overrun less vigorously spreading plants and therefore require containment. My technique makes use of a round, brown, plastic dishpan. Drill some holes in the bottom for drainage and sink the dishpan in the soil up to its rim. The aggressive herb will be kept within bounds, the round shape forced upon it will not be unnatural in appearance, and the dishpan's brown color will fade into neutrality. If your soil is red clay or black loam, a layer of mulch will serve to disguise the dishpan.

The appearance of different herbs is another important consideration. Unless the garden is concerned primarily with production and herbs are simply grown in a row, plant combinations must be taken into account. The herbs Paul Gervais mentions do flower, but it is their foliage for which they are grown (with the exception of alpine strawberries). Instead of creating a hodgepodge of this and that, try planting herbs in a way that shows off their ornamental value. You'll still be able to harvest leaves for flavoring. Sweet woodruff (*Galium odoratum*) makes a superb groundcover that can also be used to flavor May wine. Sage (*Salvia officinalis*) has pebbly, soft gray leaves and looks elegant beside the finely textured gray foliage of *Artemisia schmidtiana* 'Silver Mound', the glaucous blue foliage of rue (*Ruta graveolens*), or the crisp green foliage of parsley (*Petroselinum crispum*). Ornamental selections of *S. officinalis* include 'Icterina' with pale green leaves and an irregular soft yellow margin, 'Kew Gold' with yellow leaves, 'Purpurascens' with red-purple leaves, and 'Tricolor' with gray-green leaves featuring white and purple zones. *Thymus* includes upright shrubby plants as well as prostrate ground-hugging sheets.

FRAGRANT FOLIAGE

As previously mentioned, I once studied Japanese garden art with Nakamura-sensei, who spoke with passion of the amenity garden. The simple act of walking from cool shade into warm sunlight was, to him, very much a part of experiencing a garden. In an amenity garden one plants to include the sounds of grass blades bending in a breeze and the soughing of wind in tree branches. The tactile qualities of leaves are taken into account—the furriness of lamb's ear (*Stachys byzantina*) or moth mullein (*Verbascum blattaria*), the velvety fuzz on the underside of yellow-stripe bamboo (*Pleioblastus auricomus*). Olfactory considerations are equally important: the scent that rises from peppermint geranium (*Pelargonium tomentosum*) when you stroke its large plushy leaves, the citrus aroma of lemon balm (*Melissa officinalis*) when a few leaves are crushed. Fragrance is the most evocative of our senses. It functions as a trigger, storing up current happenings and awakening dormant memories. Once, during a winter visit, my father became suddenly overwhelmed by a powerful sense of nostalgia. The cause? Birch logs in a wood-burning stove. The aroma roused memories of his boyhood in Russia.

Some plant families are more likely to have fragrant foliage than others, the mint family (Lamiaceae or Labiatae) being a prime example. Members of this family have square stems and flowers arranged in two lips. Those with fragrant foliage include *Agastache*, *Calamintha* (calamint), *Cunila*, *Hyssopus* (hyssop), *Lavandula* (lavender), *Marrubium* (horehound), *Melissa* (lemon balm), *Mentha* (mint), *Monarda* (beebalm), *Nepeta* (catmint), *Ocimum* (basil), *Origanum* (oregano), *Perilla*, *Plectranthus*, *Rosmarinus* (rosemary), *Salvia* (sage), *Satureja* (savory), and *Thymus* (thyme).

Leaves keep their scents to themselves more than flowers do. For flowers, fragrance is part of an advertising program designed to lure pollinating insects. It may be an aroma we humans find pleasant, or it may be one we find distinctly malodorous, as with wild ginger (*Asarum*) and skunk cabbage (*Symplocarpus foetidus*), both pollinated by carrion beetles. The scents produced by flowers are more chemically complex than those produced by leaves, which are simple combinations of oils (sometimes even just one). But leaves don't contain pollen, so why do they carry a scent? Fragrance is often used to ward off leaf-chewing or sap-sucking insects and others who might otherwise browse on foliage. Deer, rabbits, woodchucks, and caterpillars avoid herbs with strongly scented leaves. As with flowers, some scents please us while others might be politely described as "pungent." Boxwood (*Buxus sempervirens*), for example, smells like a cat's well-used litter pan, especially when freshly pruned. Savin juniper (*Juniperus sabina*) carries the same aroma, though perhaps not as powerfully. The bottom line: flowers use fragrance to attract, while leaves use fragrance to repel.

The essential oils that create foliage fragrances are held within glandular trichomes. Volatile oils, resins, sticky mucilage, and gums fill storage pockets between cell wall and surface cuticle. When foliage is pinched, rubbed, or stroked, the cuticle ruptures, releasing the fragrance. This does not damage the leaf, however, which will release its fragrance again and again. Mint (*Mentha*), rosemary (*Rosmarinus*), and thyme (*Thymus*) need only the lightest touch to release the essential oils from their easily shattered trichomes. In contrast, the leaves of bay laurel (*Laurus nobilis*) are stiff and leathery, with a hard cuticle, and must be broken, crushed, and crumbled for their fragrance to become apparent. Wintergreen (*Gaultheria procumbens*) also has a leathery leaf that needs heavy bruising to release its oils, which are used in confections, soft drinks, perfumes, and pharmaceuticals.

More potent foliage fragrances may waft on a stiff breeze or become most apparent in the heat of the day. A heavy rain will release the apple blossom scent of *Rosa rubiginosa* from glands on the underside of its leaves. On a hot, sunny day eucalyptus may smell strongly of eucalyptol, found in high concentrations in its leaves. Warm conditions will also free the spicy, pungently sweet scent of prairie dropseed (*Sporobolus heterolepis*)—something like the smell of slightly burnt buttered popcorn with overtones of crushed cilantro. Late in summer this odor floats over the grasslands of the Shaw Nature Reserve in Gray Summit, Missouri. Harlequin glory bower (*Clerodendrum trichotomum*) also carries an interesting fragrance. When fondled, its ovate, pubescent leaves smell a bit like peanut butter. Though some reference books assert that harlequin glory bower is only hardy to zone 7, it does quite nicely in my zone 6 New Jersey clay. Deer walk right by it, too. A suckering upright shrub, it grows 5 to 6 feet tall. Small, starlike white flowers with red calyces open in late summer, followed by metallic blue-black fruits.

Spicebush (*Lindera benzoin*) is a familiar shrub native to wet woodlands from Ontario and Maine to Florida and Texas. The ovate to lanceolate medium green leaves have a spicy scent when crushed and can be used to make a fragrant tea. Sweet fern (*Comptonia peregrina*) is also native to North America. Found from Nova Scotia and Manitoba to North Carolina, this shrub is cold hardy to zone 2. Fragrant, deeply incised, fernlike leaves make a pleasant tea. Despite its undemanding nature, sweet fern is generally neglected by all except native plant enthusiasts. It thrives in sandy, acid soil that is low in fertility, and prefers sun or light shade. Plants are difficult to transplant except as smaller, container-grown specimens. Sweet fern is a good filler plant as its suckering habit means it will grow from 4 to 8 feet wide yet only half as tall.

Hay-scented fern (*Dennstaedtia punctilobula*) is, admittedly, a thug. Beware if it ever creeps into a stone wall. The only way to evict it will be to disassemble the wall and remove every scrap of invading rhizome. That said, this spreading, deciduous fern does have desirable attributes: it will grow in full sun if given enough moisture and will tolerate dry conditions if grown in partial shade. Where moisture is available, hay-scented fern will spread and produce new fronds all summer. The new-mown-hay scent is quickly apparent when a few fronds are crushed. Just like other gardeners, I have my own prejudices, and at one time I declared I would never introduce this invasive plant into any garden. But then I visited a garden on Long Island designed by Thomas Reinhardt. He had used hay-scented fern to carpet an area of sandy soil in open shade. Restrained by the dryness of the site, the fern was not as aggressive as it would be in a richer, moister location. Yellowish green fronds about 18 to 24 inches long made a beautiful groundcover, and those that spread onto the path were crushed underfoot, emitting their lovely fragrance. Thomas had assessed the attributes of hay-scented fern and used it appropriately—a more skillful way to design a garden than by just grabbing the latest trendy plant.

The fragrant foliage of sweet woodruff (*Galium odoratum*) develops its strongest aroma when dried. One of the few herbs that grows in shade, sweet woodruff has a delicate appearance and a rugged constitution. Whorls of airy, light green leaves cover creeping stems that extend far and wide. Clusters of small white flowers appear in midspring. One or two flowering stems should be sufficient to perfume an entire bottle of Rhine wine in a few hours, which can then be served chilled with a sliced strawberry in each glass.

Scented geraniums (*Pelargonium*) are the mimics of the plant world, including such cultivars as the strongly rose-scented *P.* 'Attar of Roses' and the robust, strongly lemon-scented *P.* 'Mabel Grey' with its rough, raspy leaves. The lemon-scented *P.* crispum includes several cultivars. *Pelargonium crispum* 'Variegatum', also lemon scented, features cream-edged leaves. Ruffle-leaved *P. crispum* 'Prince Rupert' has more of an orange scent, as does *P. crispum* 'Prince of Orange'. The large, velvety, grapelike leaves of peppermint geranium (*P. tomentosum*) smell more like mint to me than does mint itself. There are several rose-scented geraniums, including *P. graveolens*, whose broadly cut leaves give off an old-fashioned roselike aroma (old-fashioned merely because so many modern roses are sadly lacking in this regard). *Pelargonium graveolens* 'Lady Plymouth' has cream-edged leaves, and *P. graveolens* 'Rober's Lemon Rose' has soft gray-green, irregularly cut leaves with a rose to lemon scent. The leaves of *P. radens* also have a rose to lemon scent. *Pelargonium capitatum* has velvety rose-scented leaves with crinkled edges. Less frequently available is southernwood geranium (*P. abrotanifolium*), whose aromatic leaves are finely divided and gray-green. Pine geranium (*P. denticulatum*), also called balsam geranium, features triangular, deeply cut, sticky leaves that smell like balsam pine. Apple-scented geranium (*P. odoratissimum*) has small, roundish, light green leaves.

These geraniums differ in more than just the scent of their leaves. Peppermint geranium (*Pelargonium tomentosum*) is a large sprawling plant with big hairy leaves. *Pelargonium crispum* 'Variegatum' is a small upright plant with dainty, crisp, variegated leaves. They each require different placement in the garden, whether in the ground or in a container. Find them partners to suit their varied habits, keeping in mind that all scented geraniums need full sun and reasonably good drainage. Scented geraniums and their kin are native to South Africa and will not tolerate harsh winter conditions. In places likely to experience cold and snow, take late-summer cuttings of the more boisterous geraniums. The young plants are better suited to houseplant conditions. More refined types can be potted and brought indoors for the winter.

Anise hyssop (*Agastache foeniculum*) and Korean mint (*A. rugosa*) are two more examples of herbaceous plants with attractively fragrant foliage. Both will cross-pollinate, and their hybrid offspring can be difficult to distinguish. Beebalm (*Monarda didyma*), also called bergamot or Oswego tea, smells to some people like Earl Grey tea. Or should it be the other way around? Oil of bergamot is used to flavor the black tea leaves of Earl Grey. You can brew a cup of minty beebalm tea using either fresh or dried leaves. Just be careful to pluck clean leaves, since mildew rarely adds anything positive to the experience.

Lavender (*Lavandula*) has a wonderfully clean, hot fragrance. A universally appealing herb, it has been popular since ancient times. Romans used it to scent their baths. Hildegard von Bingen mentioned it in her twelfth-century book about materia medica. People have used it as a stimulant, a carminative to relieve gas and digestive colic, an antiseptic, and an insect repellent. At one time small bags of dried lavender were tucked under bed pillows to soothe headaches and induce a more refreshing sleep. Though the strongest scent is found in the flowers, lavender leaves are also scented. We commonly think of this herb as possessing gray leaves, but the color varies among different species and cultivars from gray to gray-green, light green, or medium green. Moreover, color often shifts during the growing season. *Lavandula lanata*, a Spanish species not especially common in cultivation, has beautiful, dense, silver-gray foliage. *Lavandula ×intermedia*, a hybrid of *L. angustifolia* and *L. latifolia*, includes several cultivars with delightfully gray foliage, most especially 'Grey Hedge' and its less floriferous counterpart, 'Chaix'. Both cultivars are French. *Lavandula ×intermedia* 'Chaix' would be the better choice for low hedges and parterres. *Lavandula buchii* is a beautiful lavender with deeply cut, pinnate, glowing silver leaves. It is native to the Canary Islands and therefore hardy only in zone 9 or above. My own specimen makes a charming potted plant that winters alongside rosemary and bay laurel in my cool greenhouse, where night temperatures are around 50° Fahrenheit. Lavenders need full sun and a gritty, well-drained, limy soil for best growth. Regular pruning each spring just as the buds break into growth after winter dormancy will go a long way to keep plants from maturing into gnarled woody shrubs with a naked base. English lavender (*L. angustifolia*) and *L. ×intermedia* are the most cold hardy, down to zone 5. However, both require good drainage, especially in winter, and an airy winter covering of pine boughs or salt hay.

I sometimes see rosemary (*Rosmarinus*) offered for sale around Christmas time, sheared into tidy little trees. These discount store and supermarket specimens are a marketing ploy. Rosemary is unhappy as a houseplant unless you can provide cool (even nearly freezing) temperatures at night and a careful hand with watering. As mentioned, I keep mine in a cool greenhouse. I also had good results once using a box bay window, kept shut off from the bathroom at night with a pull-down shade. Ice would form at the bottom of the window, melting away each day. The rosemary appreciated its chilly microclimate, but I still nearly lost it before I learned how to water—too little water and it nearly died from drought, too much and its leaves became fat and white with mildew. When the surface soil of a potted rosemary is dry, give it a modest drink. Wait for the plant to use its water up before you water again. Rosemary will survive as a garden plant in zone 6 if provided good drainage, a protected site, and a milder-than-usual winter, but it grows more reliably in zone 7. In warmer areas such as California it grows as a 6-foot-tall shrub. Rosemary is a vigorous shrub and needs regular pruning throughout the growing season if it is to be kept in a manicured, topiary shape. Oil of rosemary contains a complex mixture of pinene, cineol, borneol, and camphor, and is used in scented soaps and perfumes.

Thymes (*Thymus*) are useful in both the kitchen and the garden. Leaves are green, gold, gray, or variegated, and flowers are anything from carmine to pink to white. Cultivars cover a surprisingly wide range of scents, from caraway and citrus to mint, oregano, and the traditional aroma of culinary thyme. The mat-forming varieties make excellent groundcovers for sunny places with good drainage. They are perfect for rock gardens, for example, where they make an outstanding covering for small bulbs such as crocus. Creeping thyme can also be used as a carpeting plant between paving stones, where light bruising from occasional foot traffic will release its pleasing scent. Many creeping thymes are forms of mother-of-thyme (*Thymus serpyllum*), which features dark green, gold, or variegated leaves tinted olive-green or bronze. Leaves may be completely gold, as with *T. serpyllum* 'Aureus' and *T. vulgaris* 'Aureus'. The variegated leaves of *T. serpyllum* 'Carol Ann' are green and yellow. *Thymus* ×*citriodorus* 'Doone Valley' is a prostrate thyme whose dark green leaves are splashed with yellow. There are a couple of white-variegated thymes: *T.* ×*citriodorus* 'Argenteus Variegatus' and *T.* ×*citriodorus* 'Silver Queen'. *Thymus pseudolanuginosus* is a lovely fuzzy gray. *Thymus herba-barona*, a creeping species, is named caraway thyme for the very strong caraway scent of its leaves. A possibly apocryphal tale of its discovery relates how a hiker in the Alps sat down to eat his lunch, which was packed by the hotel where he was staying. Smelling caraway, he expected to find seedcakes, but found none. Searching around him, he discovered that the odor was emanating from the 2-inch-high mat of thyme he had sat upon.

Upright, shrubby French thyme (*Thymus vulgaris*) is the species used in the kitchen. Typically, it bears gray-green foliage. However, *T. vulgaris* 'Aureus' features yellow leaves, and the leaves of *T. vulgaris* 'Argenteus' are edged in white. It is important to pay attention when shopping for these cultivars. If you simply grab the first thyme labeled 'Aureus' you may end up with a creeping thyme rather than the little upright shrub you meant to purchase.

I am not alone when it comes to the problems I have with various true mints (*Mentha*). I want to grow them for their great-tasting leaves, which I use for making teas, chutneys, and other things, but they happen to be among the most rampageous plants to take over a garden. I once made a tire planter for my daughter and she declared that at last she had something sturdy enough to contain true

Plate 56. The elegantly tidy, crisp white variegation of *Hemerocallis fulva* 'Kwanzo Variegata' lasts throughout the growing season, as opposed to its flowers, each of which lasts for only a day.

Plate 57. There are many options when it comes to variegation, and even the simplest form can create an interesting display. A thin white edge added to the fuzzy green leaves of *Plectranthus madagascariensis* creates a pleasing pattern.

Plate 58. The white-edged, gray-green foliage of *Pittosporum tobira* 'Variegatum' creates a soft, cloudlike effect in a shady woodland garden.

Plate 59. The ghostly white new leaves on this *Acanthopanax sieboldianus* 'Variegata' are nourished by the partially green, chlorophyll-containing leaves located elsewhere on the plant.

Plate 60. A splashy pattern of light green, cream, and white enhances the bold, tropical-looking foliage of *Alocasia* 'Hilo Beauty'.

Plate 61. The luscious leaves of *Symphytum* ×*uplandicum* 'Axminster Gold' are creamy yellow irregularly blotched with apple-green and forest-green, the result of an absence of chlorophyll in the outside layer of its leaves.

Plate 62. The sunny golden foliage of *Canna* 'Pretoria' is enhanced by a simple tracery of thin green lines.

Plate 63. An almost painful grouping of conflicting colors: the vivid pink flowers of *Catharanthus roseus* screech at the long, narrow, gold-brushed scarlet leaves of *Amaranthus tricolor* 'Illumination'.

Plate 64. A lovely, quiet planting for the shady garden pairs the silver-blotched foliage of *Lamium galeobdolon* with the white-edged leaves of *Hosta* 'Albomarginata'. The nicely cut green foliage of a white-flowered form of *Geranium macrorrhizum* adds to the display.

Plate 65. Tom Mannion's shady garden is enlivened by tousled mounds of white-striped *Acorus gramineus* 'Variegatus' and *Hosta* 'Great Expectations', its large leaves irregularly center-blotched with creamy white. *Chasmanthium latifolium* forms a backdrop, and *Begonia grandis* takes shelter among the hosta foliage.

Plate 66. In a shady garden the lacy fronds of Japanese painted fern (*Athyrium nipponicum* 'Pictum') make a lovely partner for white impatiens.

Plate 67. The bold, green-veined white leaves of *Caladium bicolor* 'Candidum' are also used effectively with white impatiens.

Plate 68. When *Cornus alba* 'Elegantissima' is grown in combination with a few white impatiens, the shrub's leaves, neatly margined in white, produce a cool, refined effect.

Plate 69. A charming spring scene: the swordlike leaves of *Iris pallida* 'Aureomarginata' and Johnny-jump-up (*Viola tricolor*). The creamy yellow variegation of the iris sets off the dainty purple and yellow flowers.

Plate 70. Sometimes disease can be beautiful, as demonstrated by the exquisite gold-speckled foliage of *Abutilon pictum* 'Thompsonii', caused by a virus.

Plate 71. Imagine using the showy foliage of *Pelargonium* 'Skies of Italy' in a mix-and-match summer container planting. The flamboyant leaves adds interest regardless of whether the plant is in or out of bloom.

Plate 72. In this kitchen garden, red cabbage (*Brassica oleracea*) and purple sage (*Salvia officinalis* 'Purpurascens') provide a simple partnership with great visual appeal.

Plate 73. Both edibles and ornamentals offer attractive foliage for the discerning gardener. A display bed at the New Orleans Zoo contrasts the purple-flushed blocky leaves of red mustard cabbage (*Brassica juncea* 'Red Leaf') with the delicate silver lace of *Senecio cineraria* 'Silver Dust'.

Plate 74. Red mustard cabbage (*Brassica juncea* 'Red Leaf') pairs up equally well—though with a very different feel—with an unidentified velvety red coleus with gold-edged leaves. *Hylotelephium sieboldii* adds to the display.

Plate 75. A sturdy, frost-proof combination: the elegantly ruffled purple foliage of kale (*Brassica oleracea* 'Redbor') and the rusty-hued seed heads of *Hylotelephium spectabile*.

Plate 76. A window box provides an excellent display case for this fabulous combination of herbs put to ornamental use. *Artemisia stelleriana* 'Silver Brocade' cascades over the edge in front, as licorice plant (*Helichrysum petiolare*) splays out against the wall in back. Lemon-scented, rose-scented, and nutmeg-scented geraniums add their small scale, fragrant green leaves, and modest flowers to the display. The white-flowered form of *Heliotropium arborescens* also lends its perfume to the combination.

Plate 78. This corner of a vegetable garden is as pretty as a picture. Perilla, ruby Swiss chard, and curly parsley create a pleasing interplay of texture, shape, and color.

Plate 77. Ruby Swiss chard is a popular vegetable, both for its slightly sweet taste and the elegant appearance of its red-veined leaves.

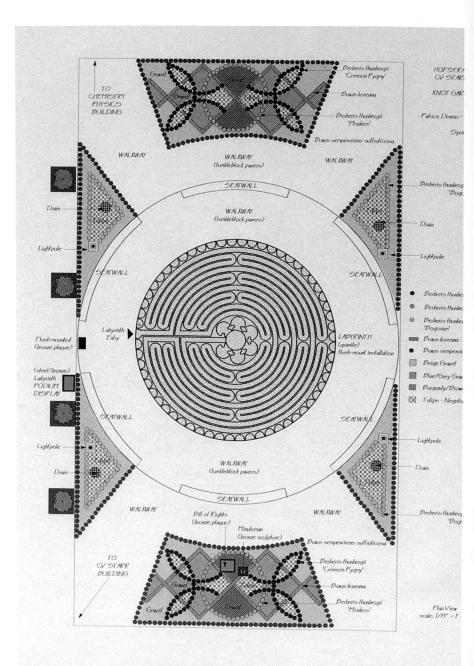

Plate 79. This plan drawing of the Hofstra University labyrinth garden demonstrates how elegantly the labyrinth itself is incorporated into the courtyard and planting beds. Drawing courtesy of landscape designer Patrice Dimino and Hofstra University.

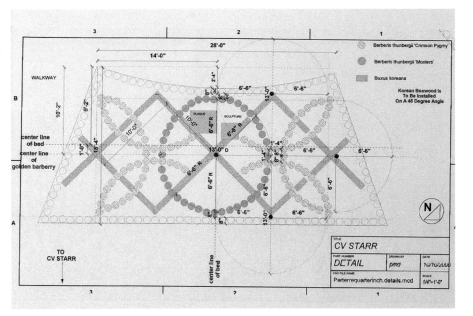

Plate 80. A detailed plan for the elegant knot garden that accompanies the labyrinth. Notice the severe geometry and restrained selection of plants. Drawing courtesy of landscape designer Patrice Dimino and Hofstra University.

Plate 81. The green walls of a geometric boxwood maze at Afton Villa Gardens, St. Francisville, Louisiana, are low enough to peek over.

Plate 82. Low hedges of germander (*Teucrium chamaedrys*), lavender cotton (*Santolina chamaecyparissus*), and lavender (*Lavandula*) create the traditional interweaving ribbons of a knot garden.

Plate 84. Another style of formal geometry: these meticulously clipped yews (*Taxus*) provide a basic embellishment to a simple country house.

Plate 83. The formal patterns of these boxwood (*Buxus*) parterres, filled in with sage (*Salvia*) and lavender (*Lavandula*), were designed to be viewed from an upper floor of the Het Loo Palace in Apeldoorn, Netherlands. When they were new, at the end of the seventeenth century, Queen Mary and her ladies undoubtedly admired them as much as tourists do today.

Plate 85. This lovely, simple hedge echoes the lines of the adjacent pergola.

Plate 86. A spirally clipped juniper provides a corner accent for the narrow planting bed in front of this charming bungalow. The juniper was already fifteen years old when it was planted seven years ago. Regular pruning has maintained its form, though a dry summer has caused some problems.

mints. Peppermint (*M. ×piperita*) is a hybrid of watermint (*M. aquatica*) and spearmint (*M. spicata*). Leaves are smooth or wrinkled, sometimes slightly hairy, dark green, intensely scented, and savory. Peppermint tea is more powerful than tea made from spearmint, and it is often suggested that children not drink it. *Mentha ×piperita* 'Citrata', called lemon mint, bergamot mint, or eau de cologne mint for its distinguishing light, citrus-accented, monarda-like scent, has fat, heart-shaped leaves. *M. ×piperita* 'Lime Mint' features lime-citrus overtones. The peppermint-flavored leaves of *M. ×piperita* 'Crispa' are crinkled, while those of *M. ×piperita* 'Variegata' are dark green with cream mottling. Spearmint (*M. spicata*) is alternately known as lamb mint or, in the South, julep mint, suggesting its culinary appeal. Leaves are wrinkled or pebbly, shiny, and dark green. *Mentha spicata* 'Crispa' has strongly curled leaves with crimped and twisted edges. Peppermint and spearmint can be easily distinguished by looking at the edges of the leaves: those of peppermint are smooth, while those of spearmint are spiked or serrated. Apple mint (*M. ×villosa* 'Variegata') is one of the most attractive ornamental mints. Rounded, wooly apple-green leaves are bordered and spattered with white. When crushed they smell of apples and spice. Apple mint will accept light shade, and it is not as determined a spreader as many of its relatives—two attributes guaranteed to endear it to gardeners. Golden ginger mint (*M. ×gracilis* 'Variegata') is another decorative mint, featuring serrate leaves flecked with yellow and cream, a fruitlike scent, and the taste of ginger. True mints readily cross-pollinate, something you have no doubt already deduced from *M. ×piperita*, *M. ×villosa*, and *M. ×gracilis*.

In *The Food-Lover's Garden*, Angelo M. Pellegrini lovingly describes a dish from his boyhood in Italy, which consisted of "frogs cooked in a sauce whose fragrance lived in my memory for years." The herb used in the dish was *puleggio*, none other than English pennyroyal (*Mentha pulegium*), a marginally hardy creeping mint. Pellegrini bought a bunch of English pennyroyal at a vegetable market in North Beach, San Francisco, and brought it home to Seattle. The sprigs rooted with the same ease of other mints. Even though English pennyroyal will not survive hard winters, Pellegrini discovered that it reseeded, so he need never be without it again. (The frogs were a different story, but English pennyroyal seems to be just as good with fish.)

The scent of Corsican mint (*Mentha requienii*) seems somehow even more the essence of mint than mint itself. At less than 1 inch high, this is the tiniest species of the genus. Forming a dainty, ground-hugging mat, it needs a damp site if it is to thrive, and even then patches of it often die over the winter in zone 6. An airy covering of pine boughs will help it through the winter. Should it die back anyway, it will replenish itself from the roots the next spring.

Mountain mint (*Pycnanthemum pilosum*) is not a true mint, but it does belong to the mint family. I remember this plant from my childhood summers in rural, quiet Brookfield, Connecticut, where mountain mint could be gathered from roadside meadows and used for making tea. This 2-foot-tall, stiffly upright plant has small, rather narrow, grayish green leaves that smell of peppermint with a hint of thyme. Well behaved, it does not go rushing around in the garden. Mountain mint is not wildly exciting to look at, but its fragrance intensifies in late summer when frumpy off-white flowers appear, looking more like small, white leaves. This species does not get a lot of mention in books concerned with native plants, herbaceous perennials, or herbals, but this may soon change. I recently saw mountain mint used to great effect at Green Spring Gardens Park in Alexandria, Virginia, where a mass planting made a subtle, intensely fragrant accent in combination with the vivid colors of goldenrod (*Solidago*), sunflower (*Helianthus*), and ironweed (*Vernonia*). Wolfgang Oehme used another native species and close relative, *P. muticum*, in his splendid design for the Towson Courthouse Garden in Towson, Maryland, where again the understated coloration served as a grace note in an otherwise colorful display.

There are other plants whose fragrant foliage forms an indelible part of my garden memories. Marigolds (*Tagetes*) have a strong spicy scent when their leaves are crushed. Some folks find the fragrance objectionable, which explains the development of unscented cultivars. However, the scented cultivars repel nematodes in the soil around their roots, while the unscented marigolds do not. Mexican mint marigold (*T. lucida*) is a perennial with a sweet scent to its leaves, something like a blend of anise, licorice, and tarragon. Tolerant of hot, dry summer weather, it thrives in the arid Southwest as an acceptable alternative to true French tarragon (*Artemisia dracunculus*). Tomato leaves also have a pungent odor when crushed, though this does nothing to deter tomato hornworms, large juicy green caterpillars that can decimate a plant to bare stalks overnight.

LEAFY VEGETABLES

We often put objects in categories and then create difficulties for ourselves by confining them there, keeping them from crossing over to another group. Agriculture is for production. Horticulture is for decoration. When tomatoes were thought to be poisonous they were grown as ornamentals. When was the last time you saw tomatoes grown as ornamentals?

My brother, Benjamin Orlove, is a professor of anthropology at the University of California, Davis, in the Department of Environmental Studies.

Years ago he did field research in Mexico, and these were some of his observations: "The villagers around Lake Pátzcuaro in Michoacán often talked about how their fields were *bonito* (pretty) when they were free of weeds and the maize plants were all of uniform height (as opposed to having patches of scrawny plants). Beans and squashes intercropped with maize were okay; the fields could still be pretty. I was especially struck when the same people spoke of remodeling their houses (adding a room or repainting) as *mejoras*, literally 'betterings.' I realized that Americans, including the few farmers I know, would be more likely to say that a field was good and a house pretty, rather than the other way around."

Gardeners make a distinction between plants grown for their good looks and those raised for food. Anyone who has had a vegetable garden understands the appeal of the huge, fuzzy, silver-spotted leaves of zucchini or the airy veil of mature asparagus stalks. Dark green spinach, tender green or red lettuces, feathery carrot tops: vegetables can indeed be visually attractive. For the sake of efficient production we grow each kind of vegetable in a separate row. Flowers grown for production are also planted in rows. A row of sunflowers may be stately but it is also boring unless the sunflowers form a background to other plants. A row of hostas or astilbes is monotonous, suggestive of a nursery's production field. The appeal of an ornamental garden is created by its mixture of plants, whether this entails a simple combination of just a few plants or a glorious diversity of many plants.

The Ballymaloe Cookery School in County Cork, Ireland, is run by Darina and Tim Allen. Darina has created a few gardens at the school, including a potager, a French-inspired vegetable garden laid out in a formal, ornamental manner. Enclosed with high brick walls, the garden is entered through a large green gate. Beds are laid out in a series of diamonds and squares separated by paths of old brick set in a herringbone pattern. I visited this garden one June and was delighted by its assortment of plants, including scarlet-stemmed ruby chard, lettuces of many kinds, smooth to lacy *frisée*, asparagus beginning its transition from smooth fat spears to feathery clouds of needlelike foliage, edible flowers such as calendula and squash blossoms, borage and chives, delicate shoots of green onion, purple-flushed artichokes, and sea kale. The forcing pots for the sea kale confirmed that the garden was meant to be practical as well as pretty. Some were elegant terra-cotta. Places

> Anyone who has had a vegetable garden understands the appeal of the huge, fuzzy, silver-spotted leaves of zucchini or the airy veil of mature asparagus stalks.

where they'd run short on pots were served just as well with clay sewer tiles topped with plastic nursery pots held down with rocks. According to Darina Allen, the potager's only drawback is its very beauty—it seems a shame to spoil the design by picking vegetables.

Several leafy vegetables have earned a place among ornamentals (see Plates 72–78). Collard greens, ruby Swiss chard, kale, lettuce, and mustard cabbage are both edible and attractive, making them especially useful where space is limited. They can even be tucked in here and there among perennials in a sunny herbaceous border or used as foliage accents in a container.

Kale (*Brassica oleracea*) is a good choice for the fall vegetable garden, offering a tasty, elegant alternative to ornamental cabbage and ornamental kale (both of which also belong to *B. oleracea*). *Brassica oleracea* 'Nero di Toscano' is a laciniato or dinosaur-type kale with long, narrow, savoyed, blackish green leaves. It is mild in flavor and tolerant of hot or cold weather. *Brassica oleracea* 'Red Russian' has deep gray-green leaves with jaggedly toothed edges and purple veins and stems. This cultivar is especially tender compared with other kales; its young leaves are excellent served fresh in salads or lightly steamed or sautéed. The well-curled, ruffle-leaved *B. oleracea* 'Winterbor' grows 2 to 3 feet tall and is quite cold hardy. When the leaves are cut, rather than the entire plant, it grows back quite vigorously. In gardens from Maine to South Carolina, seed should be sown from mid June to early July for an autumn crop. Adjust for regional differences elsewhere in the country, keeping in mind that hot weather will cause kale to bolt.

Lactuca sativa 'Red Sails' makes a nice edging in spring, a colorful foliage partner for violas (*Viola cornuta*) of any hue. The green leaves of this versatile lettuce are heavily overlaid with deep burgundy red. The heart is green, but what you see is richly colored. I particularly like 'Red Sails' because it is slow to bolt and grows well into summer without developing much of a bitter taste. *Lactuca sativa* 'Red Lollo Rossa' is a dark red Italian specialty lettuce with heavily frilled green leaves that develop their strong color even under lower light conditions. This cultivar is compact, slower growing than other types of lettuce, and more deeply colored than 'Lollo Rossa'.

'Osaka Purple' is an attractive Japanese variety of mustard cabbage (*Brassica juncea*) that grows 12 to 14 inches tall. Medium green, somewhat curly leaves tinged with purple-red feature purple-red veins. A mild peppery flavor makes young leaves useful in salads. Light cooking is all that is needed to mellow the flavor of older leaves.

Orach (*Atriplex hortensis*), also known as mountain spinach, is popular abroad as both a foliage annual and a salad green. Typically green hastate leaves are sometimes purple-brown. Either way, leaves appear dusted with a fine crystalline farina. Orach reaches 5 or 6 feet tall and makes a great back-of-the-border filler plant. It does self-sow, but is not much of a nuisance. *Atriplex hortensis* var. *rubra* has purple-red to crimson leaves, *A. hortensis* 'Cupreatorosea' has red leaves with a coppery luster, and *A. hortensis* 'Rosea' has pale red leaves accented with more deeply red veins and petioles. The deep crimson-purple leaves of *A. hortensis* 'Oracle' are four to five shades darker than the usual red orach and painted a vibrant fuchsia on the underside. Some will come green, but these can be easily detected and weeded out as young seedlings.

The purple basils, *Ocimum basilicum* 'Dark Opal' and *O. basilicum* 'Purple Ruffles', have beautiful red-purple leaves that can lend their color to any pesto or flavored vinegar you might make. These cultivars are readily available at most garden centers in spring, along with other herb and vegetable seedlings. If you intend to raise them from seed yourself, remember that they will need a head start indoors before frost-free planting time arrives.

Shiso (*Perilla frutescens* 'Atropurpurea') is a Japanese herb. It is used to color *umeboshi* (pickled plums), served with sashimi, and shredded as a flavoring for rice balls. A slight metallic tint enhances the deep reddish purple leaves, which fade to greenish purple as the plant starts flowering in late summer. Shiso grows in full sun or light shade and seeds about with abandon. Goldfinches enjoy the seeds in winter. One little bird, weighing in at only half an ounce or so, will sway back and forth as it perches at the tip of a 2- to 3-foot-tall withered shiso stem, eating a few seeds and scattering the rest. Unwanted plants are easily weeded out, but these will be numerous.

Tampala (*Amaranthus tricolor*), also known as Chinese spinach, is a heat-tolerant vegetable that reaches 4 feet tall. Several cultivars with richly colored leaves are used for summer interest. The narrow, willowlike leaves of *A. tricolor* 'Flaming Fountain' are vivid carmine and crimson-red. The broader leaves of *A. tricolor* 'Molten Fire' are brown-red to maroon with a glowing red blotch at the base that extends towards the tip of the leaf. *Amaranthus tricolor* 'Splendens' also features broader leaves, which are a deep red when young, turning a brilliant light red with age.

CHAPTER 9

❧

Geometry in the Garden

Gardening is, by its very nature, a manipulation of plants. We want this to grow here and that to grow there. Nowhere is our dominance over plants more clearly displayed than in the woody plants we clip, shear, and trim into rigid forms quite unlike their natural habit of growth. But we have a Jekyll and Hyde dichotomy in how we feel about this. Consider the geometrics of a foundation planting wherein yews and azaleas are precisely shaped into cubes and spheres. The self-same shape that is seen as lacking in taste when a plant is wedged up against a house in an urban or suburban setting is appreciated when the plant is isolated. It is then called topiary and perceived as garden art. In Japan azaleas are clipped into exact rounded forms and called "brocaded pillows." We sigh, "Ah, so beautiful—the Japanese have such an exquisite love of nature," all the while ignoring the identical mounds created by our unsophisticated neighbor back in Brooklyn, Newark, or Pittsburgh.

This push-pull, love-hate attitude is nothing new when it comes to topiary. In *The Essayes or Counsels of Francis Lo. Verulam, Viscount St. Albans*, Francis Bacon wrote that he despised images cut in juniper and other plants, saying these were only fit to amuse children. William Lawson, writing in the same period, had quite the opposite view. In *A New Orchard and Garden,* he states that "your Gardiner can frame your lesser wood to the shape of men armed in the field, ready to give battell; or swift running Grey Hounds to chase the Deere or hunt the Hare. This kind of hunting shall not waste your corne nor much your coyne."

What do these geometric shapes, topiary forms, and, most commonly, hedges, offer the gardener, other than exercise with a hedge trimmer?

Many people recognize the manicured edges of a landscape as a sign that it is maintained. By simply mowing a border around the perimeter of an uncut lawn, you salvage it from weediness and restore it to garden status. Mow a path through it from one front corner to the opposing rear corner (a nice, gently curving Hogarth curve, please) and the distinction is sharpened. You might add a martin house on a pole in one grassy area, a gate at the start of the path... But I digress.

When a shrub is pruned into a geometric form—whether a hedge, cube, sphere, or even more elaborate shape—it announces to the viewer, "This is a garden. Someone is taking care of these plants." Clip a line of forsythia into a hedge and it becomes gardenesque, even though flowering will probably be sparse and irregular. Prune a yew into a flattened globe and it adds a sense of orderliness in contrast to the unpruned, natural shape of the surrounding shrubs. The geometry need not always involve sharp edges and crisp corners, either. Low mounds and curving, swirling shapes are also possible, if perhaps more difficult to maintain with accuracy.

HEDGES

A hedge is created as a boundary or barrier, the living counterpart to a wall or fence. To create a hedge, shrubs are planted closely together so as to create a continuous line. A hedge may be purely decorative, serving to screen out an unsightly vista, create a garden room, or frame a focal point. It may also function as a windbreak, creating shelter for plants less tolerant of exposure.

As with any other type of gardening, the key to the successful creation of a hedge is thorough preparation. Digging individual holes for each shrub, whether there are six or sixty, is a difficult task and will not get the infant hedge off to a very good start. Create a trench row instead, which will encourage roots to spread more quickly. In the 1914 edition of *The Standard Cyclopedia of Horticulture*, Liberty Hyde Bailey suggests "thoroughly plowing and cultivating an area 6 feet wide and the length the hedge is proposed to extend; or else to dig a trench 2 feet deep and 2 or 3 feet wide, and fill it with good top-soil thoroughly enriched." The old-fashioned method of double hedging was considered practically obsolete in Bailey's time, and the same is true now. A single row allows for more balanced growth and easier maintenance of the ground beneath and around the hedge. Pruning is necessary from the first and will continue to be an annual necessity, and it must never be omitted in the summer. As Bailey notes, "This work can be greatly accelerated and consequently cheapened by shearing when the plants are young and tender, say during the month of July."

The cross section of a hedge is critical to its continued health. Should the top be wider than the bottom there will be shading and subsequent dieback along the sides, resulting in a shabby appearance. A hedge with a flat top may collect snow in winter, causing branches to break. A triangular shape—or even, as Liberty Hyde Bailey suggests, a "curvilinear or Gothic arch"—is more desirable. The sun will reach the sides and base of the shrubs, keeping them covered with foliage right down to the ground. I have also seen truncated triangles, hedges that are narrower at the top than at the base, with just a small portion of the tip removed.

When it comes to selecting plants for hedges, keep in mind that it doesn't matter whether a shrub is evergreen or deciduous so long as it will tolerate close clipping and shearing. The most popular of the coniferous evergreen hedging plants are the various yews (*Taxus*): English yew (*T. baccata*), Japanese yew (*T. cuspidata*), and the hybrid of the two species, *T. ×media*. Yews respond especially well to pruning. I had just such a hedge of yew at a house I once lived in. In the beginning it served to screen the road and muffle traffic noise, but with the advent of deer the base of the hedge became "pruned" into graceful open arches, as high as the deer could reach when balanced on their hind legs. Yew is, unfortunately, eminently popular with deer.

Box (*Buxus sempervirens*) has been used in gardens since Roman times and is another classic shrub for hedges and topiary. Though slow growing, it will eventually reach 20 feet tall. This shrub is native to southern Europe, northern Africa, and western Asia, and is hardy in zones 6 through 10. Unfortunately, while it grows well in warm, moist climates, boxwood dislikes extremes of heat or cold. It is also susceptible to a number of diseases and insect pests. Shallow rooted, boxwood resents drought and is easily damaged if cultivation disturbs its root system. It prefers partial shade when planted in hot climates. In warm-summer regions it can tolerate full sun, though partial shade is still suitable. Box has been used for hedges in the United States since colonial times. A gardener in Virginia once told me she thinks every Welcome Wagon comes equipped with pots of boxwood—how else to explain the pair of shrubs gracing every front walk? *Buxus sempervirens* 'Northern Find' and *B. sempervirens* 'Vardar Valley' are hardier than the species, down to zone 5. *Buxus sempervirens* 'Suffruticosa', a dwarf form, is appropriate for low hedges.

Several species of holly (*Ilex*) make good plants for hedges. Japanese holly (*I. crenata*), for example, is an excellent alternative to boxwood. Useful for hedges 4 feet tall or lower, it is hardy in all except the most northern states. Small, oval evergreen leaves create a fine, tight texture. American holly (*I. opaca*) can be used for green screening hedges up to 30 feet tall. English holly (*I. aquifolium*) is not as hardy but is useful south of Philadelphia and St. Louis. Its glossy leaves are a brighter green than the olive-hued leaves of American holly. It may be used for hedges up to 6 feet tall.

California privet (*Ligustrum ovalifolium*) is so amenable to shearing that it may be used for hedges anywhere from 12 feet tall down to 6 inches. The drawback is its rapid growth, which calls for pruning every week or two.

Hornbeam (*Carpinus caroliniana*) is an excellent choice for deciduous hedges. It is rarely used in this manner in the United States, however, because it is both unfamiliar to gardeners and difficult to obtain. European hornbeam (*C. betulus*) is widely used abroad for hedges and other clipped and trained applications. A magnificent example may be seen at the Het Loo Palace in Apeldoorn, Netherlands. Built in the last third of the seventeenth century, Het Loo was home to William of Orange (later King William III of England) and his wife, Mary. The Queen's Garden included marvelous pathways of trellis and greenery, what they called *berceaux*. (A *berceau* is a cradle, specifically the old-fashioned sort with a rounded top.) Arbors were covered with European hornbeam to create a cloister, the result being an arcade where ladies could stroll without exposing themselves to the sun. I was fortunate enough to visit Het Loo soon after it was restored and opened to the public for its three-hundredth anniversary in 1984. Young European hornbeams were tied into place and beginning to form a covering on the supporting lattice structure. I could clearly see the framework and envision the bosky shade that would be created when the plants had more growth. Contemporary offices and work spaces for the museum required space of their own, so only half the *berceaux* could be replaced, but even so the result was enchanting.

Beech (*Fagus sylvatica*) is another hedging plant more popular in Europe than in the United States. Though beech is deciduous, it's chestnut-brown autumn leaves are retained late into the year. This aspect, coupled with its smooth gray bark, adds winter interest. This naturally tall tree requires regular attention from the start in order to be dwarfed into a densely branched tall hedge.

Barberry (*Berberis thunbergii*) is popularly used for deciduous hedges no more than 4 feet tall. Its naturally tight, dense habit allows it to be formally clipped into a hedge or left unpruned for a more billowy, casual look. Purple-leaved cultivars such as *B. thunbergii* f. *atropurpurea* can be used for a colorful effect. The dwarf forms of purple-leaved barberry, *B. thunbergii* 'Atropurpurea Nana' and *B. thunbergii* 'Bagatelle', are useful in knot gardens, their colorful foliage creating a fine contrast to the silver leaves of lavender (*Lavandula*) and the green leaves of germander (*Teucrium chamaedrys*) or dwarf box (*Buxus microphylla*). Golden yellow *B. thunbergii* 'Aurea' grows 3 to 4 feet tall. In my own garden it makes a great accent plant in the herbaceous border, setting off the blue columbines (*Aquilegia*) in spring and softly blending with the chartreuse leaves of golden feverfew (*Chrysanthemum parthenium* 'Aureum').

Hedges are something within reach of most gardeners. They can define and delineate a small garden, separating it from the world beyond and providing a backdrop for flowers. They can also keep small children and wind-blown debris—or the neighbor's chickens, depending on your circumstances—from passing through.

FEDGES

The first fedge I ever saw was in Maura Sheahan's garden in Bray, County Wicklow, Ireland. The rear of her property, an acre in size, is very cleverly divided into garden rooms by simple wire fences concealed with vines. A fedge, you see, is a space-saving combination of fence and hedge. Place the fence posts, string the wire, and plant the vine. The thin, flat, hedgelike result is far more attractive than a wire fence and much less laborious to install and maintain. It is a quick way to create green walls. Do be sure to use sturdy fencing, though: once it is covered in vines, attempts to remove and replace rusting, sagging wire will be most tedious. For this reason I'd recommend using plastic-coated wire fencing for 3- to 4-foot-high fedges, and the dreaded industrial-strength chain-link fencing for tall fedges. In fact, if you have a chain link fence that cannot be removed for some reason, this might be the ideal way to conceal its presence.

Where it is hardy, ivy (*Hedera*) is the best choice for a year-round, evergreen fedge. Keep in mind, though, that ivy trailing out along the ground will be less subject to winter burn than the very same plant growing on a fence. More shelter will be required in zones approaching the limits of ivy's hardiness. It especially needs protection from drying winds and early morning sun in winter. It would also be a good idea to apply an anti-desiccant spray in early November and again during the January thaw. A plain green-leaved cultivar will provide the most neutral appearance, *H. helix* 'Baltica' being the most cold-resistant selection (it was discovered in the early 1900s growing on the eastern edge of the Baltic Sea near Riga, Latvia). Variegated ivies have a livelier appearance. The pale green to buttery yellow leaves of *H. helix* 'Buttercup' appear greener in shade but brighten up in sunny sites. *Hedera helix* 'Goldheart' has dark green leaves with an irregular, clear yellow central blotch, and is considered one of the best climbing ivies. The gray-green leaves of *H. helix* 'Glacier' feature narrow white to cream edges. This cultivar is usually listed as hardy to zone 7. I have seen it in New Canaan, Connecticut, zone 6, happily climbing up a tree.

Other options for fedges include Virginia creeper (*Parthenocissus quinquefolia*), Boston ivy (*P. tricuspidata*), and climbing hydrangea (*Hydrangea anomala*), all of which are deciduous.

The same concept can be employed around a swimming pool. Building codes require secure fencing to protect small children from accidental drowning. If a sturdy wire fence is hidden inside a hedge, security is maintained along with aesthetic design objectives. Keep the hedge sufficiently taller and wider than the fence to avoid cutting into the wire when using hedge trimmers.

LABYRINTHS AND MAZES

A labyrinth can be a couple of things, the first being essentially the same thing as a maze. The winding passages Theseus made his way through to slay the Minotaur are one example. In a garden labyrinth or maze, this type of intricate puzzle is replicated with plants, using tall hedges for passage walls. The designer creates twists, turns, and dead ends that must be overcome if participants are to reach the center—which, of course, is not visible.

There were two mazes at Het Loo Palace. After becoming king of England, William III had a maze built at his new home outside London. Today you can visit Hampton Court Palace and see the maze, approximately a quarter-acre in size with half a mile of pathways. In 1935 a reproduction half this size was fashioned in Colonial Williamsburg, Virginia, at the gardens of Governors Palace.

In *The Standard Cyclopedia of Horticulture*, Liberty Hyde Bailey describes labyrinths and mazes as "intricate and confusing networks of walks and passages within hedges of evergreen, formerly employed as a garden entertainment and conceit. They are still kept up in some Old World gardens as relics of the past. They were popular in the sixteenth and seventeenth centuries." Bailey includes an illustration of the maze at St. Catherine's Hill, Winchester, England, from a plan made in 1710. He continues, "It would be vandalism to destroy so fine an example of a style of gardening no longer fashionable, but folly to copy it in a modern garden." He was both right and wrong: mazes were indeed admired in earlier times, but they have also made a comeback, especially those in the United Kingdom. In 1906 William Waldorf Astor commissioned the design and construction of a circle in a square yew hedge maze for the grounds of Hever Castle, which dates back to the thirteenth century. A 1962 hedge maze planted at Chatsworth, Derbyshire, was based on an earlier design. Longleat, Wiltshire, added a huge maze to its public attractions in 1978. It includes hairpin turns and spirals as well as bridges to provide an overview for bemused wanderers. In 1990 Randoll Coate, a noted contemporary British maze designer, planted a stepped ziggurat maze in yew at Blervic House in Elgin, Scotland.

Contemporary American mazes tend to be more transient. They are cut into cornfields. Why? Well, why not? Corn grows quickly compared with the length of time it takes to establish a hedge, so a maze can be created within a matter of weeks. These kinds of mazes, with their inherent flexibility, are sprouting up everywhere. Once the maze season is over (around the end of October), the standing corn can be harvested for animal feed.

The Great Maze in North Danville, Vermont, covers five acres. Participants of the first maze, created in 1999, took an average of forty-five to sixty minutes to complete the course. In 1994 British maze designer Adrian Fisher designed the first Amazing Maize Maze in a Pennsylvania cornfield. In 2001 Maize Quest, a consortium of thirteen individual farms, produced mazes in Pennsylvania, Ohio, Arkansas, Virginia, Tennessee, Missouri, Vermont, and New York. The mazes provide entertainment for visitors and an additional source of income for farmers. Twelve of the mazes created by Maize Quest are cut into corn, with about two miles of paths cut into four- or five-acre fields. The remaining one, located in Warwick, New York, is cut into Sudan grass (*Sorghum bicolor*). I remember reading about one maze (in Pennsylvania, I believe) that was planted with tall cannas, but I found myself wondering how they could store the requisite number of rhizomes over the winter.

Adrian Fisher also designs the corn maze at Howell Living History Farm in Titusville, New Jersey, with proceeds going towards restoration of the farm's historic barn. Since the farm is maintained as a mid-nineteenth-century historical entity, the four-acre maze is situated off site to avoid historical conflict. In 1997, the first year the maze was created, the pattern cut into the field was that of a barn. In other years the design has been that of a fiddle, Washington crossing the Delaware, a tree-of-life quilt, and the farm's logo of a plowman and his team of horses (a historically accurate twist was added when the maze field was plowed with a four-horse tandem hitch rather than a tractor). Executing the design is an exercise in geometry, as the pattern must be laid out on graph paper, then transferred to a grid in the field. Finally, towards the end of July, volunteers cut the precise pathways into approximately 175,000 ankle-high stalks of corn. Pete Wilson, director at the Howell Living History Farm, told me they always leave some corn standing in certain pathways until the morning of opening day on Labor Day weekend, to conceal the maze from small aircraft attempting a preview.

Another form of labyrinth involves a mazelike design created inside a church, such as those produced in early thirteenth-century cathedrals. Walking one is intended as a metaphor for a pilgrimage. During the crusades of the Middle Ages the penitent might crawl on their knees to complete a full

four-quadrant, eleven-circuit labyrinth. Chartres Cathedral in France contains a labyrinth built around 1200. It is often used as a model for contemporary labyrinths. Unlike a maze, this kind of labyrinth has no dead ends. While
the path does have twists and turns, leading into one quadrant and then
another, in and out, back and forth, there is only one path, so it is not possible to get lost. Participation is a meditative activity intended as contemplative
exercise. I once walked such a labyrinth. It was painted on a ground cloth.
Several of us walked at a time, following the inward-turning pattern to the
center and then following it out again.

There is a marvelous contemporary outdoor labyrinth at Hofstra
University in Hempstead, New York, modeled on the one at Chartres Cathedral
(see Plates 79 and 80). It began when James Shuart, president of the university,
read a newspaper article discussing a labyrinth. It so fascinated and inspired
him that he requested one be built on the university grounds. The project took
hold and grew, eventually involving architects, designers, curators, museum
directors, construction managers, and outside contractors as well as in-house
administrative staff and tradespeople. The labyrinth is constructed of light burgundy and gray granite laid flush with the walking paths of gray tumbleblock
pavers. Once the hardscape was complete it needed to be finished with landscaping. Landscape designer Patrice Dimino was determined that the landscape
expand upon the serene, meditative qualities of the labyrinth. She decided on a
knot design set within parterres. "Although a visitor may not be physically walking through the knot patterns," says Patrice, "the perception of the flowing lines
allows the onlooker to gaze methodically along the curves and angles of the
plant material with the same reflective manner as if they were walking through
the labyrinth itself." By choosing boxwood (*Buxus sempervirens*) and barberry
(*Berberis thunbergii*) for the interlocking diamond-and-circle pattern, Patrice
ensured the plants' low habit of growth would "not interfere with nor obstruct
the viewer's eye from sweeping and embracing the entire space."

PARTERRES AND KNOT GARDENS

Parterre (from *par terre*, meaning "on the ground") involves the formal arrangement of ornamental flower beds in a flat, often rectangular garden. The beds are
frequently lined with low-growing hedges as well. These gardens are laid out
adjacent to the house and meant to resemble embroidery when viewed from
above. Parterre became the vogue of English garden style in the 1600s, but the
style is actually much older than that. Rose Standish Nichols, author of the
delightful 1902 book *English Pleasure Gardens*, begins in the classical times of

the Roman emperor Augustus: "The *xystus*, or parterre, was elaborately laid out in figures edged with box. Sometimes these outlines were left empty, and sometimes they were filled with flowers." This is clearly an antecedent of the formal herb gardens we enjoy today.

This style, Nichols notes, was closely emulated by Tudor gardens of the late fifteenth and much of the sixteenth century, where "the four quarters formed by the main alleys which intersected the middle of the garden were enclosed by a latticework fence or striped railings fastened to posts. These quarters were subdivided into *knots*. The knot was either a geometrical pattern or the outline of some fanciful shape such as a dragon kept in place by a coping of wood, brick, stone or tiles, and edged with box or some other border plant. The design of the knot was known as *open* or *closed* according to whether it was merely outlined with a border plant and strewn inside the outlines with coloured sands, or was filled with growing flowers. Clipped evergreen shrubs accented the corners of the beds or the centre of the garden." Nichols goes on to describe Longleat, a garden of the Marquise of Bath in Wiltshire, an early example of a Tudor garden, with parterres marked by borders of yew (*Taxus*) or box (*Buxus sempervirens*). The outer border was treated like a series of closed knots, with the corners accented by a cone-shaped yew. Separated from the borders by a strip of turf and a path were quarters divided into open knots of variegated holly and yew, the golden foliage of one contrasting with the dark green of the other. These parterres were an elaboration of the more austere monastic gardens of the twelfth century, which included an open plot of grass enclosed by a cloister, called a cloister garth. According to Nichols, "Two paths crossing each other at right angles divided the grass plot into quarters." This simple beginning evolved into elaborate geometric patterns and shapes used in interrelated groups. Frequently an uncomplicated outermost boundary—a square, rectangle, or even circle—defined the area, and this seems to have remained the best demarcation. The perimeter pattern should relate to the landscape within which it is placed. Squares and rectangles are usually the easiest shapes to lay out and construct, and they frequently fall most gracefully into the overall landscape. This is not to say that a circle won't work, just that it is more difficult to produce. The Western Reserve Herb Society Garden in Cleveland is arranged in the manner of a

> Squares and rectangles are usually the easiest shapes to lay out and construct, and they frequently fall most gracefully into the overall landscape.

medieval monastery herb garden, with numerous millstones as the paradigm for circular beds of herbs.

Elizabethan flower gardens of the late sixteenth century were designed on a grander scale. Knot gardens—outlined in box (*Buxus sempervirens*) or lavender (*Lavandula*), sometimes with an edging of pinks (*Dianthus*) and daisies—were laid out with each section occupying a piece of ground from 25 to 100 feet square. Of course, these were created for emperors, kings, and marquises who had resources, space, and staff not available to commoners. The recently restored Privy Garden at Hampton Court Palace is just such an elaborate parterre in the formal garden of a historic great house. Another notable example is the formal garden at the chateau of Villandry, which inspired Darina Allen, founder of the Ballymaloe Cookery School in Kinoith, Ireland, to create her elegant herb garden. The garden at Ballymaloe is surrounded with ancient hedges of beech (*Fagus*), a remnant of Kinoith's nineteenth-century garden. These create high walls with arched openings. Parterre-style beds are framed in boxwood, with vertical accents of globe artichoke (*Cynara scolymus*), Jerusalem artichoke (*Helianthus tuberosus*), angelica, and lovage (*Levisticum officinale*). Scarlet runner beans (*Phaseolus coccineus*) vining up decorative metal tuteurs in the circular beds give height to the overall design. Herbs such as catmint, sage, rosemary, thyme, rue, lemon balm, bronze fennel, summer savory, sweet cicely, parsley, and chives are planted in patterns of contrasting color, all appearing lush in the soft Irish weather. The perimeter of the garden is lined with herbaceous borders and beds of sea kale (*Crambe maritima*), complete with terra-cotta forcing pots. Outside the garden, a sturdy wooden ladder leads to a railed platform up in a huge beech tree, an ideal spot for surveying the patterns below.

> Any child who has whiled away a rainy afternoon playing with a compass and ruler will understand the groundwork for designing a simple parterre pattern.

Published in 1699, Leonard Meager's *The English Gardner* includes a section devoted to "The ordering of the Garden of pleasure, with varietie of Knots and Wilderness-work after the best fashion." Clearly a practical gardener, Meager not only suggests "the names of several herbs etc fit to set Knots with, or to edge borders to keep them in fashion, etc," but also discusses their maintenance. Dutch box and French box, he advises, are the handsomest, most durable, and cheapest options. "It is common in the mouths of many, that Box doth take away all the heart of a ground where it grows; but the naked truth is, that it doth not draw so much vertue from a ground as other herbs doth, my reason is, because it doth not grow so fast, and so by consequence not draw so much vertue from the place where it grows; and in case it do begger or barren a place where it grows, it comes to pass by its long standing compleat and hand-some, which is part of its excellency, it being the most durable of any kind of herb wherewith Knots are made."

Meager recommends other herbs for knot gardening as well, some of which are still popular today: "Germander was much used many years ago, it must have good keeping. Some use Lavender-Cotton and Herba-grace, [they] will be handsome if kept well. Rosemary may be kept low as other herbs if oft cut. Lavender as it may be kept, will be both low and handsome." Others are less prevalent in contemporary herb gardens. I cannot recall seeing any of the fol-lowing used to form the low hedging pattern of knots: "Hyssop is handsome if cut once in a fortnight or three weeks in the growing season. Two or three sorts of Thyme will be durable and handsome if oft cut. Thrift is well lik'd of by some, it is apt to gape and be unhandsome. Grass cut often. Sage likewise." Purple-leaved dwarf barberry (*Berberis thunbergii* 'Atropurpurea Nana') is pop-ular today. Though this charming little shrub was unavailable in Meager's time, I'm sure he would have recommended it.

Italian gardens have ancient roots, dating back to the time of the emperor Augustus. Paul Gervais, who, as previously mentioned, is the author of *A Garden in Lucca*, designed a contemporary counterpart of a medieval cloister garden for his Tuscan villa. Creating a working plan on paper, he drew the pre-cise cruciform design to scale. Since the four quadrants looked a bit dull, he trimmed away the inside corners to make a few curves. (This sort of revision is quite easy on paper, much more so than waiting until after the little hedging plants are in the ground.) Traditionally there would be four paths leading to the center, but Gervais's design included eight. Instead of placing an antique foun-tain at the center, which would easily cost five figures, he selected a conical box-wood (*Buxus sempervirens*) and surrounded it with two concentric circles of dwarf box (*B. microphylla*). The boxwood circles created an effect like ripples in a pond and reflected the curves from the inside corners of the beds.

Any child who has whiled away a rainy afternoon playing with a compass and ruler will understand the groundwork for designing a simple parterre pat-tern. Create a square. Draw a line from the upper left corner to the lower right corner and one from the upper right corner to the lower left corner. Create a dia-mond by connecting the midpoint of the top to the midpoint of each side and the midpoint of the bottom to the midpoint of the same sides. You now have a plan for a parterre with twelve compartments. The lines can be translated into boxwood (*Buxus sempervirens*). If your garden space is longer than it is wide, consider placing a circle in the middle with a diamond at each end. If space and interest allow, enclose the pattern with a rectangular hedge. Create a knot garden using boxwood and lavender, gently clipping back where they intersect so the two shrubs appear as bands crossing under and over each other. Lavender cotton (*Santolina chamaecyparissus*) and lavender (*Lavandula*) are too subtle a combination since both have gray foliage. Lavender cotton and germander (*Teucrium chamaedrys*), on the other hand, provide a fine partnership, combining silver-gray and deep green. Dwarf forms of purple-leaved barberry (*Berberis thunbergii*) offer a third color for a more complex interweaving.

Simple geometric shapes form the basis of parterres. It is important to lay the design out with sturdy stakes and taut string in order to create a crisp pattern. The elaborate shapes of seventeenth-century parterres—fleurs-de-lis, dragons, Celtic knots—must have been the very devil to produce.

TOPIARY

Closely clipped shrubs may be formed into living sculptures that are either geometrical or figurative. When Rose Standish Nichols wrote *English Pleasure Gardens*, she provided more than an early twentieth-century English viewpoint. Laying a solid foundation, she created an immensely useful history of gardening, discussing the influence of ages past. The first chapter roves back to Roman times. At Pompeii, she notes, fantastically clipped evergreen trees and shrubs were the principal "vegetate ornament" of the garden. This kind of sculpture "is said to have been invented by Matius, a friend of the Emperor Augustus. The chief gardener was known as the *topiarius*, and it was his none too easy task to see that the evergreens were artistically shorn. Under his supervision pyramids, cones, wild animals, hunting scenes, and even a whole fleet of ships might be shaped by skillful shears. Of shrubs there were fewer species then, but the variety in form given by the topiary's art made up for any deficiency in their natural diversity." One superb display in a public garden is that at Longwood Gardens in Kennett Square, Pennsylvania. The geometric topiaries add precisely the appropriate formal accent to the adjacent water garden with its Italianate stonework of balustrades and statuary.

Another notable contemporary example can be found at the Ladew Topiary Gardens in Monkton, Maryland, where topiary is formed from yew (*Taxus*), box (*Buxus sempervirens*), privet (*Ligustrum*), and hemlock (*Tsuga*). The hemlocks, alas, like so many hemlocks elsewhere in the Northeast, have succumbed to woolly adelgid and must be replaced. These sap-sucking insects, which look like tiny masses of cotton on the underside of hemlock needles, cause the needles to yellow and fall prematurely, weakening the tree and sometimes killing it. If an infestation is discovered early on, spraying with horticultural oil or insecticidal soap may provide sufficient control. Established populations are more difficult to eradicate. In order to kill newly hatched larvae, it may be necessary to apply contact insecticides once a week for several weeks, using hydraulic spray equipment to completely drench the infested trees in mid to late spring. Manitoga, designer Russell Wright's former estate in Garrison, New York, suffered the traumatic loss of significant numbers of its hemlocks. These trees, planted by Wright, were key to transforming what was originally a quarry into a sublime garden.

Nothing shouts "sloppy maintenance!" louder than topiary gone fuzzy around the edges. At Ladew Topiary Gardens there is a continual effort to keep things tidy. The privet is most demanding and requires pruning every couple of weeks throughout the growing season. The boxwood only needs shaping once or twice a year. The yew is sheared once a year, receiving a second touch-up if needed. When necessary, it can be cut back hard, right into old wood. The remaining hemlocks are trimmed once a year, in September, after summer's heat ameliorates. Keep in mind that these are not simple foundation plantings to be tidied up by a quick pass with electric hedge trimmers. One design involves regal swans surfing the waves of a billowing high hedge, their necks supported by strong wire framework. Most notorious are two huntsmen on horseback, one leaping a hedge, following a pack of hounds across the lawn in pursuit of a fox on the other side of the road. All of them—hunters, horses, fox, and hounds—are rendered in topiary.

Maintenance is the key to elegant topiary, whether you're working with a cube, a sphere, or a more elaborate shape. Contemporary nurseries are fond of selling spirally clipped junipers (*Juniperus*, see Plate 86), though all too often these become blurred and fuzzy through infrequent trimming once they are planted in a garden. It is trickier to maintain a boxwood or yew clipped into a conical form than one given the precise but simple geometry of a hedge. It is very easy to go astray, tilting to one side or adding a curve where one is not wanted. Paul Gervais discovered a simple solution. Set a bamboo pole or lightweight iron rod vertically and adjacent to the shrub's main trunk. This will keep the shrub from swaying as you prune. Tie a long piece of twine to the crown, attaching a weight to the free end (a lead fishing sinker would probably be ideal). The twine now provides a straight guideline from the shrub's crown to its base and you can clip away in confidence. Gervais uses four spheres clipped from *Buxus rotundifolia* and set, two by two, in his courtyard. In *A Garden in Lucca* he notes that although these simple topiaries were focal points and accents in Roman gardens, boxwood fell out of favor during the Renaissance. Apparently, sixteenth-century English gardeners believed the cat pee smell of boxwood to be damaging to the brain.

Successful topiaries, hedges, parterres, and such are achieved through precise control. The more formal the garden, the better these disciplined, though artful, shapes will fit in. Even in casual country-style gardens a hedge makes an appropriate formal boundary. If the hedge provides a backdrop to an herbaceous border, remember to provide a grass path between the two. This will allow maneuvering room for maintenance of both the hedge and the perennials, and create space for the roots of the hedge. A trimmed shrub lends a grace note of tidiness to the spontaneous garden. It will only be out of place in the most naturalistic garden.

CHAPTER 10

❧

The Seasonal Garden

Foliage has an important role to play in garden design. I am not suggesting you garden sans flowers, merely that you give leaves the same kind of consideration. Leaves can function like a supporting cast, scarcely noticed for the stars of the performance, or they can work together with flowers in an ensemble production. We think of certain showy flowers as seasonal signifiers. The first daffodils and pussy willows are exciting reminders of spring, just as chrysanthemums are a sign of autumn. (At least they used to be. Clever manipulation of day length and temperatures now make chrysanthemums a year-round affair, and tulips are getting there too). Pity. Foliage can be just as powerful an indicator of seasonal change—sometimes blatantly so, as when leaves turn bright colors in autumn, and sometimes in a quite subtle manner, as when the pink-flushed fuzzy white leaves of oaks unfold from winter's resting buds. Winter flowers, so popular in English gardening, are scarce to nonexistent in much of the United States. Evergreen foliage can provide a quiet contrast to gray or brown twigs and bark, and to white winter snow.

Traditional Japanese garden design relies very strongly on foliage. Gardens tend to be small, so there isn't space for short-lived flowers. Rather, a potted herbaceous perennial or bulb—a chrysanthemum in fall, a lily in summer—is brought on stage when in bloom and then discreetly retired from view. The technique is similar, albeit more intensive in magnitude, with the great English estates. Passing moments in the garden see flowering plants removed and understudy replacements brought from the wings to be planted out for the next act.

Japanese poetic traditions strongly associate plants (sometimes flowers, sometimes foliage) with the cycles of their seasons. Keeping in mind that the classical Japanese calendar has a lunar cycle, unlike the arbitrary months of the Gregorian calendar, it is interesting to note these associations. Tree buds (*ko no me*) signify midspring, early March to early April, while young green plants (*wakamidori*) allude to late spring, early April to early May. Bamboo autumn (*take no aki*) is another poetic reference to late spring, that time of year when the leaves of evergreen bamboo turn yellow. Sprouting grasses and forbs (*shitamoe*) and fiddlehead ferns (*warabi*) are also used to manifest early and midspring.

With early summer comes young leaves (*wakaba*), yellow fallen bamboo leaves (*take ochiba*), new green trees (*shinju*), and cherry trees (*hazakura*). Other references to summer mention green leaves (*aoba*), myriad green leaves (*banryoku*), and the particular luxuriance of leaves (*shigeri*).

In keeping with the idea of an amenity garden, early autumn brings the voice of reeds rustled by wind (*ogi no koe*). Falling willow leaves (*yanagi chiru*) signify midautumn, as does the sound of one falling paulownia leaf (*kiri hitoha*). Empress tree (*Paulownia tomentosa*) has large, long-petioled leaves as much as 12 inches long by 10 inches wide. I don't grow this tree, but sycamores (*Platanus occidentalis*) grow wild along the drainage creek that runs through my garden. The crisp brown leaves of these trees are smaller than those of empress tree, about 9 inches wide, but I can hear them falling when autumn brings them down. The large, delicate leaves of the banana plant (*bashoo*) make a sound when tattered by autumn wind and rain, another notable signifier of the season. The poet Bashō took his name from this plant. In late autumn, from early October to early November, come the *momiji*, the red leaves of Japanese maples (*Acer palmatum*). The leaves of Japanese ivy (*tsuta*) also turn red, as do those of Boston ivy (*Parthenocissus tricuspidata*). The withered, frosted tips of both herbaceous and woody plants (*uragare*) allude to late autumn.

From early November to early February, both fallen leaves (*ochiba*) and winter greenery (*fuyuna*) have significant poetical connotations, as do winter grasses and forbs (*fuyu kusa*).

AUTUMN

As days diminish in length, the year's journey turns around to autumn, the season we associate with leaves and their fall. It matters not whether the trees are evergreen or deciduous. Even conifers change in autumn, spreading fragrant straw-gold skirts beneath their green needles. Where seasons revolve around wet and dry cycles, leaves will turn brown and fall off the trees. Then there is the fantastical change that sets New England forests on fire without a single flame—such a remarkable sight that early European travelers were accused of exaggeration by those who stayed at home. A friend of mine who had moved to the Denver, Colorado, area from Massachusetts became very excited her first autumn there when she heard the foliage was at its peak. The whole family got in the car and drove to the mountains, where they saw golden aspens (*Populus*) against dark green conifers. It was a lovely sight, but not the burning display they had anticipated.

Fall foliage color is one of the most magical effects produced by plants. Tourists interested in catching a glimpse of this foliage flock to New England, Michigan, and Wisconsin. The U.S. Forest Service Fall Color Hotline (1-800-354-4595) even apprises visitors of local conditions as Jack Frost and his paint pot move down the coast. Those living along the eastern coast of Canada or the United States, in north-central United States, or in Japan, can enjoy a spectacular fall display without leaving home by selecting appropriate plants. It is important to find the right trees and shrubs, as not all woody plants are capable of turning scarlet, red, burgundy, or orange. And even when they are, the particular season's display will depend on weather conditions.

In late summer, plants get the message that it is time to stop growing. As days become shorter and temperatures drop, chlorophyll production declines and a barrier membrane, called an abscission layer, forms between the leaf stem and the branch. If the leaf carries xanthophylls and carotenes, it will change from summer green to autumn yellow—as with the Colorado aspens, for example. The color yellow is present during the summer but disguised by chlorophyll; it only becomes evident when chlorophyll production stops.

Perhaps you have noticed a sugar maple (*Acer saccharum*) as it changes color in autumn. The sunny side of the tree turns bright red, especially the outermost leaves, and then more and more leaves follow suit. Yet some years the very same tree has a more muted appearance. This is the interplay of chemistry and climate. Mild sunny days and cool nights produce better results than overcast days and mild nights.

The colors red and purple form when anthocyanins are present in a leaf and sunny days have provided the energy needed to trigger the reaction. Unlike chlorophyll and carotene, which are attached to cell membranes, anthocyanins are found in the cell sap, and their expression is moderated by pH. If the sap is acid, the pigments that develop will have a bright red color. If the sap is less acid, the color will be purple. Sugar concentration in the sap must be high. Low temperatures destroy chlorophyll, revealing yellow. When temperatures stay above freezing, anthocyanin production is enhanced. The sugars produced as nutrients move from the roots to the leaves become trapped in the leaves as the abscission layer forms. Sugar production is increased by dry weather. In soft weather—mild nights, cloudy wet days—color will be poor.

The way in which you view autumn foliage will also influence the intensity of its display. When you stand with the sun at your back, leaves appear vivid but opaque. Try coming under the branches of a tree and looking towards the sun through a screen of leaves. When seen in this way, leaves light up like the stained glass inside a cathedral.

TREES

Sumacs (*Rhus*) such as shining sumac (*R. copallina*), staghorn sumac (*R. typhina*), and smooth sumac (*R. glabra*) turn red even when conditions are less than ideal (see Plates 104–107). For this reason they are popular ornamentals in England, where mild, frequently cloudy weather is the norm. They get less respect in eastern North America, where they are native, and where numerous other trees display blazing autumn colors.

Not all gardens must be intensively planted and highly maintained. Amaskisensi, vice president of the Kyoto University School of Art and Design, taught me that gardening is about finding the proper balance between wildness and control. If you were to select a portion of a natural landscape and begin to maintain it, the site might not be a garden in the conventional sense, but it would have the style of a garden. The raking up of fallen leaves in autumn, the pruning and shaping of existing trees and shrubs—these traditional garden chores would create the ambience of a garden, even though you hadn't planted anything. Consider a rough field of native grasses, with sumacs as the first invading woody species. Installing a fence along the boundary and mowing the grass outside the fence would announce that this is a tended area. The naturalistic meadow grasses and flaming autumn foliage of the sumacs would form a garden.

Red maple (*Acer rubrum*), also called swamp maple, is a variable species found in wet swampy places and drier uplands. Its natural range extends from the chilly zone 3 gardens of Newfoundland and Minnesota to the balmy zone 9 gardens of Florida and Texas, but this does not mean the plants are interchangeable from one place to another. Over time, plants adapt. Trees that have evolved to survive in the cold and snow of Minnesota are unlikely to make it in Florida. Look for trees of local provenance. After all, red maple is a long-lived tree. You'll want one that will be around long enough to reach its 40- to 60-foot-tall potential. Indigenous trees growing wild on a site can turn a vibrant rich red or clear pure yellow. Planting cultivars is a dependable way to get the same outstanding fall color. *Acer rubrum* 'Autumn Flame' turns red earlier than other selections and has a more compact, rather rounded form. The fact that it develops color before other cultivars indicates that it has adapted well to cold winters, making it a good choice for zones 3 and 4. *Acer rubrum* 'October Glory' reliably develops bright scarlet-red to orange-red color, but this appears rather late, making this cultivar a better choice for warmer zones. *Acer rubrum* 'Red Sunset' is somewhere between these two: its autumn color develops later than 'Autumn Flame' but it is more cold tolerant than 'October Glory'.

Acer ×freemanii 'Autumn Blaze', a hybrid of red maple (*A. rubrum*) and silver maple (*A. saccharinum*), also has superb clear red fall foliage. It is available at nurseries offering a wider selection of woody plants, up to 5- to 6-inch-caliper specimens. Due to its silver maple heritage, 'Autumn Blaze' grows more quickly than red maple.

Sugar maple (*Acer saccharum*) produces the sweet sap that, when boiled down, provides maple syrup. Alternative common names are rock maple and hard maple, owing to the sturdy quality of its wood. This is the tree that fires October roadsides with warm orange-red foliage. The slow-moving blaze travels with cold weather, from Vermont and Massachusetts through Connecticut, New Jersey, and Pennsylvania, continuing westward into Indiana. Not as heat tolerant as red maple (*A. rubrum*), sugar maple grows well from the warmer portion of zone 3 to zones 7 or 8. At maturity a specimen tree can reach 60 to 75 feet tall and 40 to 50 feet wide, so give it room to spread. Sugar maple dislikes road salt, compacted soils, and conditions that are dry or poorly drained.

Several small maples feature excellent fall color and are suitable for either small gardens or large landscapes. Japanese maples (*Acer palmatum*), of course, turn a lambent, glowing clear red, regardless of their summer color. Paperbark maple (*A. griseum*) is another lovely small tree with multi-seasonal interest. Its shaggy exfoliating bark peels away in thin, papery curls. Unlike most maples, it features three-parted leaves, and these turn a pleasing clear red in fall. Paperbark maple is only 20 feet tall at maturity, small enough to duck under power lines. This species is planted along streets in Clinton, New Jersey, where its attractive spring and autumn foliage and peeling winter bark really pay the rent. Trident maple (*A. buergerianum*) has three-pointed, lobed leaves and a more substantial appearance than the delicate-looking paperbark maple. It also grows a bit taller, from 25 to 35 feet. Flaking bark breaks away in plates on older trees, creating a snakelike gray, orange, and brown patterning. In autumn the leaves turn a deep red, accented by their glossy, light-reflecting surface.

Many oaks have leaves high in tannin, a metabolic by-product that accumulates in some leaves and causes them to turn brown in autumn. Northern red oak (*Quercus rubra*) is a different story, its leaves turning a deep russet to bright red each fall. Unlike the majority of oaks, which have deep taproots, northern red oak is relatively easy to transplant. It is hardy from the warmer

portion of zone 3 to the cooler portion of zone 9, but look for local or region-
ally adapted trees. One of our more stately forest trees, northern red oak is
capable of growing 60 to 75 feet tall with an equal spread. It is readily available
in a range of sizes to fit different budgets—from $350 for a 2½ to 3-inch-
caliper specimen to a more expensive 9- to 10-inch-caliper tree. Scarlet oak (*Q.
coccinea*) resembles northern red oak in overall habit of growth and great
autumn color, which is maroon to bright scarlet red. It is, however, more difficult to transplant and less cold tolerant, growing only to zone 5.

A few other native trees feature classic autumn color. Flowering dogwood
(*Cornus florida*) is a modestly sized, shade-tolerant
understory tree with purple-red leaves. Sweet gum
(*Liquidambar styraciflua*) has five-lobed, star-shaped
leaves ranging in color from a very deep purple to a brilliant clear red or yellow. Trees from northern stock usually change color earlier than those of southern origin.
Reaching 70 feet tall or more at maturity, sweet gum
makes a fine specimen tree. Unfortunately, large specimens can be difficult to transplant successfully. Trees
produce round fruits 1 inch in diameter and covered
with little projections that make them quite painful to
step on. Sweet gum is hardy from zones 5 to 9. Sour gum
(*Nyssa sylvatica*), also called tupelo, pepperidge, and
black gum, has bright cardinal-red, oblong to obovate
autumn leaves. While it prefers moist soil, sour gum is
adaptable to average conditions anywhere from zones 5
to 9. It is difficult to transplant and for this reason it is
best to choose a smaller tree, preferably container
grown. Sourwood (*Oxydendrum arboreum*) is yet
another great native tree. Elliptical, finely serrate leaves
from 3 to 8 inches long turn dark plum-red to bright red. Younger trees change
color much earlier than mature specimens. Sourwood can grow upwards of 60
feet tall but has a relatively narrow silhouette. Transplant smaller, container-
grown specimens in spring for best success. Well-drained acid soil is preferable.
Sassafras (*Sassafras albidum*) is a wonderful midsized tree. It can have the feel
of a shrub, depending on the number of stems you permit it to produce. Leaves
are quite variable: simple oval leaves, leaves with one lobe, and leaves with two
lobes all turn up on the same branch. Fall color ranges from an intense yellow
to an orange-red. Sassafras is dioecious, only female plants bearing the fleshy
black fruits that are so popular with birds. Again, older specimens move poorly,

> After all the vibrant shades of purple, red, and orange, yellow might not sound very exciting, but that would be like saying apples are tastier than pears.

so choose younger, container-grown specimens. If it were easier to transplant, this tree might be more popular.

Like flowering dogwood, *Amelanchier arborea* is an all-season tree that pays good rent in the garden. In autumn its serrate, oval leaves turn a lovely yellow overlaid with a rich russet. It produces numerous small white flowers in spring and delicious blue berries in early summer (if you can manage to beat the birds). Smooth silver-gray bark provides winter interest. A wide, well-branched, rounded crown and low trunk give this shadbush a shrubby feel. At fifteen years of age it will be 15 feet tall, taking forty years to reach its mature height of 40 feet. *Amelanchier arborea* is hardy from zones 3 to 8.

Wind and salt tolerance and resistance to extreme heat and drought make Chinese pistachio (*Pistacia chinensis*) a very adaptable, trouble-free tree. In autumn the 2- to 3-inch-long leaflets of its compound leaves turn a rich golden orange to red—and they do so year after year. This color shift is a rarity for gardeners in the milder climate of zones 7 to 9.

After all the vibrant shades of purple, red, and orange, yellow might not sound very exciting, but that would be like saying apples are tastier than pears. They're different, that's all. And you might feel differently when you see the fan-like leaves of ginkgo (*Ginkgo biloba*), which turn a uniform yellow in autumn, then drop all at once on a frosty afternoon, leaving bare branches above a pool of gold. Ginkgo reaches perhaps 25 feet tall at twenty-five years of age. It has been around for more than 150 million years and is a durable survivor, free from problems with diseases and insect pests. About the only problem is the gagging stench of the attractive, pinkish gold, plumlike fruits produced by female trees in autumn. For this reason, male specimens are preferred and are propagated by cuttings or grafts. *Ginkgo biloba* 'Autumn Gold' has excellent fall color and a fuller form that run-of-the mill ginkgo. There is a pendulous form, but it is quite rare.

As C. Ritchie Bell and Anne H. Lindsey note in *Fall Color and Woodland Harvests*, "For many people the clear yellow leaves of the birches and aspens …are the essence of fall color." Paper birch (*Betula papyrifera*) has coarsely twice-serrate, ovate leaves that taper to a long point. In autumn these 2- to 5-inch-long leaves turn a clear yellow, making an attractive accent against the white bark. Hardy from zones 2 to 6, paper birch will grow but not thrive in warmer regions. This is a short-lived tree. It will appreciate being planted in cool-summer regions in an open but shady site, such as on the north side of a building. The foliage is sometimes blemished by leaf miners, especially in Canada and northeastern United States. Quaking aspen (*Populus tremula*) has finely serrate, cordate leaves up to 3 inches long that turn a bright yellow in autumn, contrasting nicely with its smooth, pale, greenish gray bark. The pedicel is pinched in one direction at the leaf and 90 degrees opposite at the twig, so that leaves flutter in the slightest breeze. Like paper birch, quaking aspen is a short-lived tree hardy from zones 2 to 6. As is typical of other quick-growing trees, it has soft, weak wood.

It is the combined effect of tannins and carotenoids that gives beech (*Fagus*) leaves their characteristic golden color in fall.

SHRUBS

Shrubs, like trees, are available with spectacular purple, red, orange, or clear yellow foliage. Some, such as spicebush (*Lindera benzoin*) and witch hazel (*Hamamelis*), have lambent yellow foliage that will glow in the golden light of an autumn afternoon. Burning bush (*Euonymus alatus*), also known as winged euonymus, turns a vivid red when sited in full sun but has only a soft pink color when grown in shade. Oak leaf hydrangea (*Hydrangea quercifolia*) turns purple-red even when placed in a lightly shaded area. *Fothergilla major* (sometimes called witch alder, though I call it fothergilla) needs a sunny site to grow well, and turns yellow, orange, and red or maroon, sometimes all at once on the same 2- to 4-inch-long obovate leaf. A witch hazel relative, fothergilla is a popular shrub for spring landscapes due to its squat white spikes of bottle-brush-like flowers. Highbush blueberry (*Vaccinium corymbosum*) features excellent red fall color, attractive white urn-shaped spring flowers, and tasty summer fruit, making it an excellent choice for an ornamental shrub with edible fruit. Growing up to 12 feet tall and wide, it can be pruned up so that you can walk beneath the fine twiggy canopy. Highbush blueberry is hardy from zones 4 to 8 and requires an acid soil. Lowbush blueberry (*V. angustifolium*) is a low-growing stoloniferous shrub that produces extensive tangles of 2-foot-tall twiggy stems. Lustrous bluish green to dark green leaves turn a brilliant scarlet to crimson in autumn. The bluish black summer berries are, to some folks, even sweeter than those of highbush blueberry. Plants prefer a sunny or lightly shaded site low in fertility and with an acid pH. They are hardy anywhere from zones 2 to 6. Hobblebush (*Viburnum alnifolium*), linden viburnum (*V. dilatatum*), mapleleaf viburnum (*V. acerifolium*), and arrowwood (*V. dentatum*) also have good red fall color.

Bottlebrush buckeye (*Aesculus parviflora*) turns a clear lambent yellow, the obovate palmate leaflets seemingly lit from within (see Plate 100). A suckering shrub, it is appealing for its display of, well, bottlebrush-like white flower spikes in early summer, followed by smooth, glossy, chestnut-brown nuts in early autumn. The coarse green foliage is quietly pleasing, transmuting in autumn to a golden treasure. Spicebush (*Lindera benzoin*) turns a clear, cooler yellow. An excellent choice for moist, shaded sites, spicebush also offers small green flowers early in spring, clustered on bare branches before the leaves unfold. *Hamamelis virginiana*, a fall-blooming witch hazel, also turns clear to golden yellow. Spicy scented yellow flowers frequently appear as the leaves change color, so you'll want the shrubs that drop their leaves promptly, allowing the flowers to make a better show.

All leaves, whatever their color, should be collected after they fall and added to the compost heap. I keep one heap especially for leaves, finding the resultant leaf mold a special source of humus for certain fussy herbaceous woodland plants. Whether or not you utilize fallen leaves (and I certainly encourage you to do so), they must be raked from where they fall on lawns and low mat-forming groundcovers, or wherever they collect too thickly for the healthy growth of perennials in spring.

PERENNIALS

Whatever the reason, we generally associate autumn foliage color changes with trees and shrubs. It is as if the herbaceous perennials just quietly withered away. While it is true that many do just that, there are others that contribute quite nicely to the seasonal cycle. There comes a time in autumn when every hosta looks like *Hosta* 'Piedmont Gold'. It matters not whether it started off green, yellow, glaucous blue, or variegated—after the first few light frosts it finishes the growing season a pleasing golden yellow. Visualize a lovely autumn vignette with a hosta and a highbush blueberry, the larger yellow leaves at ground level contrasting with the smaller burgundy red leaves on the tall shrub. Cinnamon fern (*Osmunda cinnamomea*) turns a straw-yellow color, most attractive if a group of the ferns happens to be growing in the shade of a swamp maple (*Acer rubrum*). The first few maple leaves to fall will become caught in the 3-foot-tall fronds, looking like red stars on the lacy background of the golden ferns. Balloon flower (*Platycodon grandiflorus*) is a sturdy addition to the late-summer flower garden. In autumn the leaves strung up and down the stem turn a pleasing clear yellow—a visual benefit as well as a clue that a gentle tug will separate stalk from root for fall cleanup. Solomon's seals such as *Polygonatum biflorum*, *P.* ×*hybridum*, and *P. odoratum* turn an attractive yellow, their oval leaves gracefully arrayed on an arching stem. Pair them with Christmas fern (*Polystichum acrostichoides*) for a pleasing partnership.

Herbaceous peonies (*Paeonia*) sometimes turn a wonderfully warm, glowing orange-red. These can make an elegant background for chrysanthemums in shades of yellow or warm red, but avoid pairing them with cooler pinkish mauves and lavenders.

ANNUALS

Ornamental cabbages and ornamental kales (both comprised of *Brassica oleracea* cultivars) are, with chrysanthemums and pansies, the fall annuals most often sold at garden centers. Hardy to about 28° Fahrenheit, they can last through the winter in Washington, D.C., and sometimes well into December where I am, in New Jersey. When they first became available, I noticed cabbage patches sprouting up in many gardens. The mere idea of cool season annuals with fuchsia or white markings on glaucous blue-green leaves—leaves that are smooth on cabbages, attractively frilled on kales—was enough to set everyone to planting. But cabbages are cabbages, and we have fortunately moved beyond mass planting to some forethought and design (see Plates 94 and 95). I've coaxed one local nursery into making small 4-inch pots available in addition to the usual 6-inch pots, which I find awkward for use in window boxes and mixed containers. One year I used three fuchsia ornamental cabbages in a large planter at the bottom of my driveway. A nice clump of *Calamagrostis* ×*acutiflora* 'Karl Foerster', with its feathery panicles, provided some height while three wine-colored chrysanthemums disported themselves unequally, two on this side, one on the other. The cabbages went the other way, one with two chrysanthemums, two with one chrysanthemum. A largish *Euphorbia amygdaloides* 'Rubra' filled in and trailed over the side while four pale wine-colored pansies (all I had space left for) finished things off. The cabbages had lost their lower leaves and looked rather spindly, but this actually worked out well, as it allowed me to tilt the cabbages when planting them, placing them up where I wanted them in relation to the other plants.

The larger ornamental cabbages and kales are more suitable in the garden proper. Fuchsia cabbages will combine well with chrysanthemums of a similar color and a nice cardoon (*Cynara cardunculus*), whose toothy silver leaves will play off against the glaucous edge of the ornamental cabbage leaves. Try pairing white cabbages with the narrow blades of a white-variegated *Miscanthus* species. Ornamental cabbages and kales are edible. However, having been bred for good looks rather than good taste, you will find the flavor lacking and the texture rather tough and chewy.

Summer cypress (*Bassia scoparia* f. *trichophylla*), also known as burning bush, is an annual that looks like a conifer, growing 3 feet tall with an upright, rather columnar form and finely textured foliage of a warm light green (see Plates 92 and 93). Try planting one as an accent, or plant two in a pair of pots to stand sentinel at a path or flight of steps. Plant several in a row as a summer hedge, which can even be clipped to a more formal outline. The real display comes in autumn when the foliage turns a bright, slightly rusty, pinkish red.

Plants may be raised from seed, sown indoors approximately six weeks before the frost-free planting-out date. Seeds need light to germinate, so do not cover them. Space the young plants 2 feet apart, as they will average about 2 feet wide at maturity, and make sure they have good drainage, which they will need to grow and color well. *Bassia scoparia* 'Evergreen' does not turn red in autumn, which seems rather a waste.

WINTER

Sometimes it is tempting to fill the winter-interest garden with conifers and broad-leaved evergreens, but this results in a rather static presentation. Sure, new spring growth will add a softer green and winter too may experience shifts in color, but the form and outline of the plants will not alter. I prefer to embrace seasonal alterations, and the counterpoint of evergreen and bare branches provides a strong sense of winter.

Conifers such as yew (*Taxus*), pine (*Pinus*), and spruce (*Picea*) add their finely penciled-in needles and dense forms to the landscape. Whether they are trees or shrubs, and whether they are closely shaped into hedges and topiaries or allowed their natural forms, their thick habit makes a solid addition to the garden. The reduced surface and resinous nature of the needles help conifers limit their energy losses in winter. Gardeners can create visual interest by contrasting conifers with broad-leaved evergreens and deciduous shrubs. Broad-leaved evergreen options are limited or nil in colder climates, moderate in zone 6, and increase in variety the milder the winters become. Even in winter, broad-leaved evergreens lose water from their leaves. When the ground is frozen, it is difficult for the plants to replenish moisture. One common result is winter burn. When large-leaved rhododendrons experience winter burn, their leaves curl up like green cigars. Small-leaved lepidote rhododendrons are less at risk. Gardeners can help by siting broad-leaved evergreens where they are not exposed to morning sunlight or excessive wind. It may also help to use an anti-desiccant spray. It must be applied when it can dry on the leaves before freezing, when temperatures are around 40° Fahrenheit. Where I live in New Jersey the general rule is to spray once in mid to late November and again during the January thaw, since repeated snow and rain will remove the protective coating. You may also swaddle shrubs in burlap, though I have never seen much sense in the practice. Wrapping shrubs will protect them quite nicely, but one of the more desirable attributes of broad-leaved evergreens is their winter appearance, and this is effectively concealed when plants are wrapped up like mummies (see Plate 103). If the burlap provides an acceptable appearance, why bother planting the shrub?

One evergreen woody plant that disguises itself as a perennial is the denigrated yucca, which has been referred to by at least one snobbish writer as a "trailer park plant." Yucca is a sturdy survivor needing little in the way of upkeep. About the only drawback I have found is that deer occasionally dine on it, though perhaps just using it as a floss after eating juicier, more succulent plants. Still, deer don't seem to like yucca as much as they love yew, English ivy (the deer trots away with banners of ivy dangling from its mouth), tulips, and dahlias. Perhaps what we need is not another repellent spray but some new, absolutely irresistible spray, one that could be applied to poison ivy, multiflora roses, Japanese stilt grass, and kudzu so that deer will nibble these weeds into little dead nubbins.

Since yuccas keep their trunks hidden below ground, what we see is their nice tufts of swordlike leaves. While I agree that a row of these clustered bayonets leaves something to be desired, I do think a single specimen can work quite nicely as an accent in the winter landscape. Try combining yucca with a coniferous shrub such as a yew clipped to a softly mounded form, an ornamental grass gone sere and beige, or a small deciduous tree with bare branches. Yuccas are drought and heat tolerant, prefer a well-drained sunny site, and are generally able to accept humid conditions. Adam's needle (*Yucca filamentosa*) is hardy from zones 4 to 10. Leaves are 24 inches long and 1 inch wide, the edges embellished with unraveling, threadlike fibers. Overall, Adam's needle grows 4 to 6 feet tall. Though the species is typically a grayish blue-green, the leaves of *Y. filamentosa* 'Bright Edge' have golden yellow margins. *Yucca flaccida* is just as hardy, grows 4 to 7 feet tall, and has straight threads emerging from the leaf edges. The 2-foot-long leaves frequently arch over at the tip. Soapweed yucca (*Y. glauca*) is even more cold tolerant, down to zone 3. As is typical of other yuccas, it grows smaller in colder regions and larger in milder ones, ranging from 3 to 6 feet tall. Narrow gray-green leaves grow 1 to 2½ feet long and ½ inch wide, featuring paler edges and the usual marginal threads. *Yucca filamentosa*, *Y. flaccida*, and *Y. glauca* are all native to southeastern or central United States.

Beeches (*Fagus*) and oaks (*Quercus*) often hang on to a fair portion of their brown leaves until these are pushed loose by new growth in spring. There is a folktale in which Daniel Webster sells his soul to the devil on the condition that it be collected "when the last leaves drop from that there oak tree in fall." Because the oak kept some of its leaves, the devil could not collect on his deal, and so he tore the edges off the leaves in a frenzy. This is one explanation of why oaks have lobed leaves. Beech trees planted in a row and pruned as a hedge from the time they are saplings make an attractive, if less frequently seen, deciduous hedge.

Plate 87. This nursery bed of *Astilbe* cultivars clearly displays the color variation in spring foliage (and makes the copper-hued rogue in the third row easy to pick out).

Plate 88. A lush tropical look is created when papaya (*Carica papaya*) is used as a backdrop to a familiar summer planting of begonias.

Plate 89. The wonderfully jagged, palmate leaf of papaya (*Carica papaya*).

Plate 90. Surrounded by grasses, red coleus (*Solenostemon scutellarioides*), and the variegated foliage of *Polygonum virginianum*, the backlit leaves of blood banana (*Musa acuminata* 'Sumatrana') boldly dominate this lush foliage garden in Mattituck, New York, owned by Dennis Schrader.

Plate 91. Ken Selody of Atlock Flower Farm in Somerset, New Jersey, created this luxuriant summer border, with Abyssinian banana (*Ensete ventricosum* 'Maurelii') commanding pride of place. In front is palm grass (*Setaria palmifolia*), left, arching its tightly goffered green leaves, and gold-leaved sweet potato (*Ipomoea batatas* 'Margarita'), right. *Berberis thunbergii* f. *atropurpurea* grows behind the banana, reinforcing its red-flushed leaves.

Plate 92. In summertime it is easy to understand how summer cypress (*Bassia scoparia* f. *trichophylla*) received its common name. Seen here with *Solenostemon scutellarioides* 'Black Emperor' and *Catharanthus roseus*, summer cypress does indeed have a coniferous look.

Plate 93. In autumn the other common name for *Bassia scoparia* f. *trichophylla*, burning bush, becomes equally appropriate.

Plate 94. Sturdy, attractive, cold-resistant ornamental cabbages (*Brassica oleracea*), used here in combination with *Miscanthus sinensis* 'Variegatus', will ornament a garden once autumn frost kills off summer annuals.

Plate 95. A marvelous combination of flowers and foliage: ornamental cabbage (*Brassica oler acea*) dances with the jagged silver leaves of cardoon (*Cynara cardunculus*) and chrysanthe-mums of the same tender pink.

Plate 96. A shrub border at Oliver Nurseries in Fairfield, Connecticut, blends deciduous plants with conifers and broad-leaved evergreens to create winter interest. Japanese maple (*Acer palmatum*), boxwood (*Buxus*), prostrate junipers (*Juniperus*), and dwarf conifers are anchored by dragon's eye pine (*Pinus densiflora* 'Oculus-draconis').

Plate 97. The green and gold needles of dragon's eye pine (*Pinus densiflora* 'Oculus-draconis') invite closer inspection. Young trees take some time to produce a display quite this luxuriant.

Plate 98. The bright, yellow-edged, swordlike leaves of *Yucca filamentosa* 'Bright Edge' provide a strong winter contrast to pine and juniper.

Plate 99. Perennials may display autumn color as rich as any tree or shrub, as demonstrated by the glowing red-orange foliage of this herbaceous peony (*Paeonia*).

Plate 100. The luminous yellow leaves of bottlebrush buckeye (*Aesculus parviflora*) capture the essence of a golden autumn afternoon.

Plate 101. After the first frost of the season this sturdy ornamental cabbage (*Brassica oleracea*) is unaffected while the tender leaves of neighboring plectranthus have been nipped.

Plate 102. This lavender (*Lavandula*) has been unaffected by the frost that killed the tender geranium (*Pelargonium*).

Plate 103. Wrapped plants may be well protected against winter cold, but they add little visual appeal to the garden.

Plate 104. A field in Massachusetts features evergreen conifers, beige grasses, and scarlet sumac (*Rhus*): a paradigm for an autumnal garden.

Plate 105. However mild or crisp the autumn weather, staghorn sumac (*Rhus typhina*) reliably develops its bonfire-red color.

Plate 106. The oft neglected shining sumac (*Rhus copallina*) features beautifully glossy, pinnate leaves with winged rachises.

Plate 107. In autumn, shining sumac (*Rhus copallina*) turns a rich metallic bronze.

Plate 108. Some broad-leaved evergreen shrubs, such as this Oregon holly grape (*Mahonia aquifolium*), turn wonderful shades of violet-red to purple in cold winter weather.

Plate 109. *Amelanchier laevis* is a shadbush that displays lovely reddish orange color in fall, intensified here by an evergreen backdrop of the prostrate form of English yew (*Taxus baccata* 'Repandens').

Plate 111. The rich, copper-hued new spring growth of an herbaceous peony (*Paeonia*) is enhanced by grape hyacinth (*Muscari armeniacum*). As the peony foliage matures it will conceal the bare ground left by the spring-flowering bulb.

Plate 110. The new spring foliage of *Pieris formosa* var. *forrestii* is a brilliant flamingo-pink and as vivid as any flower.

Plate 112. In spring the bold, architectural leaves of *Rodgersia pinnata* are attractively flushed with a soft coppery hue, providing a seasonal bonus to the woodland garden.

Plate 113. It is not permissible to fold, braid, spindle, staple, or otherwise bundle up the leaves of spring-blooming bulbs after they have finished flowering. Instead, use the foliage of adjacent herbaceous perennials to distract attention.

Plate 114. An assortment of container plants includes *Oxalis regnellii*, with purple cloverlike leaves; naranjilla (*Solanum quitoense*), with purple-haired leaves, the veins armed with spikes like some gothic accessory; and *Setaria palmifolia*, whose finely pleated blades are stained with reddish purple down the center.

Evergreen herbaceous plants are more common in mild-winter regions than in regions where cold weather is the norm. It really is a dilemma: a nice reliable snow cover protects plants, but it also conceals them from view. For the plants' sake I would rather have a nice fluffy blanket of snow a foot or so deep. Plants can survive cold temperatures more easily when swaddled in this way. Even so, there are evergreen herbaceous perennials that make it through the irregular winters of zone 6, Christmas fern (*Polystichum acrostichoides*) being one example. *Liriope muscari* is another popular perennial, with linear, grasslike evergreen leaves. *Arum italicum* 'Pictum' waits until autumn to send up its arrowhead-shaped, slightly ruffled leaves, which bear the brunt of winter's cold before the plant goes dormant in spring. Do not be dismayed by the unadorned dark green leaves. White veining does not always appear the first winter after the tubers are planted. 'Pictum' is hardy from zones 6 to 10. Its leaves may reach 1 foot or more in length. If a cold, snowless winter turns the leaves to mush, tubers will send up a second flush of leaves in spring and the plant will be nourished through the efforts of spring flower and autumn seed production. *Arum italicum* ssp. *italicum* 'Chamaeleon' has larger, broader leaves distinctively marbled in gray-green and yellow-green. With their lacy, linear, and bold shapes, *Polystichum acrostichoides*, *L. muscari*, and *A. italicum* make fine partners for a winter grouping.

SPRING

As the three-parted leaves of paperbark maple (*Acer griseum*) unfold in spring they have a lovely soft coppery hue. It is a transitory color shift, and more subtle in its unfolding than that of autumn, just the sort of detail that can elevate the spring season. *Rhododendron* 'Stewartstonian' may be planted beneath it, with its fire-truck-red flowers.

Although all forms of *Astilbe* mature to green, the foliage of several deep pink- or red-flowered varieties is rich copper or bronze when it first appears in spring. Try combining these with violas (*Viola cornuta*) featuring yellow or clear blue flowers. White-flowered violas form a more intense combination. Herbaceous peonies (*Paeonia*) display strong coppery red hues as they emerge. Add a handful of grape hyacinths (*Muscari armeniacum*), whose smoky blue flowers blend nicely. Later the peony shoots will conceal the tattered, aging foliage of the bulb (see Plate 111).

Some herbaceous plants start off variegated but settle down with all-green leaves in summer. This is true of hostas such as *Hosta fortunei* var. *albopicta*, whose white- or yellow-variegated spring leaves turn completely green by the beginning of summer. The leaves of *H. ventricosa* var. *aureomaculata* have an irregular dark green margin and a bright yellow center that darkens to green with a tinge of yellow. *Hosta* 'Aurea' emerges in spring with yellow leaves that soon turn to a pale, flat green. The leaves of *Iris pseudacorus* 'Variegata' are attractively striped with creamy yellow in spring, maturing to an even green as summer arrives. This habit of shifting from variegated to green would be especially appropriate in naturalistic gardens, which are based on plant communities but not restricted to a selection of native plants. In temperate regions we expect plants to have green leaves during the growing season. It is in the tropics that variegated and other non-green leaves are more typical. Thus, herbaceous plants whose non-green juvenile leaves mature to green provide the naturalistic gardener with an extra element of design with which to play.

SUMMER

Summer is the time when gardeners in cooler climates gravitate towards transient plants. These plants turn up in the garden as nights become reliably mild and settled, and depart when killing frosts return. These may be true annuals or they may be herbaceous perennials, bulbs, or woody plants that are useful only for a single season. In my New Jersey garden winter cold is the most familiar limitation. In the heart of the South it is summer heat, which can fry plants. In this region snapdragons (*Antirrhinum majus*) and other vulnerable plants are grown as winter annuals. My brother lives in Davis, California, near Sacramento, and misses the lilacs (*Syringa*) he remembers from our Brooklyn childhood. Without winter chilling, lilacs cannot set flower buds, and so they are not grown where he lives. On the other hand, eucalyptus is so familiar in Davis that he overlooks it. For me, eucalyptus is a specialty plant sold at nurseries as a trendy accent for large containers. I appreciate these differences. Unlike malls and restaurant chains that push our cities towards homogenization, climate imposes regional distinctions. Yes, I keep a banana plant, but it is an outrageous exception to local conditions, and it makes my neighbors laugh.

Gardeners always like to push the envelope, growing plants that cannot carry over from year to year without assistance. These include a number of familiar summer plants that happen to be perennial in some places. Impatiens, coleus (*Solenostemon scutellarioides*), and fibrous begonias survive where winters are mild. Snapdragons (*Antirrhinum majus*) walk a fine line between winters cold enough to kill them (north of Philadelphia in some years) and summers hot enough to fry them (in the southern states). Dusty miller (*Senecio cineraria*) is another plant that is sometimes perennial. There is a push towards calling tropical plants that need a good deal of assistance to survive chilly winters *temperennial*. I'm not sure if this is a contraction for "temporary perennial" or "temperamental perennial." But we can all agree that the tropical look is popular in nontropical locations. Cannas and bananas add their bold foliage and sultry influence to suburban Westchester and the shores of Long Island, far from their hot and humid homelands.

A handful of foliage plants have long held a place among the plethora of familiar flowering annuals. Their popularity waxes and wanes. Coleus (*Solenostemon scutellarioides*), for example, was once out of favor, considered a boring plant to be used in shady places where the sun did not shine strongly enough to grow something better. Now coleus are in style, and varieties have been developed that thrive in the hot sun. There are many *S. scutellarioides* cultivars offered at nurseries, from 'Alabama Sunset' (see Plates 39 and 40) to 'Zap Knarly'.

Elephant's-ear has moved beyond the green giants of the past. *Colocasia* and *Alocasia* cultivars feature leaves with matte black or white splotches, offering bold accents for the summer landscape. *Caladium*, their smaller cousin, includes cultivars with foliage in whites, pinks, and reds for use in shady summer gardens. Various *Canna* cultivars are available in garden centers. Besides those with green and burgundy leaves, there are cannas featuring crisp yellow stripes or the hues of a tropical sunset.

Papaya is appealing for its seasonal interest (see Plates 88 and 89), but mention *Carica* and only a handful of gardeners in Florida and such places will know what you are talking about. Papaya (*Carica papaya*) is just not that familiar in most of the United States. I first saw it used in a cool-climate garden in 1991 during a visit to Elizabeth Park in Hartford, Connecticut. The tall plants had lush, green, palmate leaves, deeply cut and lobed, and were very tropical in appearance—quite unlike anything I had ever seen before. With their rich texture and interesting shape, they made a fabulous background for more traditional summer annuals. A single plant could serve as a bold accent in a bedding scheme or be used as a container plant. Papayas grow so quickly that a large plant can be produced from seed in just one growing season.

Technically a pachycaul, papaya has a simple, erect, herbaceous stem that can reach upwards of 20 to 30 feet tall, and orbicular to ovate leaves over 2 feet

> Cannas and bananas add their bold foliage and sultry influence to suburban Westchester and the shores of Long Island, far from their hot and humid homelands.

across on a petiole up to 3 feet long. Papayas are normally unbranched, but if the stem is damaged the plant will develop multiple stems. Plants adore hot weather and moist soil, but not a flooded site.

While the cultivars of *Carica papaya* are the way to go if fruit production is the goal, plants for purely ornamental use may be raised from the seed. I tried this out, unsuccessfully, using a supermarket papaya. Perhaps refrigeration during transport was the problem, or maybe the fruit had been treated to prevent sprouting. If you do obtain viable seed, February is a reasonable time to begin, but remember that this quick-growing tropical beauty wants heat and lots of light. Providing a heating mat or heating cable and grow lights should help. It might be wise to begin with enough seed for about twice the amount of plants you want to grow, so as to allow for possible mishaps (and in order to have a few extra to share with friends). Fill a small thermos with hot tap water and add your seeds. They will float. Change the water morning and night to flush away inhibitors that retard germination and to keep the seeds hydrated. In a few days, when the seeds have sunk to the bottom of the container, it is time to sow. Use a mix of half peat moss and half perlite, saturated with hot water. Plant the seeds about ½ inch beneath the surface. Use individual deep pots in order to reduce the risk of damage when transplanting. Seedlings should begin to appear in about ten days. When it is safe to plant tomatoes in the garden, papayas can go outdoors as well.

ANNUALS

On a visit to Holland I saw a plant growing in a *hofje*, as the Dutch call their courtyard gardens. This *hofje* included a nice bunch of vegetables—tomatoes, zucchinis with bold silver-splotched leaves, and so forth. There was one lovely foliage plant, the size and shape of a large shrub. I wandered in through the gate for a closer look and discovered that it was a well-grown marijuana (*Cannabis sativa*). I do not suggest you try growing this, however. The hemp that is raised for fiber and birdseed may be very low in THC, but drug enforcement agents are unlikely to appreciate such fine distinctions.

Snow-on-the-mountain (*Euphorbia marginata*), also known as snow-in-summer, is an interesting annual relative of poinsettia (*E. pulcherrima*). It is native to central United States. Do not be concerned when the gray-green oval leaves of young plants show no signs of variegation. Though less than impressive in spring, the bushy branching plants mantle themselves with "snow" in summer, their upper leaves appearing white with only a thin green stripe down the center. Plants prefer full sun in average to dry sites and will accept neglect.

Seed may be sown outdoors, though this should be held off until just a week or two before the last frost. By the time seed germinates, the weather should be frost free. If you want to jump-start the season, seed may be started indoors approximately six weeks before tomato planting time. When seed is allowed to form, self-sown volunteers will usually make their appearance in following years. Plants grow about 2 feet tall and should be spaced about 1 foot apart. *Euphorbia marginata* 'Summer Icicle' is shorter, at 18 inches high, while *E. marginata* 'White Top' grows to 3 feet tall. Though pruning should not be necessary, remember that snow-on-the-mountain, like other euphorbias, will ooze a thick white sap whenever it is cut. Sensitive individuals may develop a poison-ivy-like rash if the sap comes into contact with their skin.

Castor bean (*Ricinus communis*) is a here-you-love-it, there-you-don't kind of plant. In places where cold winters kill it off, castor bean becomes a popular statuesque plant for summer interest. It is best not to grow it in mild-winter regions such as southern California, where it lives from year to year and reseeds, or in parts of the Southeast, where it provides for another generation before it dies. If small children play in the garden, be careful: the speckled beanlike seeds of this plant are highly poisonous. That said, there are few other plants that reach 6 feet tall, sometimes more, in one season from seed. The large palmate leaves of castor bean lend a tropical look and pleasant contrast to cannas and other plants in the summer garden.

"When the world wearies and society ceases to satisfy, there is always the garden"—so said Minnie Aumonier, author of *The Poetry of Gardens* and other books. As I write, it is a week and a half into October. The first light frost arrived last night, laying a silver skin on the lawn and turning the tips of canna leaves brown. Poison ivy (*Toxicodendron radicans*) has already turned a rich, warm yellow-orange, and non-itchy sumacs (*Rhus*) are shifting to scarlet. Emulating the frenzied digging of squirrels, I plant bulbs for spring bloom, making sure to include foliage partners that will conceal the aging bulb foliage next spring. Cuttings of coleus (*Solenostemon scutellarioides*) that have rooted and been potted will remain under grow lights for the winter, to come back outdoors when summer returns.

Gardening is a never-ending story, one that takes us from the here and now and lets us look ahead to the next season. We look back to what happened last week, last month, last year. The small tree has grown into a sturdy specimen, the beebalm has no doubt encroached upon its neighbors, and the pachysandra, in defiance of visitors approaching the front door, has occupied half the front walk. The view out my study window is obscured by a hardy banana, grown 10 feet tall with 6-foot fronds. Though sheltered next to the house in a protected microclimate, it will soon enough be cut down by a heavy frost.

Garden visitors always seem to have their timing out of kilter, arriving a day too late or a week too early for the best display, but gardeners have the luxury of seeing their own garden morning, noon, and night. There is always something to notice: dew droplets resting on a hosta leaf before the sun dries them off; leaves gradually emerging in spring, clothing a tree in tender, unblemished green before time and pests take their toll; a fern crosier unrolling as the symphony of spring tunes up; the woodcut-like simplicity of winter, with its few green leaves against its many bare branches, providing an intensity altogether different from summer's lush display. Foliage can be appealing in so many ways, providing a foundation for the garden that is both practical and attractive, and helping gardeners fulfill the dreams and aspirations they have for their own gardens.

Metric Conversion Chart

INCHES	CENTIMETERS		FEET	METERS
⅛	0.3		¼	0.08
⅙	0.4		⅓	0.1
⅕	0.5		½	0.15
¼	0.6		1	0.3
⅓	0.8		1½	0.5
⅜	0.9		2	0.6
⅖	1.0		2½	0.8
½	1.25		3	0.9
⅗	1.5		4	1.2
⅝	1.6		5	1.5
⅔	1.7		6	1.8
¾	1.9		7	2.1
⅞	2.2		8	2.4
1	2.5		9	2.7
1¼	3.1		10	3.0
1⅓	3.3		12	3.6
1½	3.75		15	4.5
1¾	4.4		18	5.4
2	5.0		20	6.0
3	7.5		25	7.5
4	10		30	9.0
5	12.5		35	10.5
6	15		40	12
7	17.5		45	13.5
8	20		50	15
9	22.5		60	18
10	25		70	21
12	30		75	22.5
15	37.5		80	24
18	45		90	27
20	50		100	30
24	60		125	37.5
30	75		150	45
32	80		175	52.5
36	90		200	60

$$°C = \tfrac{5}{9} \times (°F - 32)$$
$$°F = (\tfrac{9}{5} \times °C) + 32$$

Bibliography

Bacon, Francis. 1625. *The Essayes or Counsels, Ciuill and Morall, of Francis Lo. Verulam, Viscount St. Alban.* Newly enlarged. Hanna Barret, Richard Whitaker: London.

Bagust, Harold. 1992. *The Gardener's Dictionary of Horticultural Terms.* Cassell: London.

Bailey, Liberty Hyde. 1914. *The Standard Cyclopedia of Horticulture.* Macmillan: New York.

Bell, C. Ritchie, and Anne H. Lindsey. 1990. *Fall Color and Woodland Harvests: A Guide to the More Colorful Fall Leaves and Fruits of the Eastern Forests.* Laurel Hill Press: Chapel Hill, North Carolina.

Bir, Richard E. 1992. *Growing and Propagating Showy Native Woody Plants.* University of North Carolina Press: Chapel Hill, North Carolina.

Bowles, E. A. 1997. *My Garden in Spring.* Timber Press: Portland, Oregon.

Brickell, Christopher, and David Joyce. 1996. *American Horticultural Society: Pruning and Training.* Dorling Kindersley: New York.

Capon, Brian. 1990. *Botany for Gardeners: An Introduction and Guide.* Timber Press: Portland, Oregon.

Clair, Colin. 1961. *Of Herbs and Spices.* Abelard-Schuman: New York.

Clarke, Ethne. 1995. *Herb Garden Design.* Macmillian: New York.

Clarkson, Rosetta E. 1972. *Herbs and Savory Seeds: Culinaries, Simples, Sachets, Decoratives.* Dover: New York.

Clausen, Ruth Rogers, and Nicolas H. Ekstrom. 1989. *Perennials for American Gardens.* Random House: New York.

Conder, Susan. 2001. *Variegated Plants: The Encyclopedia of Patterned Foliage.* Timber Press: Portland, Oregon.

Darke, Rick. 1999. *The Color Encyclopedia of Ornamental Grasses: Sedges, Rushes, Restios, Cat-tails, and Selected Bamboos.* Timber Press: Portland, Oregon.

Feininger, Andreas. 1984. *Leaves: 199 Photographs by Andreas Feininger.* Dover: New York.

Foley, Daniel J., ed. 1974. *Herbs for Use and for Delight: An Anthology from the Herbarist, a Publication of the Herb Society of America.* Dover: New York.

Foote, Leonard E., and Samuel B. Jones, Jr. 1989. *Native Shrubs and Woody Vines of the Southeast: Landscaping Uses and Identification.* Timber Press: Portland, Oregon.

Gervais, Paul. 2000. *A Garden in Lucca: Finding Paradise in Tuscany.* Hyperion: New York.

Greenwood, Pippa, et al. 2000. *Pests and Diseases.* Dorling Kindersley: New York.

Grenfell, Diana. 1990. *Hosta: The Flowering Foliage Plant.* Timber Press: Portland, Oregon.

Griffiths, Mark. 1994. *Index of Garden Plants.* Timber Press: Portland, Oregon.

Hersey, Jean. 1965. *The Woman's Day Book of House Plants.* Simon and Schuster: New York.

Hirose, Yoshimichi, and Masato Yokoi. 1998. *Variegated Plants in Color.* Varie Nine: Iwakuni, Japan.

Iversen, Richard. 1999. *The Exotic Garden: Designing with Tropical Plants in Any Climate.* Taunton Press: Newtown, Connecticut.

Lawson, William. 1660. *A New Orchard and Garden.* G. Sawbridge: London.

Meager, Leonard. 1699. *The English Gardner: Or, A Sure Guide to Young Planters and Gardners.* M. Wotton: London.

Mickel, John. 1994. *Ferns for American Gardens.* Macmillan: New York.

Nichols, Rose Standish. 1902. *English Pleasure Gardens.* Macmillan: New York.

Pellegrini, Angelo M. 1970. *The Food-Lover's Garden.* Knopf: New York.

Riffle, Robert Lee. 1998. *The Tropical Look: An Encyclopedia of Dramatic Landscape Plants.* Timber Press: Portland, Oregon.

Rose, Peter Q. 1996. *The Gardener's Guide to Growing Ivies.* Timber Press: Portland, Oregon.

Schmid, Wolfram George. 1991. *The Genus Hosta: Giboshi Zoku.* Timber Press: Portland Oregon.

Smittle, Delilah, ed. 1999. *The Garden Problem Solver.* Reader's Digest: Pleasantville, New York.

Stern, William T. 1983. *Botanical Latin: History, Grammar, Syntax, Terminology, and Vocabulary.* Third edition, revised. David and Charles: North Pomfret, Vermont.

Thomas, Graham Stuart. 1982. *Perennial Garden Plants, or The Modern Florilegium: A Concise Account of Herbaceous Plants, Including Bulbs, for*

General Garden Use. Second edition, revised and enlarged. Dent: London.

Thomas, Graham Stuart. 1992. *Ornamental Shrubs, Climbers and Bamboos.* Timber Press: Portland, Oregon.

van Gelderen, D. M., P. C. de Jong, and H. J. Oterdoom. 1994. *Maples of the World.* Timber Press: Portland, Oregon.

van de Laar, H. J, et al. 2000. *Naamlijst van Vaste Planten* (List of Names of Perennials). Boomteeltpraktijkonderzoek (Applied Research for Nursery Stock): Boskoop, Netherlands.

Veblen, Thorstein. 1899. *The Theory of the Leisure Class: An Economic Study in the Evolution of Institutions.* Macmillan: New York.

Waters, Alice. 1996. *Chez Panisse Vegetables.* HarperCollins: New York.

Plant Name Index